How Materials Matter

How Materials Matter

Design, Innovation and Materiality in the Pacific

Graeme Were

First published in 2019 by
Berghahn Books
www.berghahnbooks.com

First paperback edition published in 2024

Library of Congress Cataloging-in-Publication Data

Names: Were, Graeme, author.
Title: How materials matter : design, innovation and materiality in the Pacific / Graeme Were.
Description: New York : Berghahn Books, 2019. | Includes bibliographical references and index.
Identifiers: LCCN 2018057232 (print) | LCCN 2018061542 (ebook) | ISBN 9781789202021 (ebook) | ISBN 9781789202014 (hardback : alk. paper)
Subjects: LCSH: Pacific Islanders--Material culture. | Material culture--Oceania. | Plant products--Oceania. | Handicraft--Oceania. | Design--Oceania. | Oceania--Social life and customs.
Classification: LCC GN663 (ebook) | LCC GN663 .W47 2019 (print) | DDC 306.4/60995--dc23
LC record available at https://lccn.loc.gov/2018057232

British Library Cataloguing in Publication Data

A catalogue record for this book is available from the British Library

ISBN 978-1-78920-201-4 hardback
ISBN 978-1-80539-122-7 paperback
ISBN 978-1-80539-387-0 epub
ISBN 978-1-78920-202-1 web pdf

https://doi.org/10.3167/9781789202014

Contents

List of Illustrations vi

Acknowledgements viii

Introduction Materials and Design 1

PART I. MATERIALS UNDER THE MICROSCOPE

Chapter 1 On the Materials of Mats: Thinking through Design in a Melanesian Society 21

Chapter 2 Materials on the Move: Exploring the Shifting Material Identities of Barkcloth 49

Chapter 3 What's in a Plant Leaf? A Case Study of Materials Innovation in New Zealand 68

PART II. MATERIALS, DESIGN, TRANSFORMATION

Chapter 4 Of Canoes and Troughs: Materials Computation and the Nature of Social Relations 89

Chapter 5 Enclosures and Disclosures: Materials and Difference 111

PART III. MATERIAL FUTURES

Chapter 6 Returning Cultural Knowledge in a Digital Design Context: Collecting Legacies and Archival Futures 139

Chapter 7 Material Histories and the Changing Nature of Museum Collections 160

Conclusion Towards a New Understanding of Materiality 174

References 187

Index 201

Illustrations

Figure 1.1	Discarded stitched mat araazira by the side of the road, New Ireland	25
Figure 1.2	Harvesting the prop roots of the azafna pandanus	34
Figure 1.3	Mrs Waika showing amotmot pandanus leaf, used for making stitched mats	36
Figure 1.4	Vaazufnalik, ceremony to 'wash the baby', Panafao village, New Ireland	39
Figure 1.5	Awoiwoi pandanus in village hamlet	41
Figure 1.6	The late Mrs Cathy Kombeng drying awoiwoi pandanus in her house ready for mat making	43
Figure 2.1	Selian Kambau wearing her aruaai basket, New Ireland, 2009	58
Figure 2.2	Malina Kambaxal stripping the kapiak of its outer bark, New Ireland, 2011	62
Figure 4.1	Western Solomon Islands war canoe in the British Museum storage facilities	96
Figure 4.2	Food trough from Roviana, Western Solomon Islands, in the British Museum storage facilities	104
Figure 5.1	Bikmaus cemetery enclosure, Kosinai, Madina village, New Ireland	121
Figure 5.2	Tamun's men's house, Madina village, New Ireland, after the tidal surge	129
Figure 5.3	Details of rafter lashings inside Tamun's men's house, Madina village, New Ireland	130

Figure 6.1 Adam Kaminiel demonstrating the Mobile Museum software at awareness meeting, Lugagun village, New Ireland 149

Figure 6.2 Martin Kombeng and Adam Kaminiel select malangan carvings at the Queensland Museum, Australia 151

Figure 6.3 Distributing the Mobile Museum CD-ROMs amongst the Nalik community, New Ireland 153

Figure 7.1 Technician Mona Hess scanning the war canoe in the storage facilities of the British Museum 165

Figure 7.2 Detail of the scanned canoe hull appearing as a model on computer screen in the British Museum storage facilities 167

Figure 7.3 Detail of shell inlay on the hull of the war canoe 168

Acknowledgements

This book would not have been possible had it not been for the kind and unwavering support of the Nalik community in New Ireland, Papua New Guinea. I first conducted fieldwork in the village of Madina in 2000 towards the award of my doctorate degree, and since then, I have returned to the Nalik community almost annually. The close friendships I have developed over this time have provided me with privileged insights into Nalik society, including a window into understanding the role of plants in a rapidly changing society. I would like to thank my close colleagues in the community, in particular: Martin Kombeng, Adam Kaminiel, Richard Waika, Bob and Alice Kaminiel, the Batu and Lupai families, the Sabutan family and Professor Craig Volker for their unerring generosity in the field.

There are those friends and comrades who passed away during the writing of this text who deserve a special mention: Simon Waika, Walter Sisia, Kambarenges Benuona Luapoi, Cathy Kombeng, Dostain Homerang, Paul Lupai, Augustus Tumat and Rambana Wandalu.

I would like to thank Professor Roger Newman and Professor Alan Fernyhough at Scion Research for their support of my project during fieldwork in Rorotua, New Zealand. In the storage facilities of the British Museum, Jill Hassel and John Osbourne (now retired) were instrumental in providing access and knowledge of collections, as were Dr Lissant Bolton and Dr Ben Burt from the Department of Africa, Oceania and the Americas. Professor Edward Hviding (University of Bergen) provided me with access to and valuable insights into the Western Solomon Islands war canoe, including his draft manuscript, which I greatly acknowledge. Dr Mark Nesbitt at Kew Botanical Gardens in London provided some important insights into botanical collections and their histories. Professor Stuart Robson, Dr Mona Hess and Sally MacDonald (all UCL) worked tirelessly with me on the 3D war canoe scanning project as did PhD candidate Francesca Simon Millar. Their technical understanding of 3D scanning contributed to Chapter 7. Thanks also to the staff at the Queensland Museum, particularly Nick Hadnutt, Imelda

Millar and Michael Westaway, as well as the University of Queensland Anthropology Museum, Diana Young and Jane Willcock.

I wish to acknowledge funding from various sources. Research in New Ireland, Papua New Guinea, was funded by the Norwegian Research Council through the project 'Pacific Alternatives: Cultural Heritage and Political Innovation in Oceania' in 2009. The University of Queensland (UQ) provided generous funding through various schemes: New Staff start up grant on 'The Ideas of Materials in the Pacific', which provided funding for trips to New Ireland and New Zealand as well as trips to museum collections in Australia, New Zealand and the UK; a UQ Early Career Researcher grant to conduct further research in New Ireland; the UQ Collaboration and Industry Engagement Fund 'The Mobile Museum' grant to examine digital heritage technologies in New Ireland; and the UQ Foundation Research Excellence Award for research on knowledge networks in New Ireland. I am also grateful to have undertaken a Faculty Fellowship at the Centre for Critical and Cultural Studies at the University of Queensland in 2014, which supported the research and writing towards two chapters in this book.

My work has constantly been shaped by the kind and thoughtful comments of my colleagues. Some of the work appearing in this book was presented at seminars in the Department of Anthropology, University College London; Department of Anthropology, University of Bergen; University of Oslo; and the School of Social Sciences, University of Queensland, Australia. In particular, I wish to acknowledge the valuable feedback, encouragement and comments from Kaori O'Connor on various versions of this manuscript. In addition, the following individuals gave me inspiration and feedback during the theoretical framing and writing of my research: Mike Rowlands; Susanne Kuechler; Nick Stanley; Gay Hawkins; Paul Memmott; Martin Holbraad; Ian Lilley; Annelin Eriksen, Bruce Kapferer, Ludovic Coupaye, Eric Hirsch, Knut Rio, Cato Berg and Anna Pertierra. This manuscript also benefited from the comments of two anonymous reviewers, who provided rich and constructive feedback. There are also countless others who have also been generous in their positive engagement with my work.

Chapter 1 of this book is based on the 2013 paper 'On the Material of Mats: Thinking through Design in a Melanesian Society' *Journal of the Royal Anthropological Institute* 19 (3): 581–599 and which formed the basis for my Curl Lecture presented at the British Museum, 3 October 2011. I am grateful for Wiley for granting permission to reproduce this paper. Chapter Two extends my work on barkcloth and innovation, which was first published as 'Reviving Kapiak: Exploring the Material Identity of Barkcloth in a Melanesian Society' published in Janis Jefferies, Diana Wood Conroy and Hazel Clark (2016) *The Handbook of Textile Culture* (Bloomsbury). Chapter 3 is based on a chapter I wrote titled 'What's in a Plant Leaf? A Case Study of Materials Innovation in New Zealand' in Adam Drazin and Susanne Kuechler (2015) *The Social Life of Materials* published by Bloomsbury Academic, an imprint of Bloomsbury Publishing Plc, and extends the social history of New Zealand flax or *harakeke*. I am extremely grateful to Bloomsbury for granting me permission to reproduce these papers.

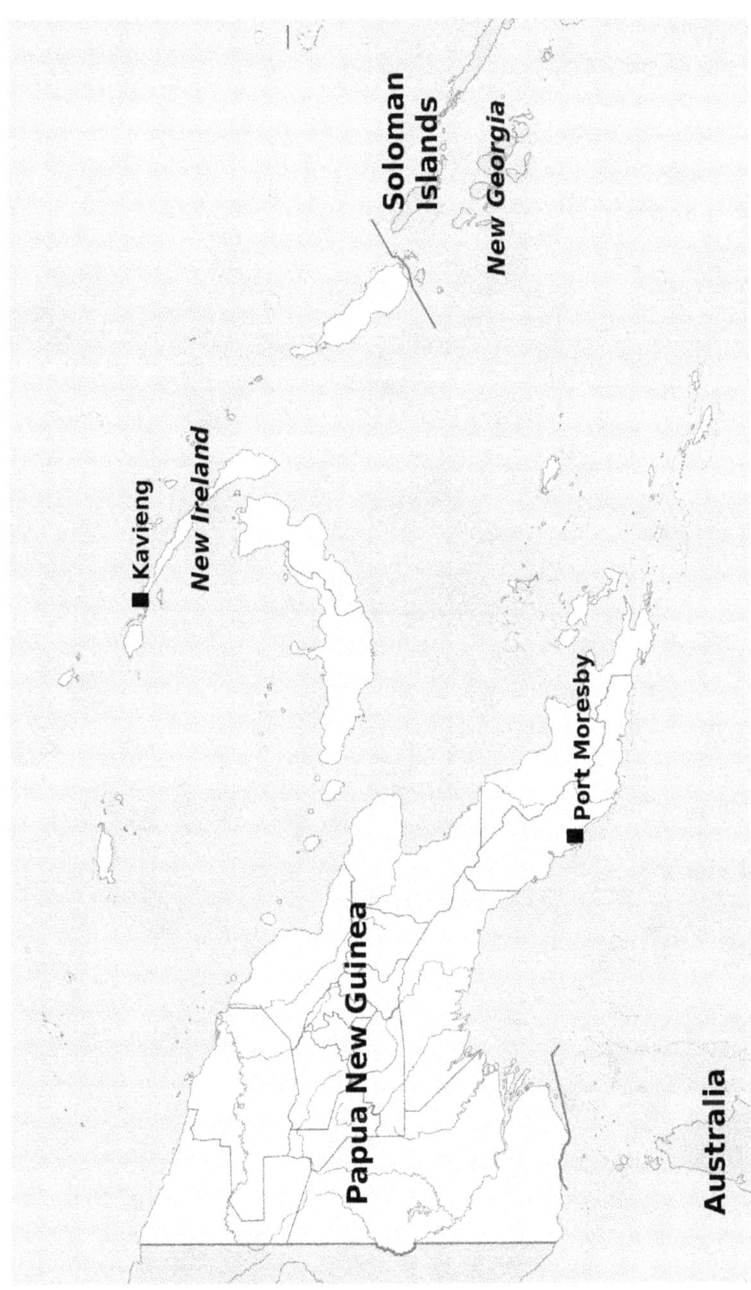

Papua New Guinea and Western Solomon Islands. Map created by the author using material from Wikimedia Commons (https://commons.wikimedia.org/wiki/File:Papua_New_Guinea_location_map.svg by NordNordWest). Published under a GNU Free Documentation Licence.

Introduction

Materials and Design

We live in a world where there are now more materials than ever before. We expect products that will improve our quality of life, incorporating materials and technologies that are efficient, cost-effective, aesthetically pleasing and sustainable, and compliant to the demands of the twenty-first century consumer. And yet, at the same time, we still know very little about how materials are used or developed, or even the processes by which these materials emerge in the world we live in. Many car drivers do not know what the steering wheel of their new car is made from, let alone the history of this material's development in laboratories and amongst users, and when it first began being used by car manufacturers and for what reasons. Seeking answers to these questions reveals important information about the complex lives of materials and their place in our society. In effect, we readily take materials so much for granted that their importance in shaping how we think and what we do is often overlooked.

Until recently, most periods of technological development were linked to changes in use of materials (Boivin 2008; Wengrow 1998). Now, it is becoming increasingly apparent that the driving force for materials innovation and design has been information technology. A range of smart materials such as temperature-responsive fabrics or self-cleaning glass are now able to process data and respond in real time to stimuli in the environment. The impact of materials innovation on our lives is that materials do more and more of the work.

In this book, my concern is to extend these stories of technological development and materials innovation beyond the world of Western societies. I go beneath the surfaces of these taken-for-granted constituents of everyday life and explore how materials innovation impacts on people's lives in the Pacific. The Pacific is an ideal region to observe and explore materials innovation because there is a long history of materials innovation continuing to the present day: from Papua New Guinea to New Zealand, driven by a variety of actors, such as local craft-makers, builders and artists or those who have visited the region, such as colonial botanists or materials scientists. Like engineered materials of Western technoscience, which were developed precisely because of their inbuilt capacity to respond to certain environments, my goal is to argue that plant materials used in design projects in the Pacific are selected on the basis of their informational capacities and so are productive of thought and action. Their selection is optimized for specific uses in the environment and to a range of contexts to which they will be exposed; and so the technical aspects of biophysical structure together with their aesthetics and design have direct outcomes in the social world.

This book, therefore, concentrates on the way materials innovation helps Pacific societies to manage their lives better, and this is an objective of human-material interaction everywhere. I delve into their rich histories in development and product design because so little is known about materials and their role in social innovation in the Pacific. Moreover, the book reveals the historical and changing nature of materials of a region, probing their complex relation to transformation and display in design activities through a diverse range of case studies from Papua New Guinea, New Zealand and the Solomon Islands. Utilizing an ethnographic framework to explore diverse contexts – such as the laboratory, the village hamlet and the museum storage facility – this book explores the complex relationship of materials to shifting boundaries and interfaces relating to culture and tradition; their relation to personifications of power and human agency; and the ideas, perceptions and associations embedded in the materials themselves, whether pandanus, bark or even digitally augmented. It breaks new ground in understandings of materiality and sociality in the Pacific by bringing the emerging theoretical literature on Western technoscience and materials innovation in direct conversation with the anthropology of material culture in the Pacific.

Game-Changers and Enablers

Western cultures have a lot to learn from indigenous engagement with plants and materials, and this book explores the role of materials as constituent elements in the formation of people's lifeworlds in the Pacific. The book highlights how through the processes of informed selection, transformation and display, plant materials in Pacific society offer the capacity to create situations and events through their integration in projects of design, whether worn on the body, in architectural design or as 3D digital objects. Plant materials such as leaves, lianas, woods, stems and sap are understood as game-changers, not simply in terms of creating form and function; they are also 'enabling' and so enact forms of sociality through their transformation and the responses these elicit. Following Elizabeth Shove et al. (2007), who introduced the notion that Western materials such as plastic are 'co-productive' (simultaneously productive of new consumer products and new modes of living), I extend this argument to the plant materials of the Pacific to focus on the way materials are generative of certain forms of sociality and modes of being. Indeed, this book demonstrates how materials not only communicate certain ideas through forms of self-fashioning, as Strathern (1979, 1988) has famously argued in relation to articulations of personhood and power in Highlands New Guinea; it is the materials themselves that also perform certain actions in the social world by 'making themselves known' (DeLanda 2006) – information in their constitution linked to their biophysical structure and outward aesthetic.

Therefore, one of my main concerns is to recognize the natural vulnerability of plant materials and frame the performance of their biophysical structure alongside their operations and effects in the social world. I trace out their complex histories and trajectories as they move through various stages in their lives (Kopytoff 1986) before they deteriorate and decay or are recycled, repurposed or discarded. In this way, their presence as much as their fragility animates thought and action and so materials are not fixed but always in a state of becoming. I emphasize their mobility and biographies precisely because recent work has underlined how materials do not arrive in the world ready to use; rather they emerge in social worlds over time having negotiated a multitude of actors as well as other competing materials – all of which have shaped the way these materials appear in the public domain (Daston and Galison 2007). In uncovering materials, I wish to rekindle the *material* in material culture by putting matter under the analytical microscope and situating it within an expanded political, historical and social framework (Barry 2013; Bensaude-Vincent 2013; Hawkins, Potter and Race 2015). In extending the scope of analysis at the margins of Western technoscience (where studies of materiality have been focused to date) and placing the analytical microscope on the Pacific, this book reveals the active nature of plant materials in design and innovation in a region where plants have long simply been taken for granted in the anthropology of material culture.[1]

While an increasing body of work on new materialism has focused on the networked assemblages of scientists, consumers, planners, funders and environmentalists in the development of materials including plastics, aluminium and concrete (Barry 2013; Bennett 2010; Hawkins, Potter and Race 2015; Latour 1996; Meikle 1995; Sheller 2014), these studies have exclusively placed their sociological analysis in the dominant realm of Western technoscience. This somehow reinforces the assumption – through its conspicuous absence – that materials innovation does not take place outside any model of Western science; that comparable types of decisions and informational networks do not exist outside the privileged world of Western society. This narrow approach has two consequences for our understanding of materials innovation. Firstly, it prevents us from understanding the dynamic relationship between society and materiality in cultures outside our own. What are the inherent processes of materials innovation in regions of the world that seemingly appear untouched by Western technoscience? Secondly, such an approach also perpetuates an invidious distinction between non-Western/natural materials and Western/synthetic materials and suggests that there is no material, design and innovation transfer between the two categories when, increasingly, this is not the case. Indeed, we simply need to look at the rise of materials libraries and the contemporary uses of botanical collections to recognize the co-dependency of natural and synthetic plant materials and how indigenous knowledge has informed Western technoscience (Gamage et al. 2012; Miodownik 2015).

In order to adopt an integrated approach to fully appreciate the complexities of materials innovation taking place in the Pacific, this book examines a series of projects of materials innovation across the region to challenge this analytical shortfall. I demonstrate how materials are quintessential to ways of being and thinking in the world and how the ever-changing nature of materials drives social transformation of a region. Today, as in the past, I argue that materials innovation is at the vanguard of social transformation because any engagement with plant materials on the part of Pacific people requires an empathy of their potential and performance together with an intellectual engagement of 'working them out'.

My case studies reveal how materials innovation is active and ongoing, expressed, for example, in the creative attempts of women and men to revive material knowledge in order to reinvigorate traditional craft production techniques. Unlike the Arts and Crafts Movement led by William Morris in Britain in the late nineteenth century, crafting practices in the Pacific are not necessarily orientated towards some nostalgia for a bygone era, a dissatisfaction with modernism and an ideological reform of art production. Rather, as I have already demonstrated in some of my published work (e.g. Were 2010), craft revival is inspired by political and religious aspirations, led by religious movements or political followers, who envisage a better future by rekindling past forms and images and integrating them into elaborate performances and practices. As I show, they have done this in order to tap into new economic, political and spiritual sources of wealth – as a means to extend their political influence beyond their immediate locale – but now are ever more networked through the opening up of mobile phone networks, diaspora communities and cheaper air travel. Sometimes, as is the case amongst Pacific communities living in urban New Zealand or Australia, materials innovation involves radical transformation and change due to the availability or lack thereof of the raw materials necessary. Coupled with a vibrant youth generation, material knowledge is being appropriated to create new visible forms of material culture, making statements about urban identity amongst diaspora communities using fashion, art and performance (e.g. Colchester 2003b).

Like Hau'ofa's 'sea of islands' (Hau'ofa 1994), which asserts a connected model of island spaces (rather than a Eurocentric one of borders and imaginary lines), this book asks how natural resources such as plant materials connect people (rather than be classified scientifically and in terms of difference) and so act as a tangible provision as a means for mobility, communication and fashioning. Equally, given the finite constraints of island societies – manifest in rights to access to land, gardens and marine resources, the impact of development and global market forces and the threat of rising sea levels and pollution from plastics and other waste products – how does the use of plant products raise important questions about sustainability and political rites of succession? Henceforth, a key question that runs throughout this book is: in what ways are plant materials optimized to take on such a pronounced role in managing informational environments in Pacific society? I explore how materials work on behalf of persons and analyse how their tooling equips them to exert influence in people's lives. In a changing Pacific, I explore the significance of sustaining material knowledge for communities, questioning how imported materials like synthetics, metals and plastics as well as new digital technologies have impacted on local forms of knowledge and skills.

And in a shifting social, religious and political space, where access to plant materials is regarded as a valuable resource, I ask how holding onto or reviving particular technical knowledge associated to plants empowers communities in a way the use of newly available ready-made materials may not.

This book frames these questions through an examination of the diverse role of materials in social transformation, focusing on their innovative use in diverse projects that reflect the changing nature of Pacific society. The fine-grained analyses of plant materials presented in this book reveal the relational nature of materials and their connection to changing gender roles and new forms of self-fashioning, which have implications for personifications of power in the region. Probing the nature of plant materials emphasizes how material identities are constantly shifting in the region and reveals the opportunities and challenges that are opened up to persons who engage materials in this way. The questions addressed in this book appear to be central to an anthropology of material culture and of the Pacific region, which has long focused on debates of materiality and personhood that have often subordinated the role of plants as derivative of human agency.[2] More generally, the book offers a departure from such conventional approaches and leads us towards an appreciation of the capacity to which materials drive society towards transformation and change, not simply in adapting materials to new uses but through their sophisticated role in managing complex informational and social environments. In so doing, it extends the concepts and theories of new materialism and Western technoscience to the Pacific (Bennett 2010; Barry 2013; Bensaude-Vincent 2011; Hawkins, Potter and Race 2015), which by the region's very omission implies that somehow the plant materials are less worthy of serious attention, which is surprising given the region's biodiversity and contribution to colonial science.

Made to Measure

This book has been inspired, in part, by Philip Ball's landmark science text *Made to Measure* (Ball 1997). In his book, Ball uses the term 'made to measure' to refer to a class of advanced materials that have been designed with particular applications in mind; in some cases, by altering their molecular structure and so enhancing their performance. Such materials have been especially engineered in laboratories to overcome specific problems for which they are designed to solve. Through their inbuilt functionality they hold capacities to 'do things that no others can' (1997: 5) and so they possess huge potential for driving innovation and change in society. Such capacities may involve using a special heat sensitive material in a thermostatic control system or a glass composite that is resistant to dirt and so can be used in office windows. As advanced materials are unique and generally expensive to make, Ball states how they are designed to fill niches in the market rather than replacing older, cheaper materials like wood or stone.

I apply Ball's concept of 'made to measure' to plant materials of the Pacific because, I argue, materials are especially selected for their known performance in the social domain. As Bensaude-Vincent (2011) states in the context of Western materials science, materials are the machines. Materials, therefore, operate as the fulcrum between technical and social worlds. In moving beyond the assumption that materials innovation is a singular act of discovery or genius, I adopt Ball's concept of 'made to measure' in order to analyse the reasons why particular plant materials are selected and transformed in design activities for the purpose of filling niches and fulfilling outcomes in the social domain, and how, as a result, materials make things happen, driving change in a society. Such a focus on materials innovation reveals the transformations taking place in the Pacific and reflects on the shifts in material identities, personhood and modernity of a region. In doing so this book presents an ethnographic description and analysis of the intentionalities of materials in design and innovation; how their informed selection, transformation and display situates anthropological discourse on the capacities of materials beyond relations to form and function and within a discussion of the nature of human agency.

Material Agency

Over the last decade or so, there has been a growing interest in anthropology on the relation between art, material culture and agency (Coupaye 2013; Harrison, Clark and Byrne 2013; Henare, Holbraad and Wastell 2007; Lemonnier 2012; Morphy 2007). Alfred Gell's 1998 *Art and Agency* has arguably been the most influential in the discipline in recent years. Gell's approach merges persons with objects and objects merge with persons in ways that suggest objects are person-like. A central feature of his theory is his analysis of the relation between style and culture. Undertaking a formal analysis of Marquesan artworks from Polynesia, Gell argues that variations and constraints (in the application of style) in the design of objects from a given region adhere to a logical system of principles. This logic, Gell argues, not only governs how style is generated but it also extends to configure the way social relations are structured. Thus what Gell presents is a model of agency in which artefactual relations map directly onto the dynamic workings of social relations in ways that challenge conventional anthropological understandings of style and culture.

While Gell's work has had a profound influence on debates around artworks and non-human agency, his model of agency does not deal directly with the materials of material culture. Instead, as Conkey (2006) argues in relation to anthropology in general, Gell's work takes a methodological approach in which materials are presented as subordinate to form and style.

As a means of redressing this imbalance, more recent work has approached the relation between materials and agency from a cross-disciplinary perspective. For instance, the term 'material agency' has been applied by Knappett and Malafouris (2008) to refer to the fluidity of boundaries between persons and things and the capacity of the latter to embody and objectify, as well as produce, social consequences (Knappett and Malafouris 2008: x). Their cross-disciplinary approach draws out the historical, political, social and intercultural dimensions of materials and agency from an archaeological standpoint in order to explore social worlds as they emerge through human engagement with materials.

Within anthropology, two key approaches have recently developed the debate on the nature of material agency. The first argues that materials help forge human lifeworlds through the human activity of making. This approach privileges technical understandings of materials and emphasizes the situated relation between material and maker. Key protagonist Tim Ingold has examined materials adopting a focus on the relationship between maker and material in crafting activities such as basketry and weaving (Ingold 2000b; 2007). He argues through hands-on interaction with materials – bending, twisting, moulding and so forth – there is an intimate relationship that connects maker and material through which the form of the artefact emerges in the world. For Ingold, material agency is expressed by the 'field of forces' that conjoins maker and material, which shapes the way in which artefacts emerge in the world (Ingold 2000b: 342).

Ingold's approach says much about the emergence of artefact form in the process of making; however, it does so at the expense of ignoring the question as to why certain materials are selected in making – a question that is central to this book. Similar to the way Gell's (1998) analysis subordinates the role of materials in material culture, in

Ingold's analysis materials appear predisposed to making, with little reflection on their affordances, aesthetics, performance and potential. Trapped within 'meshworks' (Ingold 2011), the operational qualities of materials are subordinated to the flow of emerging forms, which Ingold foregrounds in his analysis of making. In this way, I worry that a craftswoman's intimate knowledge and experience of material properties and their biophysical and aesthetic diversity makes way for an analytical focus on emergent products and corporeal forces.

An alternative approach – which draws on archaeological and anthropological perspectives – is put forward by Chris Tilley (2004), who approaches materials in terms of their materiality. Tilley (2004) has examined archaeological sites in the European landscape, arguing that the visual and tactile transformation of stone surfaces, e.g. shimmering states when wet, moss-clad, honey and ochre tones etc., can be understood to create ancestral and spiritual connections. Stones, he claims, exert their muted agency, as they impact on persons. Stone monuments embody ideas and associations and act as material metaphors by which worlds became known and inhabited (Tilley 2004: 219). Tilley concludes by stating how prehistoric social identities were created or sustained, reproduced and transformed through the agency of stones (2004: 217).

Tilley argues that material agency brings into focus an understanding of how stone helps shape human experience of landscape and cosmology (2004, 2007). Ingold, in his critique, claims that Tilley's analysis loses sight of stone's physical properties. From this perspective, culture appears to rest on the surface of stone, not permeate it (Ingold 2000, 2007). Ingold adds that in regard to the materiality approach, the transformational nature of stone surfaces appears to stand for everything out there: 'the stone is instantly swallowed up by the landscape whose surface marks an interface not between earth and air but between nature and culture, the physical world and the world of ideas' (Ingold 2007: 14).

While I agree with Ingold's critique of materiality, one could equally argue that his own approach restricts materials to a very narrow framework of making (see Knappett 2007). Ingold's aim is to examine objects as they emerge in the world *in situ*, through a material-maker interaction. I argue, in contrast, that the creative process of design involves many forms of knowledge from material knowledge, economics, markets and branding (Norman 1988; Pye 1968). A craftswoman must know how to pick the correct tools for each job in hand, costs of sourcing materials and production as well as the appearance of the product when complete. Moreover, a craftswoman is also aware that the selection of appropriate materials is crucial to design because this provides technical functionality and product identity (Ashby and Johnson 2010; Forty 1986; Shove et al. 2007). Cultural and logical perceptions may also influence her uptake of materials as well as understandings of their performance under specific conditions (Norman 1988). Therefore, materials are laden with knowledge and experience that spills out through selection and transformation in the process of design. As Bijker (1995) has demonstrated in his analysis of the design of bicycles, materials intersect with social worlds through thought and action and are mutually constitutive.

In this book, I develop an approach to materiality that, in contrast to Ingold and Tilley, situates materials within a relational field of connected and competing materials, objects and environments. In privileging the material substance and its co-dependency with the object world, my holistic approach is distinct in anthropology because it recognizes how the process of material selection involves an intellectual engagement or 'working it out' on the part of local craftspersons, who think through how certain materials with their complex positioning within natural and cultural environments and their performance as objects can fill niches or solve particular problems in society. Thus, I focus on the affordances of certain materials (ranging from recognition of their biophysical properties to their aesthetic attributes) and how technical knowledge and experience of particular plants gives rise to projects of design and making. Therefore, the informed selection of materials, like Ball's advanced materials, involves an appreciation of how materials innovation in Pacific society can be seen as a process of 'value-adding' because, as I will show, their selection is based on the premise that the materials improve people's lives by doing all the work (the material is the machine, as Bensaude-Vincent so persuasively argues) – though they may never go away, as they undergo a continual cycle of transformation, reuse and reinvention.

Materials, I will show, never really act alone but operate within complex environments through collaborations, social forces and natural cycles (Barry 2005). As Bennett (2010) rightly states, current theories about objects have been framed in terms of individualism and to an atomistic rather than congregational understanding of agency. Following Bennett's call for a more holistic understanding of agency, I will offer an analysis of the interrelation of materials to sociopolitical environments in the Pacific. This approach is similar to Shove et al. (2007), in their examination of the emergence of plastic in Western society. Their work is important to developing my own model of material agency because it draws out an understanding of the emergence of plastic in Western society by describing how plastic had first to be framed alongside other materials in order for it to be readily accepted as an alternative to existing materials. Plastic's relation to hygiene, to comfort and ease of use was as important as its physical properties: hard-wearing, easily cleaned and heat resistant. This emphasizes the mutability of materials in the course of their history as their environments shift and change (Ingold 2012).

Materials and Social Transformation

The question as to how materials enact transformations in society is an especially important one in the humanities and social sciences. While a notable number of scholars have examined the impact of cloth and clothing as they were introduced across the Pacific (e.g. Colchester 2003a; Kuechler and Were 2005; Thomas 1999) as a means to better understand the process of missionization and colonialism, there still remains little analysis of how materials are designed to perform particular tasks in society or are 'made to measure'. As Thomas (1999) has claimed, there has been a tendency in the anthropology of material culture to argue that indigenous cultures employ conservative strategies to preserve an existing order rather than transform an existing one (a factor that is reinforced through the literature on new materialism and its focus on Western technoscience – i.e. Western materials are advanced).

And yet, there is ample evidence put forward by anthropologists and archaeologists to demonstrate that materials are at the vanguard of social transformation and change. In archaeology, for example, Boivin (2008) demonstrates how the use and application of soil transformed Near Eastern Neolithic society. Her work reveals how the malleability of soil may have enabled new forms of social transformation to take effect, particularly through the application of heat and water. Of significance, Boivin states how soil was mixed with water to make a range of material artefacts, including figurines. This led, she suggests, to the emergence of material symbols that could be transported and communicated on wider scales than previously. Similarly, anthropologist O'Connor (2011) points to the transformative potential of new synthetic materials in Western society. Focusing on the development of Lycra, O'Connor demonstrates how the emergence of this synthetic in fashion clothing has helped shape and reflect new body images and social roles for Western women. Equally, in Melanesia, the influx of new materials such as calico, iron and, more recently, plastics and synthetics radically altered material culture and fostered new forms of social being in the region (Were 2005a). Colchester has argued that the emergence of cloth transformed female gender roles and led to new modes of domesticity and deportment for Pacific women in the nineteenth century (Colchester 2003a). As Thomas (1999) points out, in his analysis of how the introduction of cloth in Polynesia radically altered the ritual economy and displaced traditional materials such as barkcloth, cloth could be understood as a kind of technology; not just an expression of a new context but a technology that created that context anew (Thomas 1999: 18).

Thomas's claim that materials, namely cloth, could be understood as kinds of technology echoes strongly the argument made by Ball (1997) that advanced materials possess the inbuilt capacity to 'do all the work' on behalf of persons. Like wood composites or biomaterials, I argue that plant materials can be understood as technologies that, through their informed selection, transformation and display and can make things happen. They are the machines that create and recreate events and relations as their materiality changes through growth, aging and decay and so are reasons for driving sociality (Coupaye 2009). My concern therefore is to investigate the emergence of 'new' materials in the Pacific context, not as a way to maintain a status quo or existing social order; but rather as a calculated means to fill a niche (Kuechler and Were 2005; O'Connor 2011). This niche, I contend, can have a pervasive effect and may lead on to social transformation.

Drawing on ethnographic research based in Papua New Guinea and New Zealand, together with in-depth analyses of Melanesian objects in museum storage facilities in the United Kingdom and Australia, I reveal the ways in which materials emerge in the world much in the same way as Ball's engineered materials: that is, they offer bespoke design and perform for specific purposes and so are 'made to measure'. I show that the processes of informed selection and calculated design are embedded in complex social, historical, political and natural environments; and how materials emerge in the world infused in these environments.

Material Identities

It is symptomatic of the global concerns of environmental impact, waste management and sustainability that product designers are re-engaging with natural materials to offer design solutions. Consider the connotations of bamboo, a natural material that grows abundantly in tropical counties. For those fortunate enough to have visited or lived in

Hong Kong or Hanoi Vietnam, now modernized concrete cityscapes, many will have noticed kitchen utensils or even scaffolding crafted from the plant material. Then imagine learning how this abundant material is now used in the design of bicycle frames. Its lightness, stability and elasticity has made it an ideal material to withstand the stresses and strains of cycling and to absorb any vibrations from the road. How have perceptions of these everyday materials shifted so dramatically and what are the factors that led this everyday plant material to be reimagined in new ways?

This question could equally be applied to the many other materials of the Pacific. There, material identities are constantly shifting as the environments change around them. Materials are situated in fluid environments that redefine their use and effect. This is evident in the way craftswomen and men alike seek out new types of materials to inspire design projects, much in the same way as bicycle manufacturers have used bamboo in their innovative design. This means that materials are not placed in any static classificatory schema: rather, they are continually redefined as new materials become available and new opportunities and challenges arise in society.

To highlight the shifting identities of materials in their historical and political context, this book focuses on the selection, use and application of traditional or 'old' materials – such as beaten bark strips and woven plant fibres – and the means by which they are reinvented in ways that allow makers to take control of modes of commodity production and so enact a new and emerging form of individualized agency in society. Indeed, I demonstrate how this transformation of the natural environment into the confines of a commodified and branded world has repercussions for their operation and effects in society. For instance, taking control of natural resources such as palms and barks is to make claims to innovation and intellectual property. In (re)claiming material knowledge as one's own and utilizing this in design projects, communities in the Pacific are enacting changes in the classification of materials and bringing processes of 'heritagization' into play. Such a process, I argue, positions old materials alongside competing new materials and provides a perspective from which to understand and explore materials innovation as a relational form of action. In this way, I extend Ball's application of 'made to measure' materials to demonstrate how, in the Pacific, this concept also applies to the way materials are 'engineered' in new and innovative ways and for specific purposes in mind. This focus on materials innovation, I believe, presents an opportunity for this book to extend anthropological understandings of contemporary Pacific identities and leads to a better understanding of the dynamic role materials play in the region and beyond.

Book Orientation

This book draws together themes and contexts regarding materials and their innovation in the Pacific, engaging theoretical literature in new materialism to explore ways in which plant materials enable diverse forms of sociality – machines of nature that drive social innovation. The collection of chapters in this volume is interested in the historical and changing nature of materials, exploring the context of their transformation and display in activities in Papua New Guinea, New Zealand and the Solomon Islands. The book also unravels the relation of materials to culture and tradition and to the forms of social power these activities elicit, and provides an ethnographic context for exploring the ideas and associations embedded in the materials themselves. Each chapter points to the centrality of materials in anthropological analysis, their enduring nature as a hallmark of personifications of power and human agency and their complex relation to shifting boundaries and interfaces relating to identity.

The book is divided into three parts around which seven chapters are organized, challenging readers to think about plant materials in Pacific society as tooling for social transformation. Part I of this book engages design theory and material culture approaches to reveal ways in which plant materials possess the capacity to manage complex informational systems in the Pacific. Focused on a study of the operations and effects of particular plant materials, this work describes how materials invoke thought and action, their propensity towards designing the future and how future forms help engineer tangible outcomes in society. Each chapter takes the case of an indigenous organic material and examines its use and application within society. The aim of this exploration is to frame materials within recent theoretical debates as to their role within society and their agentive capacity. Each chapter is focused on asking what it means to liken plant materials to machines that manage complex informational systems. What are the complex environments in which material selection takes place? And, what does the selection of specific materials in design tool and equip society for?

Chapter 1 begins by examining the affordances of a class of materials. It focuses on how small differences in the appearance of plants are understood in quite different ways as to their properties in design, drawing on the pandanus, a ubiquitous plant in the Pacific that has different varieties and whose leaves are understood quite differently in terms of the biophysical properties and their use in crafting. A theoretical focus on J.J. Gibson's Theory of Affordances (Gibson 1979) aims to reveal the material engagements on the part of local craftwomen, their material knowledge of pandanus and the plant's relation to the construction of the social body and modes of kinship and exchange. A key argument introduced in this chapter is to shift anthropological understandings of materials beyond surface and visual analysis. Whereas a great deal of Melanesian ethnography has focused on kinship through the visual articulation of certain types of material and substances (e.g. Strathern 1988), this chapter innovatively reorientates this approach towards ideas of permeability and natural decay as indexes of relations in the social world.

If Chapter 1 sets the groundwork for rethinking the relation between people and things, in which things are determined through a deeper understanding of their materiality and substance and their 'co-productive' possibilities, then Chapter 2 extends this notion further through an analysis of barkcloth or *kapiak* in New Ireland society, which has recently been revived and innovated. Once manufactured in the recent past for making garden baskets and wall hangings featuring religious symbols, barkcloth has been revived by women in crafting practices for entirely different purposes. The chapter focuses on barkcloth's use in novel forms of fashion baskets, worn over the neck or on the shoulder, and emblazoned with decorative designs and pieces of coloured wool. The reintroduction of the material as something new and distinctive is crucial to establishing the success of the basket as a commodifiable product in a market saturated with many styles of baskets. I explain how barkcloth offers the basket a niche in the market, tethering the product to place, and also asserts a new form of female agency in the community through its sale in roadside stalls or the market place and its positioning outside the male dominated sphere of ritual.

Chapter 3 examines the story of *harakeke* or New Zealand flax. As a plant associated with the production of Maori treasures (*taonga*), harakeke was also cultivated by white settler society to feed the colonial economy. This chapter explores the highs and lows of the New Zealand flax industry, focusing on developments and innovations in the global hard fibre industry. Drawing on Bennett's (Bennett 2010) notion of networked materials – the idea that materials do not act alone – this analysis of New Zealand flax focuses on the wider social and political environments in which the plant fibre has been situated. Taking such an approach demonstrates how the success of this material should not be understood in isolation; rather how its performance is measured against other types of plant fibres in the global fibre industry. In particular, this chapter extends analysis to the more recent success of harakeke as a new environmentally friendly biomaterial and how its performance has now been framed within a branded context alongside the nation-branding of New Zealand as a clean, green country.

Part II of this book introduces the concept of material computation to capture design thinking and the strategic process of selecting one type of material over another. I use ethnographic case studies to frame the ways in which various timbers and plant fibres are used to create and manage social relationships on varying scales. Taking two similar objects as a starting point, Chapter 4 examines the relations between forms in the material selection of a canoe and food trough, two iconic objects of Melanesian collections. What can the expansive additive techniques of a plank canoe construction – planks of seasoned timber stitched together to form a hull – tell us about the way connections are mapped and understood as opposed to the food trough, made by hollowing out a tree trunk using a subtractive technology? Important to this discussion are the calculative processes of scale that distinguish the construction of these artefacts. My focus is to emphasize how diverse forms of relations are built into the design of vessels through calculated technical acts of making in ways that create and manage connections in the region.

Chapter 5 maintains focus on material computation through an examination of some of the classic symbols of Melanesian material culture. It explores the men's house – a ceremonial structure – and compares this to the cemetery and garden enclosure in the Nalik-speaking region of New Ireland, Papua New Guinea. Looking at how the material identity of a newly established men's house was 'built without nails' or a clan cemetery enclosure had been erected using a special kind of fish design, this chapter explores diverse forms of design thinking and the possibilities and opportunities this presents for Nalik society. Of significance is the way in which the materials are foregrounded as a particular strategy to engage new resources such as government grants and funding to help support Nalik society and place it on a national agenda. In this way, the chapter demonstrates how shifting material identities attract new forms of connections and personifications of male power through their integration into architectural forms and positioning within political spheres of display.

Part III raises the question of the future of plant materials in the Pacific, asking how new digital technologies now present in the region offer possibilities to support or disrupt knowledge networks and so transform crafting practices. This also has implications for the future of museums, and I focus on the ways in which material knowledge is recovered from museum storage facilities, reconfigured and then transmitted to communities of origin in the Pacific. If Conn (2010) questions whether museums need objects any more, then this section interrogates the rise of digital return projects that link museums to source communities to ask the provocative question: do people still need to remember crafting knowledge? Two chapters examine the nature of material knowledge as it circulates and is transmitted, taking into account traditional modes of observation and mimicry together with new forms of knowledge transmission, such as digital technologies, that are encroaching in the region.

While metal nails, woven cloth and other materials introduced by colonial officials and missionaries had a huge impact on material identities in the Pacific, it is now digital technologies that are transforming the nature of materiality and material aesthetics in the region. Maintaining a focus on the Nalik region of New Ireland in Papua New Guinea, Chapter 6 explores how new digital technologies are transforming the transmission of material knowledge in design practices. The use of these technologies, I demonstrate, is shifting the way the ancestral past is represented and indexed to a new generation of New Irelanders. In exploring the way new technologies retrieve the material past through a collaborative museum project, this chapter explores the outcomes of accessing new digital resources for the community, who claim 3D digital objects as their own. In particular, this chapter examines the digital practices performed by community members and how this integrates into the social and political context of the management of material knowledge. In doing so, this chapter draws attention to the changing nature of museum collections and the challenges and opportunities this poses for material histories of the future.

Innovative digital practices are again under scrutiny in Chapter 7 of this book. Here, the museum is the focus for a project in which material knowledge is recoded into digital formats and returned to the Solomon Islands via digital media as a way for the museum to enter into a form of 'digital repatriation'. This chapter explores the visual limits of photographic 2D and 3D representations of artefacts for the purpose of material identification and crafting revival for the benefit of communities of origin. It asks: what are the legacies of colonial collecting in today's networked society in which digital reproductions can be hastily assembled and transmitted large distances across the world's surface? It also considers how digital images are perceived by a community in the Western Solomon Islands, who claim the 3D digital object as their own. In a similar way to Chapter 6, it explores the perceptions and understandings of engagement with the 3D digital objects and the implications of this for the transmission and sustainability of material knowledge and its innovation.

The final part of this book, Chapter 8, draws together the key issues and arguments covered by this book to present the framework for a new approach to understanding materiality. By returning to the key debate in anthropology regarding the nature of materials in material culture, this chapter sets out a new framework for acknowledging the agentive capacities of materials and their relation to human thought and action. While I have shown how materials evoke thought and action in various different contexts and situations, I hope this book clearly demonstrates how materials are entirely political substances situated in environments in which knowledge, display and action are unpacked and interpreted. In this way, we can begin to appreciate how materials are potent in Pacific society; they exert particular forms of intellectual responses and they help people create, order, manage and make sense of their social world. It is the world of materials, I argue, that embodies and expresses the richness of life across the Pacific and through which sociality takes shape.

Notes

1. There is a rich history of ethnobotanical work in the Pacific that focuses on plant classifications and their uses (e.g. Bulmer and Pawley 1991; Hyndman 1984; Kwa'ioloa and Burt 2001; Nombo and Leach 2010; Sillitoe 1983). Little anthropological analysis to date has focused on plant materials as a locus of thought and action.
2. There are, however, some notable exceptions in anthropology that have approached the way plants act as agents for human sociality. These include: Coupaye (2013), Mosko (2009) and Mackenzie (1991).

PART I

Materials under the Microscope

1

ON THE MATERIALS OF MATS

Thinking through Design in a Melanesian Society

This book begins on the small tarmac airstrip in Kavieng – lying at the north-eastern tip of New Ireland – which is the main port of entry and exit to this beautiful outlying island in Papua New Guinea, situated in the crystal blue waters of the Bismarck Archipelago. As each plane unloads its cargo, a handful of arriving international tourists walk by, many carrying surfboards and attracted to the surfing and diving resorts located at the fringes of the town, the provincial capital, or a few of the remoter resorts lying a few hours south by road along one of the Pacific's most famous roads, the Boluminski Highway. There is little doubt that tourists are lured by the opportunity to surf and dive in the pristine conditions of the tropical coastline amongst the wrecks of Japanese fighter planes and coral reefs teeming with life. Few if any tourists venture inland, most likely because the forested interior is largely inaccessible by vehicle and can only be accessed by hiking on foot in uncomfortably hot, humid and mosquito-infested conditions.[1]

To some degree, I must admit that my own anthropological fieldwork amongst the Nalik people of northern New Ireland was also shaped initially by a focus on the activities that took place along the coast. From my first visit to the region in 2000 onwards, most of my time was spent documenting life in the inhabited hamlet areas along the beach front with shade and cool breezes to enjoy – a focal point for community life and domestic residence.[2] In contrast, a lesser proportion of my time was spent in the forested parts of the community, where gardens are cultivated. The forest (*bus*) is the abode of malevolent spirits (*ges*) and where pools of fresh spring water, caves and cultivated gardens can be located as well as marsupials, birds and snakes.

In this chapter I want to look closely at how the resources of the forest bring relations to Nalik society – the focus of this chapter – and how plant materials and their performance are matters of selected understanding.[3] In Nalik society, the forest plays a pivotal role in social life because of a dualism between the forest and sea (*nambis*). Naliks trace their clan lineages from apical ancestors, who lived in the forested mountains and then migrated to the coastal areas in the recent past. Ever since pacification in the early twentieth century under German colonial rule and the arrival of George Brown and the Methodists, followed by the Catholic missionaries to the island, the hamlets have been the focal point for intense ritual activities, as this is where most clan cemeteries (*rabaarau*) are now situated and a gathering point during mortuary feasts, when hundreds converge to demonstrate their relatedness to the deceased and participate in ceremonial exchange.[4]

Nalik people also identify themselves as either 'east coast Nalik' or 'west coast Nalik'; very few refer to themselves as from the interior 'bus', though one exception is the Kuot-speaking people, who are also known as the *bus pipol* (bush people), a reference to their acknowledgement as having occupied the island before the Austronesian-speaking people, who now dominate. The coast, then, with its hamlet settlements and sea air, is naturally seen as the focal point from which to begin to understand New Ireland society.

The edge of the forested interior is marked out by the Boluminski Highway, which straddles the shoreline, drawing a man-made dividing line as it weaves through coconut groves and between village hamlets, the sea and forest never far out of sight. Built under German administration in the early 1900s and now surviving as a darkened tarmac (though once made from crushed fossilized coral (*karanas*), which illuminated silhouettes of people on the road at night), the road marks an important boundary point in Nalik life between the inland mountainous forested area and the coastal hamlets built on sand and fossilized coral that stand in small clusters.

The forest is the place where plant resources can be easily located and extracted: bamboo, fruit, creepers and medicinal leaves grow abundantly. In contrast to the secret knowledge associated with performing ritual activities, knowledge of the uses and applications of plants and leaves in the forest – for everyday building, eating and craft activities – is not restricted. This does not mean this knowledge is not valued: it is acquired at a very young age, as children learn about the forest and the properties of certain leaves through senior men and women. The maintenance of this knowledge suggests that it is important and remains significant.

The forest harbours myths and stories that document the changing landscape in New Ireland. Inland tracks stretch from the coast deep inside the interior to limestone mountain ridges: some are former logging roads while others are overgrown passes to the west coast of the island.[5] There are many accounts of journeys made between the west and east coast along these tracks, from attacks from neighbouring villages to stories of mythical lakes in the interior. Rocky outcrops, stones, caves, trees and *masalei* (clan totems) demarcate the interior landscape and reveal narratives of ancestral migrations and journeys from high up in the mountains before colonial times. The forest also harbours more recent stories: accounts of local people hiding in caves in the mountains during Japanese occupation in World War II, and searches by the Papua New Guinea Defence Force for gold bullion supposedly hidden by Japanese soldiers during their occupation. More recently, the forested area was favoured for domestic residency after the king tides of December 2008 that devastated the east coast of New Ireland and forced people to set up homes further inland on higher ground.

Exploring the Interior

During fieldwork in the Nalik community in 2009 in which I embarked on this project examining plant materials, I began joining young people on their forays into the forest, where they taught me much about the different types of leaves, creepers and barks that grew there. Having grown up in the leafy suburbs of London – a world of brick and concrete intermingled with plots of green belt land – their knowledge and insights into the forest opened a completely new world for me into Nalik sociality, a world that up until then I had been blissfully ignorant as I had focused on the ritual activities of senior men and women in pursuit of my anthropological knowledge. It reminded me of the seminal essay 'The Science of the Concrete', in which Levi-Strauss introduces a series of ethnographic studies where indigenous peoples demonstrate an 'extreme familiarity with their biophysical environment' (Levi-Strauss 1966: 5) and that their 'precise knowledge' is often taken as 'an indication of attitudes and preoccupations which distinguish the natives from their white visitors'.

Levi-Strauss's insights into plant classification and knowledge were uncannily resonant for me in New Ireland. After several of these forays into the forest, both with groups of young men and with groups of women, I realized that while many leaves, barks and creepers looked almost identical, Naliks had an unswerving capacity to identify minute differences between the performance of different plant materials and knew how these could be transformed from raw materials into objects for use in everyday and ritual life.[6] Moreover, plants were useful not because of their practical functions but because, following Levi-Strauss (1966), they were good to think with and give order to the world.

This new understanding and awareness of plant materials gave me a greater appreciation of the workings of material culture than I had possessed beforehand. It led me to refocus my attention on design activities in the community and helped me more fully appreciate contexts in which makers select materials to create and manage connections between people.

After this cursory induction to the technical properties of the forest plants, my interest was sparked in the mat-making activities that were taking place in the community during my visit. With my newly acquired knowledge, I noticed that women were weaving and stitching mats from pandanus palms. Whereas before my training I did not know there were different varieties of pandanus, I now knew there were several types of pandanus palms each with their own uses and applications in mat making. It was then, by chance, that I stumbled upon a discarded mat, left decaying by the side of the Boluminski Highway in the hot and humid environment. The reason why this mat caught my eye was not just its state of neglect – it is rare to see mats cast aside like this – but also because I noticed how its construction was unlike others I had become accustomed to seeing. Typically, pandanus mats produced by Nalik women are made from tightly woven diagonal warp and weft strips – each individual leaf cut into thin strips before being dyed and woven – a technique common to Tonga, Samoa and other Polynesian islands.[7] This mat, in contrast, showed a markedly different construction. It was made by stitching and layering pandanus leaves together side by side and on top of each other at right angles so that its surface was both expansive and thick.[8]

Given my new-found interest in materials and the reasons for their selection, I immediately set to task quizzing my Nalik friends on the significance of the mat. I discovered that its Nalik name was *araazira*. They told me that this mat had most likely been produced in Mussau, an archipelago lying off the northern tip of the New Ireland mainland.[9] Mussau has a strong association with traditional mat-making practices, and women there still practise handloom weaving to the east on Tench Island.[10] Naliks often regarded Mussau people as lacking *kastom*, a state they blame on the advent of the Seventh Day Adventist Church to the islands: '*kastom i go lus*' is a familiar retort when discussions of kastom focus on Mussau. The stitched mat, however, has prevailed and has become essentialized as Mussau kastom and is still produced for life-cycle ceremonies today.

My Nalik friends told me that in the past, Nalik women once made the same type of mat for sleeping, rain capes or as body coverings; it was used in life-cycle ceremonies and exchanged between patriclans and matriclans, much as takes place in Mussau communities today.[11] But according to Naliks, the import of new kinds of mats such as the woven mat had meant that stitched mats were rarely produced or exchanged in the region today.

The story of the discarded pandanus stitched mat – and its counterpart, the woven mat – is important to this discussion of materials because it reveals the complexities of mat-making techniques in one locality and my gradual realization that there were two important factors related to these technologies. One of these was the high degree of technical knowledge that appeared to be relevant to the selection of plant materials in design. The other was that everybody seemed to know much about the use of plant materials in design. So when I

Figure 1.1 Discarded stitched mat araazira by the side of the road, New Ireland. Photograph by the author.

discovered that the discarded stitched mat was made from a type of pandanus called *amotmot*, which grows near swamps, and the woven mats were made from a variety called *awoiwoi*, cultivated near houses, and that women made technical and aesthetic distinctions between the pandanus palms, then it seemed to me that these facts were of great significance to the people who maintained this knowledge.

The focus of this chapter is to investigate how materials are implicated in the formation of social worlds in Melanesia. I will assert that while I am illustrating two specific cases in a particular region, I believe that I am dealing with an anthropological problem, in that materials are often downplayed in the analysis of social and technical systems. As Ingold (2000b, 2007) asserts, anthropologists have tended to treat materials as substances that are acted upon and so ensuring that materials remain analytically distinct from persons. My project, then, is to engage with the social and technical aspects of materials in a way that promotes 'a sensible enquiry into materials, their transformations and affordances' (Ingold 2007: 3). Drawing attention to materials is to foster a mode of analysis whereby the 'material may itself enunciate meanings' (Henare et al. 2007: 4) in ways that make the intentionalities of material selection evident.

Materials and Design

Until recently, anthropologists had paid little attention to the materials of material culture, favouring instead explorations of style and form (Conkey 2006; Ingold 2000b). This has rapidly changed in the last decade, however, with the development of research that has focused on phenomenological approaches to materials (Ingold 2000a; Tilley 2004), the role of materials in communication and social innovation (Boivin 2008; Wengrow 1998) and how the emergence of new materials transforms body and gender images (Colchester 2003a; O'Connor 2011).

One of the most significant contributions in anthropology to deal with technical aspects of materials has been by Tim Ingold. In his essay 'On Weaving a Basket', Ingold points out that in anthropology, materials and culture do not mix. It is the form of the artefact and not its substance that is attributed to culture (Ingold 2000b: 340). That is why, he says, little attention is paid to actual materials and their properties. It is as though culture impresses itself on materials though fails to permeate them. In his counterargument, Ingold presents the case of the basket-maker: he describes how the basket-maker bends and interweaves fibres (2000b: 342). His argument establishes how an intimate relation exists between maker and material that is brought into existence through a play of forces (both internal and external because of the basket's tensile structure). Ingold's point is to argue that through the collaborative relationship between maker and material, 'form unfolds within a kind of force field' that draws the maker into a sensuous engagement with the basket's surface (2000b: 342). Thus, for Ingold, the basket-maker works within the world rather than upon it so that baskets emerge within the form-generating process rather than pre-existing as a condition for it (2000b: 347).

Ingold's work is especially important, as it demonstrates how objects emerge through a combination of natural and cultural processes. The biophysical properties of materials are as important to generating form as the skilled movements of the basket-maker's hands. While it is not Ingold's intent to focus on the process by which basket-makers choose their materials, his special emphasis on weaving as a process of world-making is at the expense of any understanding of how a basket-maker selects materials for weaving. Are there particular types of grasses that are especially sinewy? Perhaps some are water resistant whilst others can easily be dyed? It is as though materials arrive in the world predisposed to basketry, blacksmithing or pottery.

With Ingold's contribution in mind, this chapter will address the downplaying of materials by focusing on their selection and uptake in mat making in Melanesia. I will approach material selection as an informed decision-making process situated in the human activity of design. Design is an important frame through which to understand materials because, rather than simply being a meaningless exercise in style or exploration of technology, the ongoing activity of design involves the process of making decisions in order to create new possibilities in the social world by offering solutions and innovation in people's lives.

Central to design is the choice of materials (Ashby and Johnson 2010: 4). Materials are crucial to design because they provide technical functionality and product identity. Materials may be selected on the basis of the technical requirements of design, their scientific properties or their identity and classification (Shove et al. 2007). These decisions rely on our perceptions of materials as well as our understanding of how they perform under specific conditions. Through knowledge and experience, we learn about materials, we attach particular associations and we may develop classifications for their use. It is our tactile encounters with materials that influence their uptake in design and so leads to an appreciation of materiality as a complex network of design decisions (Forty 1986). Moreover, materials are intimately linked to action through their capacity to instigate social change (Boivin 2008). That is why, as I will show in this chapter, material selection is as crucial to design as it is to innovation and change in society.

Affordances of Materials

One way to think through the question of how materials are taken up in design and how they create social effect is to focus on affordances and constraints (Knappett 2005). In his essay 'The Theory of Affordances' (1979), J.J. Gibson states that affordances offer action possibilities of the environment that any person may recognize. Affordances are not just abstract physical properties of the environment but are what the environment offers – what it provides or furnishes. Materials are always relative to persons. For example, a ledge may be a barrier to an infant but not for an adult. Similarly, a snail may crawl along a tree branch, but the weight of a cat may prevent it from doing this. For Gibson, human perception is geared towards reacting to possibilities afforded by the environment; and this is always in relation to the subject.

While Gibson's theory of affordance is useful because it introduces an idea of an intellectual response to materials in the environment, Gibson has been criticized for being too radical and one-sided in his understanding of affordance. Notably, in his archaeological engagement with Gibson's theory, Knappett states that 'what Gibson succeeds in demonstrating is the reactive/executive nature of human perception and cognition in material circumstances'. (Knappett 2004: 44). Knappett utilizes Gibson's example of the letter box to critique the one-sided nature of the theory. Gibson argues that it is the physical characteristics of the letter box that announce its function in a direct and unmediated way. This raises questions about other objects such as litter bins, which resemble letter boxes. We could ask whether we could post letters in these too because the function of the letter box is not derived from its physical form alone but also its cultural associations, indirectly perceived, that constrain its function, such as its colour and positioning.

Knappett's work is important to an anthropological analysis of material selection, as it demonstrates the sociality, relationality and transparency of affordances (2004: 46). In other words, affordances are not simply directly perceived, but the properties of materials may be understood in terms of their performance, their relation to other materials and their context of production and use. This approach demonstrates, as Barry (2005) has argued in relation to laboratory-made materials, that materials are situated in complex informational and material environments.

The understanding that materials are socialized in design has been recently developed in the work of Shove et al. (2007), who engage with affordance as a means to understand how the identities and properties of materials help shape the products they produce. Through an investigation of the development of plastics, Shove et al. demonstrate how materials enter multiple arenas where plastics are framed in relation to existing materials. They show how plastics are embedded in complex social networks through which performance of materials can be measured and understood in their use and application as objects. Sociality makes the otherwise invisible properties of plastics real: its potential for colour, flexibility and mouldability (2007: 102–3). Its properties are positioned in relation to existing classifications of materials against which plastics are designed to compete. Their work demonstrates how affordances generate 'a co-production of possibilities' contingent on the performance of things both as materials and as products and provide an important explanation for innovation in society (2007: 94–95).

If Shove et al. frame their analysis of materials through a discussion of how affordances are instrumental in informing object and material relations in design, then Norman's seminal work *The Psychology of Everyday Things* (1988) brings affordances more directly in relation to action through a discussion of constraint. In his critique of Gibson's theory, Norman believes that affordances result from the mental interpretation of things, based on our past knowledge and experience applied to our perception of the things about us (Norman 1988: 219). He states how affordances provide strong clues to the operations of things (1988: 9). But there are also factors that constrain what an object affords. He cites physical limitations, cultural factors, semantic understandings and logical underpinnings as particular constraints that shape an object's possible use. Norman states that affordances refer to the perceived and actual properties of objects, primarily those fundamental properties that determine just how the thing could possibly be used. An affordance is not an independent property of the object itself, nor is it exclusive to the subject's mind; rather it is a relational property shared between the subject and the environment.

A crucial dimension to Norman's theory of design is his concept of 'mapping' as a property of affordance (Norman 1988: 23). Norman defines mapping as the relationship between two things – that is, how design decisions create visible and logical outcomes in the social world. For instance, a designer may use a spatial analogy as a form of 'natural mapping'. To control the lights in a room, the light switch panel on the wall may reflect the spatial arrangement of lights on the ceiling. Here, any user effortlessly perceives the designer's intentions. Alternatively, bad design is where the intentions of the designer do not map readily to the perceptions of the user.

While Norman's approach is developed through case studies of Western design products and is focused primarily on the finished artefact over material selection, I nevertheless want to argue that his concept of mapping has special application in Melanesia, as it captures the way in which materials are met with highly intellectualized responses in the region. My intention is to argue that amongst the Nalik people in northern New Ireland, the concept of mapping plays a fundamental role in understanding the selection, uptake and transformation of materials where there is a diversity of plant materials used in design. Mapping, as a logical property of affordance, informs how materials are imagined and acted upon through technical processes, opening design possibilities as much as constraint in the process of production. This logic, which is shared intersubjectively, emphasizes a focus on material thinking, not just on the properties of materials but also on how these properties – through transformation – connect to the social world. Moreover, mapping – as a type of material thinking – explains how social and temporal relations are condensed into objects through the incorporation of select materials, thus allowing different forms of sociality to emerge in the process. Foregrounding a notion of mapping, I believe, helps explain how materials, through the process of design, give concrete expression to the social world, as it has long been known that materials and substances play a prominent role in Melanesian sociality (Strathern 1988).

The Nalik of Northern New Ireland

The Nalik people are a matrilineal society of around 5,000 Austronesian speakers situated in northern New Ireland, Papua New Guinea. They are horticulturalists, cultivating gardens on the interior slopes that lead up to rocky limestone ridges that form the backbone of the island. Naliks also engage in the production of cash crops, such as oil palm, cocoa and copra, and many people commute to Kavieng town by a regular bus service to work in trade stores or in local government.

Amongst anthropologists and art connoisseurs, the Nalik people are famous for a complex set of funerary rites that involves the production and revelation of carved effigies known as *malangan*, documented extensively by anthropologists, museum curators and collectors (Gunn and Peltier 2006; Kuechler 2002; Were 2010). During these funerary rites, clan alliances are renewed, marriages are announced and land is transacted between clans. Such life-cycle ceremonies focus on producing an image of unity, and it is during these events that ancestral images are revealed publicly and Naliks engage in ceremonial exchange.

Nalik society is organized around a series of exogamous clans (*watbung*) named after types of birds, which are divided into lineages. Each person belongs to a clan traced through his or her mother and is *dere* (of the same blood) to persons of the same patriclan. The lineage of the mother's clan is crucial in establishing kinship and social organization. Before pacification of the region, people lived in the mountains in exogamous groups, fleeing inter-clan warfare that plagued the region. As the missionaries established control over the island, people settled in hamlets along the coast. Clan lineages identify themselves by tracing their movement (*lemlem*) from the mountains to the coast, so clans comprise of lineages determined by their journey through the landscape.

The contribution of the patriclan in shaping, nurturing and forming Nalik persons is acknowledged through a series of small feasts conducted throughout a person's life in which cooked pig and root vegetables are prepared in a stone oven (*faamatkibal*, literally 'to give food back'). Feasts such as faamatkibal acknowledge the work of the patriclan and secure land for resident children (who are of the mother's clan). In the past, Naliks say a patrilocal marriage system existed, so exchanges to secure land were crucial to maintain traditional alliances; however, they claim that the introduction of mission Christianity, colonialism and migrant plantation labourers has disrupted traditional marriage patterns so that both matrilocal and patrilocal residency now take place.

As the introduction to this chapter outlines, Nalik social life is focused on a string of small hamlets that exist along a thin strip of land bordered by the sea on one side and a steep forested interior on the other. Along the east coast, the Boluminski Highway cuts a thin line between the forest and the hamlet (the coast). The forest and the coastline sustain a rich diversity of natural resources – which Naliks utilize – including several species of the pandanus palm. The inland forest area is turned over to garden land, and there are also vast acreages where coconut and oil palm plantations have been established and, more recently, cash crop production of cocoa and vanilla. Coconuts were planted under the German colonial administration for harvesting the cash crop copra. Large plantations along the Boluminski Highway – including the large Poliamba site in Lukuramau, which is a major employer in the region – are run by international oil palm corporations.

The forest is abundant in plant materials, and on several forays with groups of men and women, I was taught how to identify, process and use different types of creepers, barks and leaves for craft production.

The Pandanus Palm

According to the ethnobotanist Jebb (1991), pandanus plants are notoriously difficult to identify due to similarities between palms making any systematic classification of the plant hard to find in Papua New Guinea. In northern New Ireland, in contrast, Naliks appear to be especially adept at identifying and classifying different plant species.[12] They differentiate between at least seven different types of pandanus palms, which they recognize by their type of fruit, the shape of the stem, the prop root system, the shape of their leaves and their place of cultivation. Their leaves – to the untrained person – appear very similar and grow in clusters right out of the ends of the branches. They are shaped like long, thin swords, some over 1.5 metres in length; others are much wider. They have two lateral pleats that fold in the opposite direction making an M-shaped section. Some leaves are stiff and point upwards, while others are soft and fold over. Leaves are green or they may be a combination of green with white or yellowish stripes. They have sharp tips and little prickles along their perimeters and midveins.

Pandanus palms are related to places in the landscape. Some women cultivate certain types of pandanus in the vicinity of their houses, especially those women who are renowned for producing woven mats. Other types of pandanus are harder to locate: for instance, a pandanus palm sometimes used for mat making is called *amazaraas*. This palm grows in swampy areas. The leaves are long and narrow with needles along its edges and midvein. Women fold the leaf under itself using a pair of tongs, so that there is a doubling of the leaf. Mat-makers say that this doubling creates a cushion effect in the mat.

Naliks utilize various parts of the pandanus palm, although some leaves, fruit and tuberous prop roots may be potent or poisonous and are thus harvested with extreme care. Prior to dealings in the ancestral domain, a small piece of the tuberous prop root may be chewed by men whilst undergoing ritual seclusion or performing magic. Or the leaves of the pandanus may be tied around the trunk of a betel nut tree to signify a prohibition on its harvest or placed on houses or plots of land to signify a dispute. Transgressing this stipulation may incur injury, as anybody moving across the leaf boundary may become afflicted with illness or misfortune. For this reason, this leaf tie – known as *gorgor* – is quintessentially referred to as New Ireland law (*lo*) and for many typifies the New Ireland character (*pasim*) of seeking resolution to disputes.

Other types of pandanus are harvested for their fruit. The pandanus known as *avadin* bears a sweet fruit and grows in grassland areas located between the coastline and the mountains. The leaves are also used for making mats and baskets. A story exists that recounts how the sweetness of avadin fruit had been kept secret by chiefly men in the village until it was finally revealed during a famine. The story explains why people today tend to eat the fruit when food is scarce. Another type of pandanus, *abulume,* is also eaten. Its coloured fruit is baked by women at certain times in the life cycle to make a red, orange or yellow paste of blood-like consistency. The palm is recognizable by its thin trunk and long thin leaves.

Men harvest the phallic tuberous prop roots of the *azafna* pandanus, which are cut down and transformed through beating and soaking in seawater, into cordage threads. The threads are then woven into circular funerary effigies known as *wawara*. These types of malangan are considered to be the most potent of all malangan effigies and are often destroyed immediately after display, as Naliks believe that incorrect use can cause death. The leaves are also used as coverings for sago; parcels of which are hung by women under the eaves of houses during mortuary feasts. This suggests, therefore, that a gendering of parts of the pandanus exists.[13]

I have mentioned several types of pandanus palms that are selected for specific purposes in the Nalik area as well as suggesting their relation to events in the life cycle. For the purposes of this argument, I want to concentrate on the two types of pandanus whose leaves are specifically harvested for making the two mats I mentioned at the beginning of this chapter. The first is called amotmot, the pandanus palm that is used for making the stitched mat araazira. The other is called awoiwoi, which is used to weave the Polynesian-style mat *amat*.

Amotmot Pandanus

The pandanus amotmot grows to a height of 30 to 40 feet in swampy areas inside the forest. It has large stiff green leaves measuring 15–20 cms in width and about 1.5m long, with needles along the edges and

Figure 1.2 Harvesting the prop roots of the azafna pandanus. Photograph by the author.

midvein. Individual leaves are rigid, waxy and fibrous, with parallel veins running longitudinally from its base to the tip. Their waxy texture makes them water resistant, and this is an important quality of the amotmot. Nalik women say the palm is a lot like the *avaum* – a pandanus with long leaves that grows on the sandy beaches – however, they prefer the leaves of the amotmot because they say the leaves feel slightly softer and thinner.

Local women use the *tok pisin* phrase: '*wok bilong em*' – literally, 'its work' (referring to the palm leaf) to describe a sequence of possible technical actions performed on each leaf. For example, Mrs Sioti, a prominent mat-maker in the Nalik community, once cut down several types of leaves to educate me on a range of techniques: scraping, cutting, stitching, heating, sun bleaching etc. She used 'wok bilong em' to express a set of possible transformations of the leaves. The phraseology depicted suggests that leaves used for crafting elicit certain actions: the leaf is approached using prescribed technical acts rather than the craftsperson imagining what could be done to a pile of freshly cut leaves.

During fieldwork in October 2009, I witnessed Mrs Waika, a mat-maker from the Nalik village of Panafao, prepare amotmot leaves for the sewing of an araazira. 'Wok bilong em' began with the harvesting of young leaves of the amotmot. She collected the leaves from a swampy forest area belonging to the matriclan where the pandanus was known to grow. Mrs Waika cut the younger green leaves using a bush knife, as the older ones were blemished or broken. She then brought the leaves back to the village and removed the leaf's needles along its edges and midvein with a sharp knife.

The next stage involved heating the leaves in order to soften them, as the leaves, I was informed, were liable to snap or break. She made a fire from dried coconut shells and leaves, and she then held each amotmot leaf over the fire for about a minute or so, kept in a state of motion in order not to burn them. Once softened, Mrs Waika then rolled the leaves with the shiny surface inwards before she pressed them together with her hands. The leaves were then left to dry in the sun.

Since araazira are rarely produced today and are considered by knowledgeable Naliks as 'of the past', Mrs Waika explained the process of stitching the mats. She showed me how women bundle several rolls of leaves before they start to stitch. She recounted how women use a fine thread sourced from a particular type of creeper (*ayaaba*) that grows in the forest and is rolled into fine cordage. Women would pierce a series of equidistant holes along the edges of the two leaves through which they thread the cordage. The two leaves would then be sewn

Figure 1.3 Mrs Waika showing amotmot pandanus leaf, used for making stitched mats. Photograph by the author.

together longitudinally using a running stitch, tacking together the adjacent edges like a hem. Each leaf would then be placed alongside an adjacent leaf of similar length, though tip to toe to preserve equal width.

Once the required surface area has been achieved, Mrs Waika explained how the mat-maker then would turn the leaves at a ninety-degree angle and layer the subsequent leaves, stitching them together to form a thick surface. A third layer is added: this would involve turning the leaves again through another ninety degrees and stitching the leaves again. The result is a piled smooth shiny mat that is highly durable and water resistant.

In addition to the technical process of stitching, the mat is also significant in the way it is folded for storage. Rather than being rolled, it is folded in half and half again after use. I will demonstrate in Chapter 4 how scaling is an important attribute of the design process in terms of material selection and how acts of calculation enable people to manage social relations.

Several references to the araazira in ethnographic literature point to its functional use as a protective covering. Anthropologist A.J. Duffield notes its use as a bonnet and a cloak in New Ireland (Duffield 1886). He observes how:

> The men go absolutely naked, but the women wear "aprons" of grass in front and behind, suspended from cinctures, made of beads strung on threads drawn from the leaves of the aloe. The women also make an excellent bonnet from palm leaves, and also a cloak which covers the back and head, used only in the rainy season; they evinced great fear of getting wet in the rain. (Duffield 1886: 117)

Similarly, the anthropologist Sidney H. Ray, writing in 1892, notes how on the island of Nusa at the northern tip of New Ireland: 'The people are nearly nude. The women wear an apron or leaf not larger than a leaf of the Australian gum tree, and long peaked hats made of pandanus leaves sewn together' (Ray 1892: 4). These hats, a concertinaed type of mat, are known by the Nalik term *arekrek*, once worn by women to the garden though still worn today when women dance the *amuna* performed at mortuary feasts. The hats carved into the malangan funerary sculpture demarcate a deceased female.[14]

Other types of pandanus leaves are also utilized as forms of protection and give an indication of what possibilities pandanus afford to Nalik people. Special types of pandanus leaves, avaum, are cut down from trees along the coastline and transformed into food parcels during funerary rites, marriages and births. To the untrained eye (such as the anthropologist's), these leaves physically resemble the amotmot leaf though of course Naliks may find discernible differences. Each leaf, measuring up to two metres, is held over a fire before its needles are cut off and the outer surface peeled back. The leaves are rolled into cylindrical bundles then flattened before then being tacked together to form a mat. The dried midrib of the coconut leaf (*nok*) is used for tacking, broken into short lengths (about 5 centimetres) and prized through the edges of adjoining leaves. Food such as cassava or taro is placed on the mat before being wrapped and then placed in the fire and covered with stones. The covering acts as a kind of membrane – thick enough to protect the food from burning and thin enough to allow heat to penetrate in the stone oven.

I will demonstrate how the amotmot leaves fulfil a similar function of permeability and protection and that this property is crucial for the leaf's selection in the design of this stitched mat. It is well-documented in anthropological literature how woven wraps of all sorts are deemed to protect the body (Gell 1993; Kuechler and Were 2005; Thomas 1999; Were 2010). Similarly, Naliks say that the design of the araazira – created through the stitching and layering of leaves – functions as a form of protection. The amotmot leaf provides a durable waterproof layer for protection from rain. Protection is required, as Naliks believe there are harmful life forces that attack when the body is in its most vulnerable state: during periods of fasting, pregnancy and birth, causing illness or even death. Rain is also said to weaken the body. *Birua*, spirits of the dead who have died unnatural deaths (e.g. murder), plague villagers in the wet season and travel in the form of rain clouds over the ocean. As a raincape, the araazira plays an important role in protecting the body from the birua.

Modelling Social Relations

To understand how the amotmot maps an image of Nalik sociality, we need to examine why the pandanus was selected in the production of the araazira. Naliks say that in the recent past, an araazira was made for a woman by her husband's clan (the patriclan of her future children) and presented to her at a marriage ceremony to cover her during periods of pregnancy and to cover her first born child. On the birth of the child, a ceremony (*vaazufnalik*) was held in the mother's resident hamlet (and this practice still continues today). The term vaazufnalik literally means to 'wash the baby'. The mother is brought out to the centre of the village hamlet, and clansmen and women who gather during the day present shell money and food to mother and child. The woman and newborn were covered in the araazira along with decorations and body paint; a chiefly man (*maimai*) removes the araazira during the ceremony.

The revelatory process of removing the araazira and exposing mother and child publicly is met with a series of exchanges in which clan groups, allied through historical alliances to the matriclan and patriclan of the mother, move towards the couple and lay gifts of shell money and root vegetables. This follows a similar pattern of events as a malangan mortuary feast, described by Kuechler (2002) and Were (2010), in which an image of clan corporatism is generated and through which processes of renewal are allowed to take place.

The technique of stitching and layering amotmot gives concrete expression to an image-based logic of clan corporatism and growth. The adding of leaves side by side and on top of each other creates an image of the expansive and co-dependant nature of relations in which Nalik persons are implicated and for which the araazira is designed to sustain through its protective envelope. This model of social relations is known by the Nalik term *vabalos* and refers to the process by which clans nurture and support each other through mutual cooperation. Vabalos acknowledges the centrality of the matriclan in rights over land

and the biographical relation of women to the land, forged through the patrilocal marriage system or the migration (*lemlem*) of women through the landscape as a result of warfare prior to pacification. Naliks explain the term much like the running of a stitch: land moves back and forth between clans, accumulating with time the names of Nalik women who once occupied the land, much in the same way as the pandanus leaves are stitched together and layered on top of one another. Thus, the araazira presented to a woman for the vaazufnalik ceremony is acknowledged as having been made by a female mat-maker from the husband's clan, using resources harvested from clan land. The material elements of the mat, as well as the mat itself, therefore elicit clan relations and enchain names of Nalik women.

Norman (1988) writes that the fundamental principles of design are to make ideas visible through the provision of a strong conceptual model. In the case of the design of the araazira, I have demonstrated how the selection of the amotmot brings to the fore ideas about biographical relations as much as the technical properties required for the product. This reflects Damon's ethnographic analysis of the materials used in the design of the Massim outrigger canoe (Damon 2004; see also Damon 2017). Damon demonstrates that what is important

Figure 1.4 Vaazufnalik, ceremony to 'wash the baby', Panafao village, New Ireland. Photograph by the author.

in understanding the design of a canoe is how the selection of materials used in its construction is as much about technical specifications and performance as it is about eliciting biographical relations to land. While the outrigger must remain seaworthy, and so the performance of the selected materials carries great risk if they were to fail, pandanus leaves are selected on the basis of their performance in different ways.

Central to Norman's understanding of affordance is the introduction of constraint in design outcomes (Norman 1988). This is made manifest in the selection of the amotmot in the design of the araazira. Naliks recognize that the araazira has a limited capacity to sustain the social relations for which it has been designed, much like human bodies. This is because after periods of usage, the amotmot leaves and the cordage tying the individual leaves together start breaking apart or decaying (and I found several stitched mats lying at the back of Nalik houses literally falling apart). Indeed, mat-makers select the amotmot pandanus precisely because of its known performance: they recognize that the leaves are water resistant and that the fibres begin to break down after a finite period of time.

This inbuilt obsolescence of the mat provides sufficient protection to the social body when it is in its most vulnerable state; but once damaged or decaying, its resistance to the elements obviously decreases. This inevitable breakdown of the mat's membrane structure – its ultimate failure – supports a renewed cycle of mat production, which in turn helps to maintain inter-clan relations through their exchange. Indeed, as DeSilvey (2006: 323) points out 'decay reveals itself not (only) as erasure but as a process that can be generative of a different kind of knowledge.' In the context of New Ireland, this knowledge is made visible in the natural compliance of the material – its operational realism as a perishable entity – and also how the materials are productive of new social relations in the community.

Awoiwoi Pandanus

While the araazira mat thrives on a notion of corporate identity and limited durability that operates through the selection of amotmot pandanus leaves, in contrast, I want to demonstrate how the woven mat made from the leaves of the awoiwoi pandanus palm resists the mapping of Nalik sociality through its transformation and instead offers a different material identity to that of the amotmot.

Like the leaves of the amotmot pandanus, the awoiwoi has parallel vein leaves that are rigid when young, and they have needles running along the edges and midvein. Nalik women say they choose the young leaves as these are more workable: they are also free from blemishes, tears or other damage that older leaves suffer. The palm leaves vary in colour: some green, others variegated with yellow streaks. Women say that the green leaves feel heavier than the variegated ones. They choose the former for mat making, as the leaves are considered to be thicker; the latter are chosen for basketry, as the leaves are considered to be lighter.

Figure 1.5 Awoiwoi pandanus in village hamlet. Photograph by the author.

Two renowned Nalik mat-makers, Mrs Sioti and Mrs Sabutan, demonstrated how to make woven mats. Both cultivate awoiwoi palms in close vicinity to their houses, where they can be propagated as runners and offshoots in sandy soil. The mat-makers transformed the leaves of the awoiwoi into materials ready for weaving through the following series of technical actions (Coupaye 2013; Lemonnier 2012), a process that could take several weeks. 'Wok bilong em' is as follows:

Step 1) Harvesting: women select the young green leaves near the apex of the leaf shoot of the awoiwoi pandanus. These are generally cultivated close to the hamlet.

Step 2) Drying: the leaves are dried in the sun. This process whitens the leaves; the leaves also shrink and become soft in texture (some women may even whiten the leaf by soaking it in bleach or spitting chewed coconut meat on the surface).

Step 3) Rolling / unrolling: the leaves are rolled around the hand and tied together in a cylinder. They are stored for several days before they are unrolled and placed out again in the sun.

Step 4) Softening: the leaves are unrolled and the backs of the leaves are scraped with a sharp knife. The leaves are rolled again and tied into cylinders.

Step 5) Unrolling / cutting: the leaves are unrolled and cut into strips to make diagonal warp and wefts.

Step 6) Dyeing: shop-bought dyes are used and the leaves are soaked in them.

Step 7) Weave: women weave the mat with a warp and weft technique. This takes place during the night when the air is cooler. The leaves are considered to be more compliant to weaving then.

Step 8) Rolling: the mat is rolled up and stored ready for use.

Unlike the araazira, these mats are not considered by Naliks to be protective or traditional by any means but are used instead for sleeping or sitting on. Naliks consider them to be products of an individual woman's agency and a materialization of her technical expertise. If the same technique of weaving mats gives concrete expression to an image of hierarchy and status in Tonga as Kaeppler (1999) explains, then what model of sociality emerges from the woven mat in Nalik society?

Almost all the mat-makers I met who were producing woven mats from awoiwoi were married into Nalik society from other parts of Papua New Guinea. They had acquired the skills to weave mats whilst in New Ireland or visiting relatives elsewhere. The fact that these women are landless in the village emphasizes, in contrast to the araazira, how the mats cannot be understood in terms of managing corporate clan relations. Instead, I contend that the selection of the awoiwoi in the production of the mat thrives on an individualized agency exercised through maintaining disparate and distant social connections. Indeed, this emphasizes my point at the beginning of this chapter where I questioned Nalik assertions that the woven mat had replaced the stitched mat.

Woven mats are exchanged informally amongst Naliks and are generally woven for a particular person in mind: for close friends, church colleagues or a relative living far away, such as in Port Moresby. It is typical to see mats loaded onto aeroplanes at Kavieng Airport or small dinghies, returning to Simberi, the island off the east coast of New Ireland. This informal gift economy serves to strengthen and consolidate social relations through the individualized productivity of female mat-makers in the community.

Knowledge of the technical processing of plant materials is competitively sought after by Nalik women. During fieldwork in October 2009, I witnessed women producing barkcloth (*kapiak*) from the inner bark of the breadfruit tree. As I demonstrate in Chapter 2, some weavers were using the material as coverings for plaited coconut

Figure 1.6 The late Mrs Cathy Kombeng drying awoiwoi pandanus in her house ready for mat making. Photograph by the author.

baskets, attaching threads of wool and other decorations to personalize their designs. Up until recently, barkcloth was considered to be 'of the past' and had ceased production altogether.[15] Today, after a sudden revival in barkcloth production, the story is very different, with women searching out old materials to design new products. Competitive rivalry between Nalik women is such that it underlines the rewards of possessing material knowledge, as it enhances their capacity to operate social networks, which in turn bring obligatory rewards and returns in the future. It also introduces an aspect of constraint in design (Norman 1988), as any restrictions of access to technical knowledge may increase the value of the product.

To understand why woven mats emerged as the solution to intellectually manage a limited resource in ways that give rise to new forms of social power in the Nalik area, I want to focus briefly on the social and technical properties of the material. Nalik women propagate their own plants by cutting and planting offshoots close to their house or along the roadside. As a non-native plant, it does not attract the biographical relations that are elicited with the amotmot. Furthermore, Naliks do not refer to the plant idiomatically, whereas other plant shoots such as banana tubers are talked about to express relations to the land and migrations of women. Rather, the fact that the makers are aware that the awoiwoi leaf – once transformed – can hold dye means that a Nalik woman can tether her productive agency to the mat she weaves through the coloured patterns she incorporates.[16] Norman (1988) refers to this as a logical mapping: the technique of incorporating different coloured patterns makes visible the relations to personhood (Were 2010). Thus, the awoiwoi supports an image of self-replication and multiplicity that is also suggested through the techniques of cutting and stripping individual leaves into many strips.

Furthermore, Nalik mat-makers know that the strips of awoiwoi leaf are far more robust and superior in strength to the amotmot. Their biophysical properties thus allow for greater mobility, and this explains their capacity to extend relations beyond the northern New Ireland mainland. It also means that the mats can be used on an everyday basis, for sleeping on or sitting on. The mat's durability was emphasized to me by several Nalik mat-makers, and from this we could infer that the awoiwoi leaves are selected precisely because they sustain a certain type of individualized relationship over an extended period of time and on a larger scale, which one day could be renewed (if at all).

To sum up then, this comparison of two different types of pandanus leaves has tried to demonstrate their separate, though connected, material identities and the outcomes of this for the design of mats. Affordances make this possible, and it is through Norman's notion of mapping and constraint that we can begin to appreciate how materials give concrete expression to the social world. The amotmot pandanus maps an image of localized, traditional social networks, sustained over a shorter, intense duration through its production and usage at life-cycle events, as a protective covering. The awoiwoi, on the other hand, maps an image of a wider network of individualized relations that require renewal less often due to the durability of the materials. As two different types of mats, it is important to state that the woven mat did not replace the stitched one. Rather, I have tried to show how a new class of pandanus is positioned with respect to existing taxonomies of performance and product and how relational schemas of meaning emerge over time.

Conclusion

In short, what this case study of mats in New Ireland emphasizes is how, in considering affordances and mapping, the performance of objects makes real the otherwise invisible biophysical properties of the materials. In this respect, we could say that the process of design is an ongoing activity orientated towards problem-solving in the social world. While the woven mat did not replace the stitched one, the search for substitutes that are in some way superior to the materials they seek to replace still provides an important explanation for innovation; as do the emergent consequences of cultural change, which have provided the impetus for renewed interest in 'old materials' such as barkcloth (kapiak) or 'new' materials such as awoiwoi as we have seen in my case studies.

The fact that the Nalik people maintain and hold on to material knowledge suggests that their engagement and participation in the environment may be a more deeply engrained strategy than I have outlined in this chapter. But what is just as clear is that the objects Nalik produce cannot be viewed as discrete entities; rather we should understand them as complex things constituted in their relation to social, political, economic and natural environments. Thus, the kinds of objects that are produced are not constituted simply of bare materials. Rather, they can be understood as combinations of different relations, entangled in natural and cultural processes.

The idea of materials accommodating certain sets of relations conveys precisely the way in which Naliks understand plants. As a Nalik woman explained, seedlings and cuttings are like kinship relations, and in planting them, you think through your kin relations.[17] And as objects, they trace out relations and so sustain the fabric of social life. In this sense, design involves the process of eliciting relations – much in the same way as Norman (1988) describes how affordances help announce the function of objects, making the intentions of objects visible – and in the handling of materials, thinking through future possibilities and performance. But, at the same time, as objects decay, we perceive their age and vulnerability, much like human skins, which shapes affordances.

Moreover, if materials are met with such intellectualized responses in Melanesian society, as I have argued, then this study offers an important new theoretical framework from which to approach debates on materials and design in society. A key debate on the theoretical framing of materials in material culture reveals how opinions are polarized between two opposing views. One of the contributors, Tilley (2007), claims that proponents of the ecological approach, e.g. Ingold (2007), foreground the trajectories of materials without due consideration to people. Ingold (2007), on the other hand, argues that a materiality perspective, exemplified by Tilley (2004), loses sight of the materials themselves. One solution to this, according to Knappett (2007), is to somehow bring these approaches together. Indeed, what I am suggesting is that an emphasis on mapping and affordances does just that. In fruitfully combining a technical focus on materials and their properties with a conceptual understanding of materials and social relations, this chapter has productively brought materials in conversation with materiality.

In examining the relation between the technical and the social through an analysis of material thinking in Melanesian society, we can begin to see how vital it is to draw attention to plant materials and their informed use in design as a means to articulate an understanding of the concrete social world. Indeed, this approach may well open up a new dialogue and understanding of the intentionalities and ideas carried by ethnographic objects in museums. But I hope this chapter may also prompt us to think a little harder about those objects we may one day happen to find lying discarded by the roadside.

Notes

1. The anthropologist Paige West has researched surfers and surfing resorts in New Ireland (West 2014, 2017).

2. See Were (2010) for further ethnographic reading on the Nalik people. This research focused on crafting practices and the Baha'i faith, examining the pervasive use of pattern designs to create links between the past, present and future.
3. The interior is secondary forest, which is used to cultivate hardwood timbers and coconut groves, small holdings of oil palm, vegetable gardens and pig enclosures.
4. See Firth (1983) and Clay (2005) for further analysis of the history of the missions.
5. For further reading on issues around land, logging and oil palm, see Filer (2011) and Gabriel et al. (2017).
6. For comparative studies of ecological knowledge in Melanesia, see Hays (1983), Schmid (1991), Kwa'ioloa and Burt (2001), Nombo and Leach (2010) and Coupaye (2013).
7. Nalik people claim that Tongan missionaries introduced these mat-making techniques along with the awoiwoi pandanus when Methodist missionaries arrived in New Ireland in the late nineteenth and early twentieth centuries.
8. Stitched pandanus mats are represented in museum collections in the British Museum. Several stitched mats were collected from Highlands New Guinea, the Massim region and the Solomon Islands. Rickard and Cox (1984) document a type of stitched mat from Guadalcanal, Solomon Islands, used as a rain covering; while Thomas (1933) describes the mat as a pandanus hood in Buka, North Solomon Islands. The Linden Museum in Stuttgart, Germany, has a pandanus leaf cape with a pattern cut into one edge from the Tigak area of northern New Ireland (see Gunn and Peltier 2006: 52–53).
9. The German colonial name for Mussau is St Matthias Islands.
10. See Matisoo-Smith et al. (2009: 471) and Parkinson (2010: 143, 148) for more details of loom weaving in Tench Island.
11. A preliminary survey of the pandanus mat collections in the British Museum in 2009 supported the view that Naliks had produced such pandanus artefacts. Stitched mats were also produced in parts of the Solomon Islands and in the Highlands of Papua New Guinea. In the Solomon Islands, elaborate designs were incised into the surfaces of mats using a pointed instrument and through burning to blacken the surface.
12. Levi-Strauss's (1966) famous essay on the bricoleur examines plants, classification and knowledge.
13. Sillitoe's analysis of the Wola of Highlands New Guinea points to the gendering of crops (Sillitoe 1983: 172).
14. Parkinson, a plantation manager writing in the early 1900s, refers to the pandanus hat as *gogo* in New Hanover. He notes its possible origin in New Hanover and its spread outwards to northern New Ireland, an observation corroborated by Nalik people during fieldwork in 2009 and 2011. Parkinson also observes how this hat would always be worn by women in the presence of men and its use in malangan carving to depict a female ancestor (Parkinson 2010 [1907]: 121).
15. See Kooijman (1972) for a survey of barkcloth in the Pacific.

16. I have argued elsewhere how pattern in fibre and fabric allows for the extension of personhood through exchange networks across the Pacific (Were 2010).
17. See also Kuechler (2002) and Coupaye (2013) for comparative examples of plants, exchange and kinship.

 2

Materials on the Move

Exploring the Shifting Material Identities of Barkcloth

Materials, and their identities, are constantly on the move. Materials are not static entities – they do not stand still – but they are continually shaped through human interaction and experience. Our understandings of materials change over time too. Their performance is not simply judged in isolation; rather, as new materials are invented or rediscovered, the benefits of existing materials are gauged by comparison to other types of available materials. Thus, we could say that materials are placed in relational schema, whereby their aesthetic and biophysical properties may be compared for value, strength and look. The qualities that designers and consumers search for in different kinds of materials are constantly changing as consumer choices and values shift. Take, for example, a shiny worktop surface made of plastic laminate Formica. For many people who experienced the 1950s and 1960s, Formica rekindles fond memories of their mother's kitchen. At the time, Formica was considered to be modern and clean before it became old fashioned and obsolete. Then imagine learning how these worktop surfaces have now undergone a complete rebranding in the twenty-first century. Formica is a material that is now regarded as sleek and desirable, a must-have for architects and product designers for use in contemporary design. Such a dramatic shift in a material's identity naturally raises some important questions about the reasons for such change. How have perceptions of these everyday materials shifted so dramatically? What are the factors that led this laminate surface to be reimagined in new ways? And, how might we reimagine laminates beyond their function as hard-wearing and hygienic, towards thinking about them as material sites for the transformation of memory and the expression of new modes of living?

This chapter approaches these important questions about the mutable nature of materials and their identities through an ethnographic analysis of a woven leaf fibre basket. The reason why I have selected a humble basket is that baskets can reveal so much about human sociality. As Lemonnier (2012: 13) states, often mundane objects 'lie at the heart of the systems of thought and practices of their makers and users: they cement the ways people live together'. Indeed, in New Ireland, this basket is recognized for a very distinctive cloth surface design and its intimate connection to place. The basket has recently been revived and innovated amongst the Nalik people of northern New Ireland. In focusing on the material identity of the basket, this chapter intends to scratch below surfaces to consider what is at stake materially by pushing beyond boundaries and interfaces (Tolia-Kelly 2013: 154). By focusing on the process of design innovation, I believe this analysis sheds important light on the role of materials more generally and the nature of shifting material identities in regions undergoing change.

I have selected this type of cloth for my analysis of shifting material identities because I believe there is much at stake in the selection of textiles in design. This is because cloth – made from stripped, beaten and layered plant fibres – has special significance in Pacific society. Its production and circulation can be understood as an expression of kinship and of gender-based power relations (Weiner 1989). Imported cotton cloth, equally, has also played an important role since the onset of colonialism and modernity in the region. It allowed Pacific Islanders to fashion themselves in new ritual and political identities through its transformation into innovative forms of clothing, coverings and wraps. In anthropology, there exists a range of studies that have addressed the social and technical capacities of cloth in its various material guises (Kuechler 2005; Kuechler and Were 2005; Thomas 1999 and others). These studies have emphasized how cloth has offered the potential for social innovation in Pacific society through its transformation into products that could be worn, presented or exchanged. Such approaches tend to rely on an analytical framework in which material precedes form and function – and thereby creates an environment in which materials (e.g. bark and leaf fibres) are placed in isolation from objects (e.g. baskets). This ignores, as Bennett (2010) has claimed, the wider environments of materials and their complex relationship to assemblages of made objects, people, events and other materials. That is, materials and objects do not enter into the world in isolation; they are enmeshed in a network of natural, political, social, historical and cultural processes that shape the way they emerge in the world. In this way, Bennett's approach draws our attention to the decision-making processes, natural constraints of materials, economic factors and so forth that govern the way materials are selected in textile design.

This chapter describes the wider environments of materials through a critical framing of recent themes and approaches in the anthropology of cloth and textiles. I explore the material environments – the natural, cultural, historical and political processes – in which barkcloth – the inner bark of the breadfruit tree, which is stripped and beaten into a fibrous surface – is manufactured specifically for the production of a special type of basket in Nalik society. I move away from anthropological analyses, where the main emphasis has been on the way materials are transformed into products (e.g. cloth into clothing), and thereby mark a distinction between the two as separate and immutable (see Norris 2005). Instead, I move towards engaging with the material environments of barkcloth and how these environments impinge on the use and application of materials and objects. I demonstrate how the materiality of barkcloth is as much about its aesthetic and technical properties – its softness and strength – that inform its use and application as it is about its relation to other competing materials, objects and persons. This is a departure from Weiner (1989), who dispenses with such an approach in her own analysis of cloth in Melanesia. From Weiner's perspective, the importance of cloth derives from its position as a social-symbolic reference point and not from any intrinsic attributes of cloth itself, such as its feel, style and colour, which are important factors in its use and application in Nalik society as is its relation to other objects and materials.[1]

In New Ireland, what is significant about barkcloth is how its production was largely thought to have died out with the onset of colonialism and missionization in the region and the ensuing availability of Western goods such as trade cloth and clothing. Scholarly narratives have thus focused on the demise of barkcloth and its replacement by other types of materials such as cloth. Indeed, in New Ireland, the arrival of Methodist missionaries on the island in 1875 (and Catholic missionaries some years later) heralded the onset of widespread availability and adopting of trade cloth and second-hand clothing for utilitarian as well as ritual purposes.[2] As I have demonstrated elsewhere (Were 2005a), new materials such as trade cloth were adopted in a highly strategic manner according to colour, texture, pattern and so forth. For instance, items of clothing as well as ritual objects, such as wooden sculptures, incorporated tangible signs of Western contact through the incorporation of red or chequered trade cloth, in discernible patterns and designs (Were 2005a). As Thomas (1999) has argued in relation to other parts of the Pacific, trade cloth became a vehicle for new ways of thinking and being and was incorporated into the material culture in often innovative ways to express links to new forms of power. In New Ireland, the introduction of trade cloth impacted on the local production of barkcloth, so much so that until recently barkcloth production in New Ireland was considered to have ceased entirely.

Yet in the past few years, and amid a thriving cultural revival movement in the region, Nalik women have once again begun producing barkcloth. While the material appears to resemble that which was made almost half a century earlier, the environment in which the cloth is produced has entirely changed. It thus provides an opportunity, as Ingold (2012) states, to understand how material identities are continually in flux in the same way the world is continually coming into being.

I examine how concerted attempts to revive the production of barkcloth in the region generate a fruitful space for examining the propensity of cloth manufacture to become productive of new social relations, cultural flows and connectivities (Appadurai 1996; Latour 1993; Miller 1987). Hence, barkcloth revival offers possibilities and outcomes in the social world (Keane 2005; Weiner 1989) that I argue can be explained through an investigation of the relational schema that link barkcloth to wider environments in Nalik society. In exploring the material qualities, values and social meanings of barkcloth and its associated products, I ask, much like Weiner, 'Why (bark)cloth?'

The 'Material' Turn

Over the last decade or so, there has been increasing attention paid to materials in the humanities and social sciences. Such approaches examine the material narratives that link material substances to objects in order to emphasize the experiential and agentive capacity of materials and objects (Boivin 2008; Knappett and Malafouris 2008; Tilley 2004). Some approaches have explored the intimate relation between maker and material in the emergence of object form and as a means to engage more widely with theoretical questions about human thought and action (Ingold 2000b, 2011, 2012). Others have employed ethnographic practices to examine how materials emerge in the social world by mapping the networks of laboratory practice and science innovation (Barry 2005), by undertaking a visual and textual analysis of marketing campaigns (Meikle 1997; O'Connor 2011), or by focusing on factory production practices and new technologies (Bijker 1995).

These ethnographic studies of production and consumption – from the factory floor into homes, schools and workplaces – reveal what Ashby and Johnson (2002) call the multidimensional qualities of materials: that is, how material identities are fashioned not just in terms of how they feel but also because of their technical possibilities such as their capacity to stretch and to remain strong under tension. O'Connor's (2011) study of Lycra reveals how a material's identity is also shaped through an understanding of its performance as a product (e.g. an item of clothing) that provides evidence of what a material can do in the real world. This demonstrates how material identities are shaped in design, not as a single progression from material testing to product design, but the two are mutually reinforcing (i.e. there are iterative stages of product performance and material selection). As Shove et al. (2007) argue, in reference to their analysis of the branding of plastic in 1950s Western society, materials are situated within shifting environments that can have both positive and negative outcomes. In the case of plastic, they show how the management of the material-object relationship was vital to the material's success and its capacity to mimic other materials, and how designers played an important role in transmitting a positive and distinctive image (Shove et al. 2007: 109). On the one hand, stylish products designed in high-quality plastic may enhance consumer attitudes to the material, while the material's association with cheap imitation goods and disposability has a detrimental impact on its image. Thus, in observing how environments impact on and help shape the performance and perception of materials and products, we can begin to appreciate how material identities emerge.

While a vast literature on Pacific objects – many of which reside in museum collections – exists (e.g. Bolton 2003; Hermkens 2005; Mackenzie 1991; Thomas 1991, to name just some), few anthropologists have been concerned with the circulation and production of materials in the Pacific even though there has been a thriving economy since the beginning of the twentieth century. One exception is the literature on cloth as an introduced material: for example, Kuechler and Were (2005) have argued how new materials such as cotton fabrics, metals and synthetics brought into the region through sustained colonial contact and missionization enacted radical change in material culture practices. Much of these transformations focused on dressing the body, through the cutting, stitching and sewing of cloth into new forms of clothing. Thomas (1999) has pointed to how cloth – introduced by missionaries and colonial authorities – could be understood as a kind of technology for effecting new forms of thinking and being in the region. Cloth brought with it the capacity to be transformed into new forms of clothing and was redolent of colonial power relations through its exposure alongside other objects of power, such as guns, ships and government outposts. Colchester (2003b) has examined contemporary Pasifika t-shirt designs in the thriving urban city of Auckland in New Zealand. Pasifika, in this context, refers to the Pacific Islander diaspora community, who feel marginalized and disenfranchised in the urban environment. She states how visual signs and symbols incorporated on printed t-shirt designs make humorous reference to Pasifika identity and act in ways to challenge prevailing gender and ethnic stereotyping. Such approaches typify the material turn in the study of clothing and textiles, whereby the central focus has shifted towards exploring how the materiality of cloth fosters connections through visual and material reference points.

One problem with these approaches that I want to highlight in this chapter is the way both materials and objects are treated in isolation, or as Bennett (2010: 20) terms their 'latent individualism'. How were new materials aligned within existing taxonomies of materials and what were the criteria through which performance and value were adjudged? I believe, therefore, to develop a deeper understanding as to why barkcloth emerged in Nalik society, the way forward to overcoming this narrow framework is to examine the material identities of barkcloth in their wider environment. As Shove et al. (2007: 114) assert, 'what materials are and how they are seen depends, in large part, on exactly what they are made into.' Through an analysis of the production of a type of barkcloth and a basket of which the barkcloth is a constituent part, I assert that materials are as much informed by the selection of product as the basket's identity is constructed through the material selected.[3] This co-constitutive nature of barkcloth and baskets, I argue, demonstrates how design activities are situated in relational schema, natural and cultural, through which identities of products and materials emerge and are modulated. I map out the complex political and ritual environments of barkcloth (see Barry 2013), the competing materials and products available to Nalik women and understandings of barkcloth performance and barkcloth products to explain its sudden resurgence in the early part of the twenty-first century. I explore how the material identity of barkcloth has shifted from one of ordinary functionality and associated labour to that of fashion, comfort and individualism. In once again taking control of the means of production of barkcloth and then positioning the material and basket within a realm that is less about dressing the body than about creating a visual effect, women are sourcing a material that evokes particular sets of connections and relationships. Nalik women, as I demonstrate, are therefore enacting transformations and so translating their control over production of cloth into political authority, as Weiner asserts, though in new ways.

An anthropological analysis of the environments of barkcloth, I contend, develops an appreciation of materiality in terms of how material and visual properties intersect with sociotechnical schema. There is no better place to examine the environments of cloth and textiles than in Nalik society, where the influx of new materials has made a huge and highly visible impact in the region.

Transformation and Change in Nalik Society

While New Ireland has undergone constant change, cloth and textile practices were and still are prevalent in northern New Ireland. Material knowledge is highly valued and many men and women hold on to the technical knowledge required to process plant materials for various processes. For instance, plant materials such as leaves, lianas, roots, barks and flowers have been used to adorn the body. These materials often denote rank and status in society, though these have been poorly represented in museums due to their ephemeral nature (Thomas 1995). In the late nineteenth and early twentieth centuries, local textiles were produced for clothing and coverings using a variety of locally available plant fibres, sometimes dyed using pigments extracted from plants or soil. Of particular significance were piled mats, made from the leaves of a species of pandanus palm that women stitched together longitudinally and perpendicularly to make coverings for newborn infants, as shelter from rain and as floor or food mats. These mats, known as araazira in Nalik society, were considered to offer protection and were exchanged for ceremonial purposes (Were 2013; Chapter 1). Other types of textiles produced in the community were small pieces of barkcloth onto which were drawn special designs relating to local cosmological understandings. Gunn (2006) speculates how these cloths may have celebrated female fertility and could depict a developing embryo or symbols from malangan carvings. Little is really known about these and their production and significance of the design remains uncertain to many Naliks today.

Missionization had a significant impact on the material culture of the region. The establishment of Christian mission stations on the island from 1875 onwards led to the widespread availability and adopting of trade cloth and second-hand clothing for utilitarian as well as ritual purposes (Were 2005a). As Kuechler and Were (2005) argue, clothing was adopted in different ways in Melanesia, often strategically. While missionaries readily saw this as a sign of conversion to Christianity, responses on the part of Melanesians to cloth and clothing suggest that local people considered introduced materials to enable persons to fashion themselves in new ways and align themselves with new forms of power. Evidence of this is located in the design of a wooden carved *tatanua* mask from New Ireland, collected in the 1880s by British colonial administrator and explorer H.H. Romilly and housed in the Queensland Museum in Brisbane. The mask is constructed using a chequered trade cloth, coloured white, red and black. This would have replaced dyed red cloth made locally by extracting the bark of a plant. Although the practice of carving tatanua masks continues today, red cloth is still used in the construction of the headpiece.

While the early twentieth century marked an era where there was an unprecedented uptake in Western goods and materials on the part of Melanesians, a process which transformed the material culture of the region, the post-World War II era has equally seen a pattern of events that have led to further transformations. Since the 1950s, the region has been swept with revival activities known as kastom (Jolly 1992; Keesing 1982; Lindstrom 1993b, and many others). Kastom is a set of practices deemed to emanate from the ancestral past. These activities are considered to be invented, revised or idealized and are generally deployed in specific contexts such as at times of death, marriage or birth. Kastom activities may be scrutinized and contested, and their enactment may be deemed overtly political. They may – as is the case of New Ireland – be construed as antithetical to mission life.

Across Melanesia, kastom activities have led to the revival of traditional cloth and textile practices. In Vanuatu, Bolton (1997) has described how ni-Vanuatu women have revitalized traditional practices such as mat-making and basketry as a means to strengthen their relation to *peles*. The term peles literally refers to 'place' though connotes locality and community of origin. In the Nalik region, a similar revival process is taking place in which kastom activities are orchestrated at life-cycle events and increasingly during visits from political dignitaries or at church opening ceremonies. I have previously described how the Baha'i faithful are key arbiters of kastom in Nalik community life (Were 2010). Senior men and women – members of the faith – commit readily to organizing performances of ancestral dances (*singsing*), the construction of special platforms and enclosures at mortuary feasting (malangan) and the enactment of calendrical rites to bring or hold off rain. The outcome of investing resources and energy into enacting kastom is it brings status to the organizing clans, revitalizes community life and so strengthens Nalik identity (which Naliks consider to be under threat of loss). Crucially, for Naliks, kastom is also understood to be a form of worship, which fulfils the Baha'i faithful's desire to transform themselves into religious adherents.

The Sudden Revival of Barkcloth

Kastom exists in Nalik community as a strong, organizing and cohesive force from which ritual activities and community identity are manifested. Kastom galvanizes the community to work together – not just the Baha'i faithful, who see this as part of their own religious practice, but also other faiths who perform kastom due to their obligation to support other clans who initiate kastom activities. Within the community, women's groups, faith groups, youth groups and so forth organize workshops to support kastom or offer support and advice in a bid to strengthen community life. For example, workshops have been held to give advice on pig husbandry or basketry techniques. In many cases, these workshops and activities promote a flurry of intense activities. Indeed, it may have been such a type of workshop that led to the production of a special kind of basket. During fieldwork in the Nalik community in October 2009, I noticed how women had revived the production of an innovative type of woven basket – termed *aruaai* in Nalik. These playful baskets – decorated with tassels of coloured wool, and some with hand-drawn designs emblazoning their surfaces – were especially in fashion with local Nalik women and used for carrying personal possessions such as mobile phones, purses and quantities of betel nuts. Some Nalik women joked how they wore their baskets over their abdomens in order to hide any early signs of pregnancy. Much like the string bag (*bilum*) from the Papua New Guinea Highlands region (Mackenzie 1991) – which is womblike in its visual form – the basket makes visual reference to the procreative capacity of women through its form, suspended around the neck and covering the abdomen.

Having worked in the community for over decade, I was accustomed to seeing many types of baskets made from locally available materials;

the most common was the leaf of the coconut palm. Constructed from the young green leaflets of the coconut palm and plaited using a simple diagonal warp and weft technique, baskets are functional items used as containers. There are some designed for placing rubbish in, those for transporting root crops from the garden and those for cooked or uncooked food. Slight variations in the weave of the basket are achieved using an open or closed weave technique, by alternating single or split leaf warps and wefts, as well as changing the form of the basket. These design variations denote the function of the basket but also its particular peles (village/locality) and are central to expressing the cultural identity of the wearer. With growing interaction between different cultural groups in the region, however, through intermarriage and urban migration, there has been ever-increasing diversity in basketry techniques and materials found in communities. Indeed, it is common to find basket-makers experimenting with techniques from outside their community to reinvigorate their own practices.

The aruaai baskets, in contrast, were especially interesting because they were based on the design of a Nalik garden basket. Such garden baskets are still made and in use. They are produced using two young palms of the coconut tree, which are heated gently over a fire and cut

Figure 2.1 Selian Kambau wearing her aruaai basket, New Ireland, 2009. Photograph by the author.

down into sections of eight leaflets. Each leaf section is cut in half along the lateral midrib and plaited using a diagonal warp and weft technique. This process is carried out for each of the two leaves. Then, the two sections are woven together to make a basket shape. The basket's handles are made either from the run-off warp and wefts of the plaited leaflets of the coconut palm or sometimes a rope made by stripping the inner bark of a liana, noted for its strength.

The design of the aruaai basket is exactly the same as the garden basket. However, the aruaai is finished using a slightly coarse barkcloth material that is wrapped around the outside of the coconut leaf plaits and secured to make a handle. This material, as I later found out, was called *kapiak* and was extracted from the breadfruit tree (Artocarpus altilis), which grows in the interior forests of New Ireland. Kapiak is used to refer to both the breadfruit tree and the processed coarse barkcloth material extracted from it. The German priest and ethnobotanist Father Gerhard Peekel entered a description of kapiak in his survey of New Ireland plants after spending nearly fifty years in New Guinea from the early 1900s onwards (Peekel 1984 [1947]). In the 1920s, according to Peekel, kapiak was then processed for making the basket wall, handle and fastenings of the aruaai. The basket was worn by women to their gardens, suspended from the forehead and over their backs as they worked. Crops such as taro could then be easily passed over the shoulder and into the basket for carrying.

It therefore appears that since then barkcloth was discontinued in the production of the garden basket, perhaps because of the time and effort required in producing it, not to mention the availability of other types of materials and baskets. However, as this chapter points out, barkcloth was suddenly revived and integrated into an innovative type of fashion basket.

Emerging Form and Fields of Forces

Ingold (2000b) reminds us how the form of objects emerges through our interaction with the world. Challenging the conventional notion that crafting follows a template, a prescribed process in which craftspersons follow a set of skilled procedures to reach their objective (the final form of an object), Ingold argues that forms actually emerge *in situ*, as a flow of forces between maker and material in the activity of making. Drawing on his insights of the basket-maker at work, his analysis reveals the intimate engagement between maker and material as the generative locus for surfaces to emerge. Crucially, for Ingold, the form of the basket emerges through a field of forces in the basket-maker's struggle with the natural resistance of the materials in the process of making.

For the purposes of this chapter, I want to argue that this field of forces – the material environment – extends far beyond the atomistic relation between maker and material. I shall suggest that what is also required is a consideration as to how material environments help shape the design of the basket and its identity in the Nalik community. As Ashby and Johnson (2002: 55–56) state, there are several steps from moving a material into a successful product. These not only include the material's compliance to shaping, joining and finishing but also the nature of the user and any cultural, legal and environmental factors that may influence the process. These constraints, as Norman (1988) refers to them, are the environments in which materials are embedded (Barry 2005) and which influence their uptake in design.

In the Nalik community, the natural environment through which kapiak emerges is the interior forests where the breadfruit trees grow. Yet these environments offer natural constraints for the selection of the plant material. This constraint emerges because the breadfruit trees are known to be quite scarce. Mature trees grow in the forested slopes of the interior of the island, a long walk from the inhabited coastal areas. In the past, cultivation was managed through planting, though nowadays Naliks state how saplings grow when seeds from the fruit are eaten by flying foxes and birds and then carried across the island. This natural constraint on the cultivation and supply of the raw material has meant that Nalik basket-makers fell breadfruit saplings rather than cutting off the branches of mature trees, a practice carried out in the past and observed by Peekel, the German ethnobotanist.

Kabariu (2013) documents how on the island of Lihir, located off the east coast of New Ireland, breadfruit feasting ceremonies once took place amongst communities. The cultivation of breadfruit was carefully managed by the communities to ensure the material resources were sustainable. However, according to Kabariu, because of wholesale felling of breadfruit trees for canoe-making and timber, mature trees became scarcer. As a result, breadfruit trees have become quite hard to locate.

Some Naliks stated that there had been a noticeable decline in the breadfruit tree population due to similar factors of non-sustainable felling practices. The natural constraint on breadfruit – which has made breadfruit relatively scare in the community – is also complicated by rights associated to the harvesting of kapiak. In general, basket-makers can only fell saplings from land belonging to their matriclan and on parcels of land apportioned to households. This further limits the trees available for use. During my visit in 2009, I accompanied a small group of women to the forested interior, where mature breadfruit trees were known to grow. Nalik women told me it can take several hours to find only one sapling, which they cut down to extract the fibrous material. Once the women had located a suitable breadfruit sapling for processing, generally measuring around two metres in height, they cut it down using a bush knife and carried it back to the hamlet before stripping off the small branches.

The process of harvesting kapiak demonstrates how the basket design is related to the natural environment and changes in cultivation practices. The scarcity of the breadfruit tree – as a raw material – increases the symbolic value of the processed material, making it highly desirable. Furthermore, the fact that barkcloth is harvested from the land, which itself carries biographies of Nalik ancestors and clan histories, means that the identity of kapiak is intimately connected to peles, much in the way that mat styles in ni-Vanuatu society are linked to particular island communities (Bolton 1997).

Material Knowledge and Natural Compliance

The production of mats, baskets, carvings, canoes, houses and so forth are considered to be specialist areas of expertise for people in the community. Indeed, this applies equally to the manufacture of kapiak, which has become recognized as a specialized skill even though it has only recently been introduced in the community. In 2009, only a handful of related women knew how to produce kapiak competently in the community. They were recognized amongst the Nalik community as specialists in making aruaai. These women all lived in the same hamlet together and were each related through the same matriclan. It appeared this material knowledge had been shared between themselves as a scarce resource.

The Nalik women employed processes of extraction, processing, drying, weaving and wrapping to make the fashion basket. The first step involved seasoning the wood. The sapling was left to stand for a few days, which allowed for the milky sap to exude (this sap was described in Peekel's ethnobotanical survey and was used, according to Naliks, as a type of glue). The next step involved searing the wood. Once the seasoning process was complete, women then seared the outer bark of the sapling. A fire of dried coconut leaves was made and the sapling was held over the flames, burning the outer bark until black.

According to women, searing the bark made the kapiak whiter, which was preferable to Nalik women. The third step involved removing the outer bark with a knife. Starting at one end, the bark was removed by cutting and scraping to reveal a white inner bark. According to Nalik women, it was considered taboo to step over the sapling, as this would make the kapiak liable to tear.

Figure 2.2 Malina Kambaxal stripping the kapiak of its outer bark, New Ireland, 2011. Photograph by the author.

After removing the outer bark, women then beat the sapling. Taking a blunt flat-ended implement (such as the back of a knife or a piece of wood), the sapling was beaten from the widest end. This was done very slowly, gradually working around the circumference of the kapiak and along its length. Women sometimes stood in the shallows of the sea to perform this task. The beating of the sapling was a laborious process and could take several hours, as the inner bark had to be worked very slowly so that it did not tear. Once the entire kapiak had been beaten it could be pulled away from the trunk much like a sock. Then the sapling was rinsed, dried and bleached. The oily fibrous material was rinsed in the sea and hung to dry in the sun. The rectangular strip of material is about a metre or so in length by twenty centimetres in width.

The entire process took just over one week from start to finish, with the preparation and stripping taking several hours to complete (and so was the most labour intensive). After the material was bleached and dried in the sun for several days, the kapiak was wrapped around the surface of the prepared aruaai (four or eight leaflets depending on the size of the basket required) and secured to make a strap.

There were three important properties of the kapiak that made it particularly sought after and compliant in the design of a fashion basket. First, Nalik women said that the kapiak was soft. By this, they mean that even though the material is slightly coarse when initially processed, after use it becomes much softer and thus more comfortable to wear around the neck. Women stated how the soft fibres did not irritate the skin as other types of plant fibres did. Second, processed kapiak was strong and hard-wearing. It stood up to everyday use and the carrying of loads. Indeed, as Peekel (1984 [1947]) observed, in the original design of the garden basket, kapiak had been used to carry heavy loads of root crops. Finally, kapiak was attractive to Nalik women because it turns white when it is bleached and dried thoroughly. Some Nalik basket-makers would spit the chewed, interior flesh of a coconut onto the kapiak to enhance the bleaching effect. No other locally available materials were known to create this effect. Its whiteness was thus a desired quality of the material, especially as it made it particularly compliant to decoration. Indeed, women sometimes tied short threads of coloured wool to the kapiak to give the basket an eye-catching and decorative effect. Occasionally, hand-drawn designs were applied to the kapiak using a coloured pen. These designs included slogans, symbols and nicknames of people. The fact that the basket could be designed in individualized ways created an emotional attachment to the product, a key aspect of what Norman (1988) regards as successful design.

Positioning Materials and Products

Since the beginning of the twentieth century, the subsistence economy of New Ireland has been transformed with the establishment of copra plantations and cash cropping. Foster (1992) describes how in Tanga, an island off the east coast of New Ireland, the introduction of cash cropping led to a transformation in the clan-based ideology of community life. As family units engaged in the cash-crop economy of copra production, they kept their revenue separate from the domain of kastom and so ensured that households were able to maintain financial resources of their own rather than claiming the benefits of the land as the corporate ownership of the clan.

A similar shift has taken place in the production of the fashion basket. Since its revival by Nalik women over the past few years, its production has remained outside of the male-controlled realm of kastom. The aruaai is not classified as kastom. One reason for this is the way the identity of kapiak has been shaped by its revived production and visibly worn in new ways. Wearing the basket on the front or side distinguishes the aruaai from the garden basket, which is worn over the back. This style has helped the basket to remain in a separate environment than that of kastom even though both the material and product were based on a design from the past. Classified in this way, the basket – much like copra production – can be marketed as a commodity, commissioned and sold in the Nalik community for a small amount of cash. This was evident during my visit in 2009: the female basket-makers in the Nalik community were busy trying to fulfil commissions from friends, relatives and acquaintances for which they received a small cash fee for their efforts. Financial return allowed them to purchase store goods for themselves and their families. Thus, the basket's shift in identity from an ordinary garden basket to a product that is conspicuously modern (a break from the past) has meant that women benefit economically from its production. Moving the production of baskets outside the domain of kastom has ensured that women are free to produce the baskets for sale and thus secure some financial reward for their hard work. By holding on to the means of production, kapiak has become an important resource for women to exert their agency in the community.

A crucial factor in understanding how the material identity of kapiak has shifted is to examine the positioning of the aruaai in Nalik society alongside other baskets. The aruaai is manufactured to compete against other types of fashion baskets available for purchase from Asian-run trade stores in the provincial town of Kavieng, a day's trip on public transport. These baskets, made from colourful cotton and synthetic fibres, are expensive to buy and are generally of low quality. Moreover, people are always complaining about the quality of imported products sold in the shops in Kavieng. The use of kapiak in the design of the basket has transformed the identity of an ordinary basket by making it fashionable and desirable, thereby creating a niche for women to market their wares. This emphasizes what Shove et al. (2007) term the 'co-constitutive nature' of materials and objects: that is, the performance of the object is made visible through the use of certain materials; and the performance of materials informs its use as an object. The basket offers Nalik women the opportunity to buy a locally produced alternative to a shop-bought basket that is conspicuously designed in a New Ireland style using local plant resources, and so they can present themselves in ways that assert their local identity. The fact that it is not mass-produced but made to order creates a niche in the market by offering a personal attachment between maker and buyer and so enables it to compete against imported ready-made baskets. Thus, much in the same way that Shove et al. (2007) state: how the public had to first understand what plastic could do as a product before it could emerge in Western society, we could say that the material identity of kapiak has been shaped through its positioning and performance as a product within the schema of available baskets (the market environment), which has allowed kapiak to be revived in Nalik society.

Conclusion

This chapter has set out to show how material identities are constantly on the move: materials are susceptible to continual variation as their environments shift too. As identities of materials transform, so do their uses and application in society. I have demonstrated how in order for a material like kapiak to re-emerge in society as novel and desirable, it has to establish a place for itself alongside other materials by shedding its identity as 'of the past'. Kapiak has arguably transformed Nalik society – its production signals a shift internal to society – as well as the material culture of the region. I have demonstrated how both kapiak as a material and in its object form as a basket is actively engaged in shaping its material identity and performance. In this way, materials and objects can be understood as technologies for remaking the local and thereby allow persons to enact new forms of individualized agency in the world (Appadurai 1996).

This chapter also emphasizes how important it is to consider the complex environments of materials from an anthropological perspective in order to fully understand their identities. These environments, I have shown, connect materials to objects, events and people through the new relations that emerge with modernity and the global flow of materials. Shifting material identities and forms of agency are central to understanding this process. As we have seen in Nalik society, self-fashioning quite often involves the process of reimagining and reclaiming 'old' materials (which are transformed into surfaces), much in the same way that architects and product designers have reframed the identity of Formica as something sleek and contemporary. Transforming surfaces into something fashionable and desirable involves thought and effort, overcoming natural and cultural forces and the reshaping of memory. Thus, this serves to demonstrate how forms are continually coming into existence around us as materials are selected and used in design. In this respect, we could say that the continual positioning of materials in relation to others provides an important explanation for innovation and change in a region. While the emergence of new colonial relations led to a new economy in materials in the form of cloth, metals, plastics and synthetics, I have also shown how old materials too are reframed in relation to existing ideas of performance (i.e. kastom) and product (local and imported baskets).

To emphasize this process of continual change and conclude, I return to New Ireland: during my visits between 2012 and 2015, the use of kapiak as an innovative material covering for baskets had slowed (possibly because of a lack of natural resources as outlined in this chapter). Its production has been superseded by the introduction of another new plant material, *mulai*, now used in the manufacture of the aruaai. This alternative type of barkcloth – once used in the production of headpieces for malangan masks before trade cloth replaced its use – is sourced from trees inside the forest. Mulai resembles kapiak, but as Nalik women told me, it has the superior benefits of producing smoother, softer and whiter surfaces. As the crafting activities of my Nalik colleagues demonstrate, this further transformation demonstrates how materials are continually shifting in the changing environment; materials that possess the qualities of strength and aesthetics can also be worked in ways to evoke place, difference and identity and thus empower women in new ways.

As I have demonstrated in Nalik society, the search for new materials quite often involves the process of reimagining and reclaiming 'old' materials, much in the same way that scientists in the biomaterials industry are returning to botanical archives in order to research and develop new kinds of sustainable materials. This serves to demonstrate how the world of materials is continually coming into existence around us as we select and design. It suggests that materials are not simply aspects of the environment but can be held in mind as much as objects.

Notes

1. See Kuechler (2005) for a further critique of Weiner's work on cloth and density.
2. The island fell under German colonial rule (Neu Mecklenburg) from 1885 and then Australian administration (renamed New Ireland) after the end of World War I.
3. See Wendrich (1999) for an excellent overview of the literature on the relation between basketry and textiles.

3

What's in a Plant Leaf?

A Case Study of Materials Innovation in New Zealand

Introduction

This chapter begins by taking a journey back to the nineteenth century to describe two failed attempts at materials innovation. The first appears in F. Dillon Bell and Frederick Young's (1842) *Reasons for Promoting the Cultivation of the New Zealand Flax,* where the authors observe how a 'change has come o'er the spirit of their dream'. Bell and Young are referring to the failure of white settlers to sufficiently develop the plant *harakeke,* the Maori term for the plant commonly referred to as New Zealand flax (Phormium tenax). They wanted the settlers to transform the long-bladed coarse green grass – recognized for the tensile strength of its internal longitudinal fibres – into an economic crop that could be used in the manufacture of naval ropes, sacking, upholstery and other fibre products. They offered 'a premium' to the colonists to design a machine that could adequately extract the strong fibres from the leaf, but it seems their efforts were fruitless.[1]

The second example describes how a sample of waste from New Zealand flax leaves – in the form of coarse brown powder mixed with fibres – was forwarded to the Imperial Institute for testing to examine its viability as a papermaking material, manure and potash (Bulletin of the Imperial Institute 1919: XVII, 486). The report concludes that after testing, the material's best potential was for its use as manure, as there was too much competition with other waste materials for it to be utilized in papermaking.

I begin with these two stories of aspiration concerning the promotion of New Zealand flax in the nineteenth and early twentieth centuries because they emphasize the spirit of entrepreneurialism that existed during the colonial era and the concerted efforts of some who searched for new and novel application of materials in order to enhance the economic productivity of a region. As Brockway (2002) demonstrates, this was characteristic of the nineteenth century, an era defined by an unprecedented growth in public engagement with new materials made possible through the exploration of economic crops throughout the world and the discoveries of colonial science (Brockway 2002). Much like Kew Gardens and other centres of botanical collecting, the Imperial Institute in South Kensington, London, was a focal point for these activities and supported lectures, exhibitions and conferences to further knowledge of the colonies and the materials and products sourced from there (Golant 1984; Worboys 1990). Its function was to assist the expansion of trade and the exploration and utilization of natural resources in a bid to boost economic productivity and colonial trade. Colonial representatives abroad submitted specimens and products to the Imperial Institute for preliminary investigation as well as exhibition in order to link scientific knowledge with industrial enterprise (Golant 1984: 15–16).

This chapter begins with stories of failed attempts at materials innovation because they underline the 'expressivity' of harakeke: the potential of a material to create outcomes in society. As DeLanda (2006) states, materials are not passive entities: instead they perform in ways that make their presence known. Harakeke, even after research and development, could not be controlled to make the desired object. For scientists, if the strong fibres could be extracted efficiently, the performance of harakeke could be calculated and the material be used as a mass object. Yet harakeke's non-compliance instead demonstrates, as Norman (1988) famously argues, how well-laid plans and designs are often tempered by constraints of a social, technical and logical nature.

In this chapter, I investigate the ways in which materials enter the social world through a socio-historical analysis of the development of harakeke in New Zealand industry. I examine what drives materials innovation, focusing on the historical processes and distributed agency that make materials innovation possible and demonstrate how the identity of harakeke is continually shifting as the world changes around it. I question the notion of materials innovation and at the same time provide anthropology with a theoretical framework to analyse materials innovation in society.

Materials, Innovation and Anthropology

Materials are ubiquitous (Ashby and Johnson 2002). They help shape – through their experiential and agentive capacity – human thought and action (Boivin 2008; Knappett and Malafouris 2008; Miller 2005; Tilley 2004). Through their innovation and use in society and industry, materials play a significant role in social change (Ashby and Johnson 2002; Boivin 2008). The innovation of materials is important, as the process makes a more efficient and effective market for industry producers as well as consumers. Materials innovation is often driven by the necessity to optimize existing consumer products by selecting suitable materials that perform better or fulfil certain requirements. It can also apply to the process of improving existing materials by altering their molecular or biophysical structure or finding new applications for well-known materials, such as plant fibres and timbers (Ball 1997). Innovation is also driven by the environments in which materials are situated. As Welz (2003: 256) states, economics is a driving factor of innovation: the capacity to innovate is a key determining factor in the competitive advantage of national economies, industries and private business. With the development of 'knowledge societies', Welz states how a 'culture of innovation' has been invented in which a plethora of policies, institutions and procedures of 'innovation management' generate new knowledges, products and services.

In my approach to materials innovation, materials are not passive entities; I show how their capacity for transformation enables social worlds to come into being and be known (Ingold 2011; Were 2013). Materials are 'expressive' (DeLanda 2006), and as Bennett's study of their vibrancy shows, materials lend themselves to a congregational understanding of agency, rather than an individualism (Bennett 2010).[2] My approach is guided by the work of Hawkins, Potter and Race (2015), who demonstrate how the research and development into plastic water bottles had a huge impact in the social world: it changed consumer habits and had unintended consequences, generating an environmental waste problem due to problems in plastic bottle disposal. Scientists undertook research and development into inventing a new form of plastic suitable for use in the bottled water industry. Their work reveals how scientists experimented with polyethylene terephthalate (PET) in the laboratory in order to find a material that was robust enough to contain water under pressure, could safely contain water without contamination and that would remain opaque like glass. Their work is important to developing an agentive approach to materials because it emphasizes how materials innovation has observable effects outside the laboratory.

What is also significant about their work is how research and development into a type of PET plastic was guided by industry demands to develop a suitable material that could perform as a water bottle. The object became the guiding principle for innovation. This illustrates how materials innovation is not solely driven by activities within the hermetically sealed space of the laboratory; rather, research and development is intimately connected to issues, agendas and networks in the outside world (Barry 2005; Latour 1996; Latour and Woolgar 1979).

This is emphasized too in O'Connor's study of research and development of Lycra (O'Connor 2011). In her ethnographic study, O'Connor demonstrates how the American science company Dupont led research and development into Lycra during the baby-boomer era of the 1950s as an alternative to the rubber girdle then worn by women. The girdle was considered stiff, uncomfortable to wear and was also prone to deterioration. O'Connor points out that a crucial factor in the emergence of the new elastane fibre for use in girdles is how Lycra came into being through executive brainstorming sessions, design meetings, consumer wear testing and new factory mass production techniques. Thus, not only does this study underline the collaborative and co-dependent nature of materials innovation; successful transmission of Lycra's qualities to the public and to industry was vital to its uptake in the global marketplace. O'Connor's study demonstrates how important intensive marketing campaigns were to its successful launch and how a new visual culture of pamphlets and adverts emerged that positioned Lycra as a superior stretch fibre for women. The effects of this materials innovation were the creation of new kinds of gender identities and body images.

While these approaches foreground the processes and practices in which new materials emerge in the world and their impact on human behaviour, I argue that materials innovation is driven by a much deeper engagement than otherwise suggested in these studies. Indeed, I will suggest that the innovation of materials provides insights into the mind at work, revealing the cognitive work of materials in world-making (Ingold 2011, 2012). Since materials innovation is a form of material engagement involving trialling, testing and brainstorming activities, I am reminded of Alfred Gell's seminal work, which draws attention to the abductive quality of material culture (Gell 1998). Of particular significance to my argument, Gell states that artefacts possess the capacity to ensnare minds through their cognitive complexities: this involves a process of 'working things out' much like the context of materials innovation. Using a stylistic analysis of Maori meeting houses to develop this claim, Gell (1998: 256–58) argues that each house instantiated an engagement of mind – house building was competitive and involved thinking through how to deploy resources to develop a new house to rival others. We are told that because meeting houses were related to ancestral power, future houses were generally built in a recognizable form to previous houses – what Norman (1988) would call a design constraint – but innovative (e.g. larger, taller etc.), and so past houses can be regarded as 'protensions towards' the ultimate meeting house. In other words, for Gell, innovation involves thinking through a set of possible transformations that can be enacted or performed on a prototype (the Maori meeting house) whilst working within a field of constraints (e.g. form, style, tradition etc.).

Gell's argument is useful for developing my own approach to harakeke because his insights reveal how scientists engage deeply with materials to develop new products and applications. In particular, his work underlines how materials innovation – through transformation, testing and comparative analysis – objectifies and externalizes the mind at work as scientists think through uses and applications in the real world. This suggests that materials innovation cannot be understood in isolation but involves a material engagement, as innovation involves thinking about other materials and objects. Situated in complex relational and context- dependent environments (Bennett 2010; Gell 1998), materials and objects are active co-agents that mutually inform possibilities on the basis of their known and observable performance. In ascribing an agentive capacity to materials, I am claiming that research and development is driven in ways in which the performance of materials cannot be separated from their objecthood or their environments. As such, how a material emerges in society is as much shaped by social, economic and political environments as it is by its transformational capacity.

In some cases, as Welz (2003) states, economics is the driving force for innovation, but in others, this may be tempered by availability of key resources or environmental issues (Sheller 2014). Such factors reveal the vicissitudes of materials: the high and low points of materials innovation as it negotiates difficult social terrain with unintended outcomes. Indeed, as I demonstrate in this chapter, a material may have been originally developed with a particular use in mind, but its eventual uptake in society may be an unintended result of a chance encounter with a designer or a shift in public consciousness. Take the fibre material spinifex, for instance, a type of grass that is native to Australia. It has been used in Aboriginal communities for generations to build traditional thatch roofs for housing. Today, materials scientists are working with Aboriginal communities to explore the potential uses of its fibre as building insulation and its resin for other commercial purposes (O'Rourke, Flutter and Memmott 2010). The issues about the material's compliance, debates about cultural rights and property as well as the technologies of extraction all play an important factor in the process of innovation and the material's future place in society.

Growth and development in the materials industry is intrinsically linked to national development and economic productivity (Kotler and Simon 2003). Now, there are more materials than ever before and a new range of functional fibrous materials – a class of materials known as 'future fibres' – are being manufactured from coir, spinifex, bamboo, hemp and other natural fibres as a response to environmental regulations and consumer demand. These new materials expand and enhance their applications in sports, aerospace, medicine, packaging and design, offering huge potential for a bio-based economy (Ball 1997).

Society's interest in issues of sustainability and, in particular, the impact of waste on the environment has revitalized interest in natural fibres and their products. These future fibres combine plant fibres selected on the basis of their performance with synthetic resins to form composites that are considered to be more environmentally friendly than fibres produced from petrochemicals. These biocomposites have time literally inbuilt, as they begin to degrade after a finite time and thus do not present the kind of long-term environmental issues that other man-made materials generate.

The rise of interest in future fibres has been met with an upsurge in archival practices. While we could point to the mid nineteenth century and colonial economic botany as an apical period in the archiving of plant fibres from around the world (Desmond 2007), new forms of archival practices are now taking place because of the establishment of materials libraries. Materials libraries are the contemporary analogue to the botanical archive, much like the Imperial Institute (though they do not necessarily command the same power dynamics).[3] They function to serve a range of clientele in the commercial sector by archiving, displaying and matching an assortment of new materials for use by designers, industrial manufacturers, architects and so forth in their design projects. Their growth in world cities such as New York, Bangkok and Beijing, where fashion designers, car manufacturers and aerospace engineers are increasingly making use of archives of material samples as a standard procedure in the design and manufacturing process, is evidence of the rising importance of archival practices and material repositories in designing the twenty-first century.

Despite the establishment of materials libraries, the problem is that many new materials fail to make the transition from laboratory to successful product. As Ball (2008) states, there is an inherent conservatism in the way designers recommend new materials to manufacturers – meaning that many exciting materials are not promoted because they may be deemed too risky. This may be related to the material aesthetic: its colour, feel or shine; or its cost of production, technical performance or environmental credentials. All these factors, and many others, potentially impact on the success of materials innovation and reveal the complex negotiations with natural, cultural and social environments in which users, designers and consumers are mutually connected and through which the futures of materials are entrusted.

Seen this way, materials innovation involves a complex engagement between minds, matter and their environments. Indeed, as I discuss, much like social networks and visual culture in which new materials like Lycra and PET plastic have emerged in society, my analysis of materials innovation reveals a comparable story of trialling, testing and transformation over 150 years, directed largely by lucrative market opportunities that reside outside of the laboratory setting and incorporate projects of colonial science, nation-branding exercises and military conquest. I show how research and development into the potential use of harakeke originally focused on its material substance – how the strong fibres could be extracted from the plant leaf efficiently. This research, however, was driven by the internal objective of transforming harakeke into an economic crop that could support the New Zealand economy; but it was also guided externally by the need to develop a strong naval rope, an object that directed research and that could compete with other fibre products on the international market. After its decline in the second half of the twentieth century, I also show how a new niche was suddenly opened for harakeke. Laboratory practice has been driven by the need to capture the lucrative clean, green market of the New Zealand economy, and so research and development has focused on developing a suitable biomaterial (a harakeke composite) to match the needs of an environmentally conscious consumer and at the same time measure up to the required performance (of object and material).

By highlighting the different pathways and relations in which material and object are inextricably intertwined in the process of innovation and design, this chapter reveals how material substances are active agents in the wider environments and infrastructures through which materials and objects emerge in the world and how these create new subjectivities, relationships and power relations.

In seeking to control the material expressivity of harakeke, I show how the intended outcome of materials scientists has been to create a range of commercial products that are intimately tied to the New Zealand landscape. This demonstrates how, as Ingold (2012) claims, materials are not static entities but are continually changing as environments shift around them, and which I believe has important implications for developing an anthropological perspective on materials and society.

Harakeke and the Manufacturing Industry in New Zealand

Harakeke (Phormium tenax) is a plant with long spear-shaped leaves that is native to New Zealand and Norfolk Island. It is well known for the strength of its inner fibres, which run parallel to the length of the leaf. The plant grows on hills and in swamps, from sea level to around 4,000 feet, though performs better (for commercial purposes) when cultivated close to rivers. It is propagated by either seeds or division of its rootstock. Its rootstock spreads horizontally underneath the soil, and from it sword-shaped leaves grow in clusters.

Harakeke is considered sacred to Maori, a *taonga* or treasured possession (Haywood and Wheen 2016). Recently, Maori groups have been fighting a legal battle to assert intellectual property rights over its use. Known as WAI262 or the Flora and Fauna inquiry, the 2011 outcome of the Waitangi tribunal ruled in favour of improved protection of indigenous knowledge, cultural heritage, environmental resources and language as well as new partnerships in education, conservation and cultural heritage (see Lai 2014).

The plant appears in many varieties and names, each with specific applications for weaving and other uses. Maoris extract the strong fibres from its leaves by hand, using a mussel shell that they scrape along the length of the leaf. Washing, drying and twisting produces a soft, pliable and strong fibre that is able to hold dyes as well as being waterproof. The fibres are almost white in colour, flexible, soft and silky. These properties of the fibre make them ideal for manufacturing textiles and clothing as well as making floor mats, baskets, nets and ropes.

Captain Cook first brought harakeke fibre to the attention of Europeans having observed its common use by Maoris (Dodge 1897: 261). Europeans quickly recognized the possibilities of cultivating harakeke for industrial purposes. Hector (1872) and Murray (1838) include descriptions of the economic value of New Zealand flax and its use and application in papermaking and rope. Such was the enthusiasm towards this new material that Murray (1838) had some of his book printed on it to demonstrate its potential application. Later, Shaw, Bicking and O'Leary (1931) conduct a feasibility study of New Zealand flax use in the papermaking industry. Their report to the United States government points to how its success would rely on its availability in large quantities. They conclude how New Zealand flax 'is a promising material for the manufacture of wrapping and writing papers' (1931: 420).

There were several reasons why harakeke fibre was considered to be a competitive fibre. First, when compared with other fibres, it had a high yield. A much higher percentage of fibre could be extracted from the leaves in comparison with its competitor, sisal hemp. Second, the plant could be easily cultivated. Each leaf was long, and the plant could easily be propagated from the roots. A third reason was its harvesting cycle. One planting could last several years, and there was no need to harvest crops, if so desired (Critchfield 1951: 177).

Commercial production and export began in the early nineteenth century, in which Maori people prepared increasing quantities of harakeke by hand for export (Brooker et al. 1989). According to Cruthers, Carr and Laing (2009: 104), dressed and partially dressed fibre extracted by Maori people was sold to settlers, who exported the fibre and used it to manufacture various products in New Zealand. Trade of harakeke flourished between 1828 and 1853 between Maoris and settlers, with most of the fibre reportedly exported to Australia and Britain. Export production was transformed by the development of machinery to extract the fibres from the leaves, replacing the labour-intensive hand extraction process performed by Maoris. 'The stripper' extracted fibrous strands from the green leaf by drawing the leaves between a metal bar and cylindrical drum. According to Jones (2003), one machine could produce about 250 kilos of fibre a day – compared with the one kilo of finer fibre that one person could create. This resulted in an increase in exports from 1,062 long tons in 1831 to 5,471 tons in 1870 (Critchfield 1951: 175).

One of the greatest impediments to large-scale production of harakeke has been the efficiency of the technology of extraction (as outlined in the opening paragraph of this chapter). Whilst the development of mechanized techniques of fibre extraction increased yields of harakeke fibre, the efficiency of the available technology impacted on the condition of the extracted fibres. This was because the mechanical stripping process – as well as removing the useful fibres – also extracted coarser fibres from the leaf (in comparison to the fibres extracted by hand), lowering the quality of the harakeke fibres for export and so increasing failure rates when tested under lower loads. This meant that harakeke fibres, tested under load, were liable to break at lower loads than other natural fibres. In contrast, the fibre dressed by Maori people was of higher quality than machine-dressed fibre, but the rate of production was slower (Cruthers, Carr and Laing 2009). In a report to the State Department submitted by the United States consul, the following assessment was made of harakeke:

> The fiber of Phormium tenax is susceptible of a much higher degree of preparation than has been bestowed upon it up to the present. This, however, is not altogether the fault of those who are engaged in its manufacture; it is for want of the necessary machinery. The hand-dressed article prepared by the natives is as fine as silk compared with the modern machine-dressed flax of to-day. This only demonstrates the fact that the fiber may be reduced to a much finer quality, and all that is necessary to do this is an improved machine. (U.S. Consular Report May 1890, cited in Dodge 1897: 265)

It appears, therefore, that the technology developed for extracting useful fibre gave the harakeke an unreliable identity, making it difficult for it to compete with other hard fibres in the international marketplace. According to Hector (1872: v), one solution to this problem was when New Zealand flax was renamed 'New Zealand hemp' in 1871 in order to account for its lower quality and so give it an advantageous position alongside other hemp fibres that were traded at the time.

To reduce the failure of harakeke to a singular outcome, as Bennett (2010) argues, is to deny it its material vibrancy: its relation to assemblages of events, persons and objects. Indeed, there were also natural factors that hindered the commercial development of harakeke fibre. For instance, harakeke was beset with cultivation problems. One of the major drawbacks to the establishment of harakeke plantations was the long harvesting cycle of the plant. Few farmers would risk investment in harakeke when their first economic returns came after at least five years. Another problem was its cultivation. Harakeke was vulnerable to disease. In the 1920s, yellow-leaf disease destroyed plants, whilst other fibres that harakeke fibre competed against remained unaffected. Once these natural factors had been taken into account, harakeke fibre had to compete commercially with other hard fibres processed throughout the world – notably sisal hemp, which was of higher quality and comparable strength.

And like all market economies, the New Zealand flax industry was susceptible to periods of economic growth and decline as market conditions fluctuated. Jones (2003) states how New Zealand flax underwent three periods of substantial growth: the first two boom periods for New Zealand were 1869–70 and 1889–90 and the third began in 1898, when the Spanish-American War cut off the supply of manila fibre from the Philippines. This underlines the relatedness of the fibre to the material vicissitudes of other fibres in the global marketplace.

The industry boomed in the first quarter of the twentieth century, when harakeke was used as a replacement for sisal, manila and other hard fibres used in naval ropes. In 1907, exports peaked when 28,547 long tons were shipped abroad (Critchfield 1951: 176). The economic depression of the 1930s sent the industry into decline. As exports dwindled, the industry switched attention to domestic markets, and processing mills began to produce fibre for use as woolpacks in the wool industry. In 1936, the New Zealand government restricted the import of woolpacks made from Indian jute in order to support the domestic flax milling industry.

During World War II, the flax milling industry briefly blossomed due to the disruption of fibre imports to New Zealand. The New Zealand government provided financial support to the industry in order to ensure that the country had enough fibre for agricultural and military use. After the war, import restrictions remained and so the government continued to support harakeke production and the fifteen to twenty mills that were still in operation. The mills mainly produced fibre to make woolpacks but also underfelt, carpets and upholstery materials and binder twine to tie up hay bales (Jones 2003). With the lifting of government protection in the 1970s, New Zealand flax could no longer compete with other natural fibres that were produced more cheaply elsewhere in the world. Moreover, the development of cheaper synthetic fibres such as polyester signalled the end of the industry and the closure of the last flax mill in New Zealand in 1985. However, Cruthers, Carr and Laing (2009: 108) claim this is an over simplification of the facts, as overall world demand for fibre – both natural and man-made – actually has increased. In any case, Brooking (2004) succinctly notes that the flax industry promised so much and delivered so little.

Clean, Green Harakeke

So far, this chapter has concentrated on the story as to how the performance of harakeke, through its application and use in the design of objects such as woolpacks, ropes and matting, was evaluated by a network of scientists, brokers and farmers. It has emphasized how harakeke was positioned, not as a material in isolation but in terms of its performance as an object and its relation to other types of fibre products that were available at the time in terms of its economic potential. Performance, moreover, was not just about its strength and stiffness under load but also its capacity to be cultivated quickly, processed easily, its resistance to disease and its capability to attract government subsidy. Thus, the material identity of the plant fibre – its potential application (as a hard fibre) and its reputation (performance) – had been constructed in line with market opportunities on an international scale.

Markets, however, are not static and neither are material identities, which are susceptible to shifting and refining. As the well-documented case of the social history of plastic in Western consumer culture testifies, its identity as an easily mouldable material that was clean and hygienic shifted to one that posed large-scale waste and environment problems (Hawkins 2011; Meikle 1997). Indeed, as I will now demonstrate, new market opportunities and social movements have meant that new possibilities have emerged for harakeke. A major factor has been the emergence of a bio-based economy and the commoditization of the New Zealand landscape. The plant's association to the land has provided a space for a new identity to be created that has been capitalized on in New Zealand by materials scientists, cosmetic companies and product designers.

Since the late 1990s, Tourism New Zealand has been running an international branding campaign as a green and clean country. Its '100% Pure' brand was developed by M&C Saatchi and established in 1999 through aggressive marketing in several countries. According to Medway and Warnaby (2014), places are increasingly regarded as brands: countries like New Zealand become commodities that are marketed with associated values and images. In New Zealand, the natural landscape has become a niche brand. The 100% Pure campaign aimed to combine New Zealand's brand essence – its distinctive landscape – with a real point of difference that no other destination in the world could possess (Morgan, Pritchard and Piggott 2002: 351). In brand marketing, it is the positioning of the brand image that is more important to the ultimate success than its actual characteristics. The outcome of this branding process was that New Zealand became recognized internationally for its green values. This has acted as a powerful marketing tool to attract international tourism, develop economic productivity and raise environmental sustainability ('Greening New Zealand's Growth', 2011). The notion that New Zealanders share green values has been pivotal for creating a new space to support renewed efforts to research the potentials of harakeke as an economic plant. While the New Zealand flax industry of the nineteenth and twentieth century positioned the material as a coarse fibre, materials scientists began to develop a new generation of sustainable materials known for their clean and green credentials. In other words, place branding has helped drive materials innovation.

Scion, a Crown Research Institute based in Rotorua, New Zealand, is currently leading research and development into harakeke and other native plants through the production of a range of environmentally sustainable products that have minimal impact on the environment. Their aim is to develop a range of biomaterials that help support a new bio-based economy in New Zealand and support the image of a clean, green country.[4] Their vision is: 'Prosperity from trees' or '*Mai i te ngahere oranga*' (Maori). The Annual Report 2013 states: 'Scion's purpose is to drive innovation and growth from New Zealand's forestry, wood product and wood-derived materials and other biomaterial sectors, to create economic value and contribute to beneficial environmental and social outcomes for New Zealand' (Scion Annual Report 2013). In addition to these vision statements, the chairman and CEO of Scion state how 'Scion is also dedicated to increasing the benefit to New Zealand from forest ecosystem services and improved environmental sustainability' (Scion Annual Report 2013: 5).

The Scion website fashionably adopts the language of environmentalism and sustainability. Its 'Manufacturing and Bioproducts' webpage points to key developments in 'wood and fibre technology', 'industrial biotechnology' and 'packaging' and is an example of a materials-focused approach to innovation. It states how 'the world is witnessing a major shift towards materials, chemicals and fuels made from renewable resources.' Scion, it states, 'offers New Zealand's leading research capability in utilizing industrial biotechnology to create new materials, energy products and green chemicals'. The website goes on to state, in relation to wood and fibre technology, how the world is increasingly seeking to use renewable and sustainable materials to meet consumer needs, and as a consequence new applications for wood and plant fibres are rapidly emerging.[5]

I visited Scion in June 2011 to investigate further why scientists had decided to conduct research on harakeke. In particular, my interest was raised by media reports of one of the products Scion had developed – a surfboard made using harakeke fibre. Scion scientists outlined three main reasons for thinking that harakeke could perform as a suitable substitute for fibreglass in the design of the surfboard. Firstly, harakeke offered an environmentally friendly alternative to glass fibre, which is made from petrochemicals. Harakeke grows wild in New Zealand, and at present there are government programmes to promote its cultivation. It was explained that by adding organic nutrients – or diallers as they are termed in the materials industry – the life of composite materials could be prolonged or cut short the time a product takes to decay in the environment and so address or conform to environmental and waste regulations. Secondly, scientists also selected harakeke because of its biophysical properties: its strength and stiffness were considered ideal for surfboard design (since they were aware that it had been used for naval ropes up until World War II). Scientists combined harakeke with synthetic resins to produce a lightweight, strong composite structure that also made the board waterproof. Lastly, the surfboard could also be coloured, giving it a unique decorative effect, owing to the fact that harakeke fibres can be dyed.

Scion had developed the surfboard (as well as a series of other prototype models of eco-products) to demonstrate how biomaterials could potentially be marketed in the design of eco-products. These bespoke biomaterials – with time built in to them, since their rate of decay is known – appear to have obvious environment benefits. But because extracting the harakeke fibres was a complicated process, as outlined at the beginning of this chapter, scientists could not scale up production to the model of mass production they desired and so the surfboard was considered to be commercially unviable.

Instead, the 'operational realism' (Barry 2005) of harakeke (as a hard fibre) meant that efforts appeared to be orientated towards developing products on a model of small-scale production. Harakeke biocomposite could not be produced commercially in manufacturing industry, but it could assume a craft potential, as it conformed to small-scale models of production required for handmade products. This was made evident when Scion formed a partnership in 2010 with David Trubridge – a prominent New Zealand designer working with sustainable materials – to create household lamps made using a specially developed composite material from bioplastic (polylactic acid) and harakeke fibre (Scion Annual Report 2011). Trubridge stated that in this design 'we are expressing our spreading awareness of, and connection to, Nature'

(Scion Highlights of the Financial Year 2010/2011). The product's value is clearly in Trubridge's innovative use of harakeke and the plant's unique place in the cultural and natural landscape of New Zealand.

Harakeke Oil Extraction and Environmental Branding

While research and development continues to explore the potential of harakeke in a bio-based economy, its unique and natural association to the '100% Pure' New Zealand landscape has created another niche within the green cosmetics industry in New Zealand. The oil extracted from the plant's leaves and its seeds have been successfully used in healing and soothing ointments and creams. This material transformation has positioned harakeke as New Zealand's answer to aloe vera. These cosmetic products, as I will demonstrate, render the actual material substance (harakeke) unrecognizable (since the raw materials are reduced, through processing, to creams or liquids), and in so doing they rely on a visual culture of labelling for promotion that situates the products in the New Zealand landscape. An analysis of two corporate marketing websites of popular cosmetic companies will reveal how harakeke products build on the success of the 100% Pure New Zealand brand and demonstrates how development of harakeke has been guided by its potential as a cosmetic product.

Living Nature

The website of Living Nature (http://www.livingnature.com/pages/harakeke) brands itself as '100% natural' and 'uniquely New Zealand'. The natural cosmetics company produce and market a range of products including skin care oils and cream, shampoos and conditioners and face, eye and lip care cosmetics. The products are packaged simply, displaying the Living Nature logo, a circular design similar to a Maori curvilinear kowhaiwhai rafter pattern. Its mission is rooted in the land and the unique plant resources New Zealand offers: 'featuring the uniqueness of our plant resources in a way that inspires the human spirit'.

Their website goes on to assert how the company has 'harnessed the purifying, healing and nourishing power of New Zealand's unique native botanicals like *Harakeke* Flax Gel, Totarol, Manuka Honey, Manuka Oil, Hallo Clay and Kelp'. Their green credentials are underlined further with the following statement about their commitment to the environment. Their facility

> uses energy from a New Zealand power supplier that generates renewable energy from wind and water (hydro) and we harvest our own filtered rainwater. Our packaging is fully recyclable, meets the highest EU environmental standards and is 100% free from harmful phthalates and Bisphenol-A (BPA). Paper and cartons are sourced from renewable, managed forests and, like our inks, are free from dioxin and elemental chlorine.

Further information on the website presents Living Nature as a pristine company that thrives on its unique environment. It asserts that because of the isolation of the islands that emerged over 80 million years, 80% of the plants found in New Zealand are unique to the region and found nowhere else in the world. It states how these unique plants are specially sourced on the basis of their bioactive ingredients from the most potent plants known for their healing, purifying and nourishing qualities.

Plants in the New Zealand landscape are marketed as bodily transformative. A number of indigenous plants are presented as 'hero ingredients' and the resulting cosmetics 'hero products'. Harakeke leaf sap is categorized under this. The sap is extracted from the plant's older leaves to make a natural gel product that helps hydrate the skin. The product description mentions the traditional uses of harakeke by Maoris as well as by early European settlers for rope and linen. The website has a close-up image of harakeke leaves behind which in soft focus is pictured a middle-aged woman with clear white skin. The image is emblazoned with the slogan 'Harakeke: Nature's Super Skin Hydrator'.

Place is important in the promotion of product and its authenticity. The website ascribes provenance, pointing out how the gel is sourced from Te Araroa on New Zealand's East Cape. It provides further details about extraction process, stating how the gel is physically removed from the base of the mature leaves so that the main rootstock and younger leaves are preserved. The company uses the harakeke leaves for the gel and the seeds for making soap. A short film provides visual testimony of the source for the gel, located at the base of each leaf.

Primal Earth

The cosmetics company Primal Earth (http://www.primalearth.co.nz/) produces natural plant-based skincare products that utilize New Zealand's natural environment to market the efficacy of their products. Their slogan 'Powered by Plants' accompanies a range of products including shaving crème, face crème and moisturiser in earthy green packaging. The cosmetics company utilize harakeke and Mamuku fern, highlighting their use as natural skin lotions and healing properties. The Primal Earth oath states: 'Just New Zealand naturally active ingredients that work'. It adds: 'This range is powered by plants. No harsh chemicals. Look and feel great, without irritating your skin. Made in New Zealand, by Kiwis.'

The company website features three images of plants (harakeke, aloe vera and Mamuku fern) situated in New Zealand's natural landscape with no signs of human intervention. In their promotional material about the different properties of plants, the website states:

> Harakeke is a striking plant that features dominantly in the New Zealand landscape. It is native to New Zealand and a handful of Pacific Islands. Harakeke is renowned for the clear polysaccharide gel exudates produced on the surface of leaves at the base. This gel is often referred to as the New Zealand Aloe Vera gel. We use it extensively in our products for its skin soothing and hydrating properties. It is a superior natural alternative to petro-chemically derived synthetic gels.

The positioning of harakeke as New Zealand's answer to aloe vera builds on the plant's existing identity as a herbal medicine. Unlike the other cosmetic companies that market harakeke, the website does not include details of how the gel is extracted, its provenance or any historical reference points relating to the importance of harakeke to New Zealand (Maori and white settler) identity.

Summary

These natural products that are produced from the harakeke plant therefore serve to underline how products are successfully marketed internationally for their association to a natural, unique and pristine environment. This branding builds on the clean, green image that has been constructed and transmitted by the 100% Pure New Zealand campaign. It foregrounds visual representations of the New Zealand landscape to assert its New Zealand identity in distinctive ways that add value to the product (see Ball 1997). It also demonstrates how materials innovation has been driven by available demand for renewable products in the green cosmetics industry and the wider environment, in which the New Zealand landscape has been transformed into a recognizable and understood brand that transmits a set of green values and visual images.

Concluding Comments

To summarize, while Maoris have for generations utilized harakeke fibre for their own ritual and social practices, colonial scientists and biomaterial experts have been unable to map their own model of mass production onto the fibre for the product they are designing. It appears that even when harakeke is repositioned as an alternative to mineral and petrochemical-based products, harakeke is still not compliant to the kinds of outcomes that the scientists so desired through their products. That is, the operational realism of the fibre material means that products like the surfboard and the woolpacks were deemed uneconomic and inefficient to produce and support once positioned alongside other products readily available and easily extractible in the global materials industry, resulting in their failure of uptake. This demonstrates that even though the material had the potential to innovate design and meet the needs of an environmentally conscious public, in its object form, the harakeke did not meet commercial expectations. In Gell's terms (1998), this suggests that harakeke lacked 'coherence' in its object form and thus failed to perform to expectations.

This story of innovation has also demonstrated how materials are intimately tied to cultural and political environments into which they emerge, and how in turn these influence users' and consumers' perception and performance of materials. The national branding of New Zealand as a green and clean economy has helped open a niche for the plant fibre and drive research and development into the harakeke plant as an alternative to petro-based materials. Its operational realism has opened opportunities for a craft-based industry due to the lack of investment to find a technical solution to extract the strong fibres. In effect, it has meant that scientists have looked for other properties of the plant, such as the gel, which draws on the known curative properties of harakeke. This illustrates how the material expressivity of harakeke shapes social worlds and guides research and development in innovative ways.

Materials innovation, I have hoped to emphasize, is not simply about discovery. Rather, as I have demonstrated, it involves a deeper engagement, as materials provoke connections that shape their substance and form, which in turn informs their use and application in society. As Ingold (2000b) rightly reminds us, this is why materials are impregnated with culture and do not exist in separate domains of experience.

Notes

1. Hector (1872) describes how in 1844, a company was formed in England that sent out specialist machines and technicians to New Zealand. The enterprise, according to Hector, failed as the machines 'proved unsuitable for the purpose' (1872: iii). Many other attempts were made to extract the fibre: experimentation with different types of machinery resulted in the fibre failing to meet the quality of other fibres. These projects, as a consequence, ended in financial disaster.
2. Although Ball (2012: 362) asserts how materials are computational and 'the material structure itself is the machine'.
3. See Schiebinger (2004) and Mueggler (2011) for further reading on the power relations of botanical archives and colonialism; and Drazin and Kuechler (2015) for branding and intellectual property of new materials.
4. See Kotler and Simon (2003) for an analysis of the impact the materials industry has on the economic productivity of a country.
5. See https://www.scionresearch.com/science/bio-based-products-and-technologies (accessed 8 October 2018).

PART II

Materials, Design, Transformation

4

Of Canoes and Troughs

Materials Computation and the Nature of Social Relations

In this chapter, I develop and apply an understanding of materials computation in the context of the Pacific. Materials computation signifies a shift in the role of materials in the design process. As the science writer Philip Ball states (2012: 362), materials computation is a process of reliance in which designers shift responsibility onto the material or the structure to do the work. This involves a fundamental rethinking of the application of materials in design processes: a method by which materials with certain biophysical properties – such as responsive to heat, light, dirt and so forth – are selected in the design process to suit its function and behaviour in the environment. This means that materials are responsive to the environment, shifting the focus from form to structure so the material is the machine.

This shift in design thinking from a focus on form deriving from external machine, tool or hand processes towards one where form is directly informed by the combination of material properties and environmental conditions signals an important change in thinking about design and production processes. Much like the new engineered materials that are 'made to measure' (Ball 1997) in Western industrial design, I argue that a comparable process is taking place in the Pacific in relation to design practices there. Certain plants and trees are selected on an informed basis for their known capacity to perform in social environments after their transformation and display. What is integral to understanding this technical knowledge is a requirement to possess a deep empathy with the performance of plant materials and their natural compliance. This knowledge involves an understanding of the biophysical properties of certain types of leaf materials and how once transformed the materials selected 'do all the work'; that is, to work on behalf of persons to create and manage the social world. I demonstrate how Pacific people understand plant materials as more than mere functional or symbolic entities that grow naturally in the environment. Instead, through acts of informed selection, plant materials perform as complex systems by acting as physical agents to create and manage connections, establish continuity and aid survival (Boivin 2008; Damon 2004). If, as DeLanda (2006) states, such materials perform in ways that make their presence known, then in the Pacific, I show how their presence communicates ideas through processes of articulation, a central vehicle for Melanesian agency (Strathern 1988).

What is so important about this study of materials computation is that I extend this beyond simply asserting that materials are productive of the social imagination; rather, I claim that materials computation is expressed in acts of scaling, a calculative logic enacted in materials through cutting, stitching, sawing, seasoning and shaping. Scaling is a logical property of materials that necessitates an intimate understanding of the potential of certain types of plants, roots, lianas, barks and timbers to be transformed through acts of calculation such as addition or subtraction, and which has implications for the way crafted products are understood in the social domain. Thus, the logic of material calculation translates across the technical and social domains of life, areas that we once understood to be separate and distinct.

Scale and Design

The articulation of scale in the design of artefacts as 'mathematics elsewhere' has been well documented in the emerging field of ethnomathematics (e.g. Ascher 2002). One of the most compelling studies that draws on the complexities of indigenous design is the highly innovative analysis of African design by Ron Eglash (1999). Here, Eglash (1999) demonstrates how scale – in the form of fractal designs – is pervasive in African material culture. Fractals are iterative scaling patterns, self-similar in form. His analysis shows how iterative scaling patterns are located in diverse forms, from wooden sculptures to settlement structures and in ritual performances. He claims that fractals have existed in many different forms before the rise of chaos theory in the 1980s, except that no one noticed them. Eglash points to African haircuts as an everyday instance of fractal design: cornrow braids feature row upon row of repetitive patterns aligned in patterned rows. Wooden sculptures of animals display different sized animals repeated with diminishing scale. Settlement structures exhibit seed-like forms that appear to be based on increasing patterns of settlement, where domestic spaces, community spaces and ceremonial areas take on identical form though increasing in scale.

What is remarkable about Eglash's study is how he extends his analysis to the scaling relations located in ritual performances, arguing that there are analogous understandings of scale and self-similarity in the way ritual potency is temporally dispersed, and bodily movements inside ritual spaces are enacted. Eglash's work is important to this analysis of materials computation because it underlines how important anthropology, as a discipline, is to locating localized understandings and knowledge systems and situating this within a framework that can challenge Western assumptions about the dominance of Western technoscience.

Similarly, this chapter also takes note of the importance of scale as set out in Alfred Gell's influential *Art and Agency* (1998). His compelling analysis of Marquesan artworks teases out the formal relationships that exist between different artefacts in the corpus of works produced in the nineteenth century. Scale, too, exists within a logical system of stylistic interrelations, which, according to Gell, maps directly on to a system of social relations that existed in Marquesan society at the time. Different types of anthropomorphic designs carved in wood and stone appear transformed, through enlargement or reduction, geometric translation or reflection, and so define a relationship that delineates the stylistic parameters that make artefacts distinctly Marquesan. This system of style – in which scale is an important parameter for articulating difference – finds its analogue in the way Marquesan society is structured; as Gell states, it is the possible transformations within the corpus of artworks that can also be traced out in the way kinship relations are organized in society.

For Gell, style is foremost the driver of the social domain, and the inter-artefactual relations inherent in the creation of artworks generates social difference. While Gell's earlier analysis of tattooing arguably provides a much richer ethnographic case study of human skin (as a medium or material) together with the workings of style and its influence and interaction with the social domain through what he calls 'the tattooing plane' (Gell 1993) – a system of historical and political relations mapped onto tattooing practices – his analysis of artworks and style also overlooks the active and important role of materials in the creation of artworks. This oversight also holds in the context of Eglash's analysis of African fractals. While it may be argued that stone and wood were the preferred materials for Marquesan artists to work with during the early colonial period when most collections were amassed, Gell pays little attention to the technical processes and knowledge implicit in the materials selected for such creativity (as indeed his analysis focuses on the relation between style and culture). It is as though the type of material existed a priori and that the material itself is simply a canvas onto which cultural ideas are applied.

As this chapter sets out to demonstrate, what is important is how a focus on materials computation draws anthropological attention towards an appreciation of the capacity of materials to intervene in environments, both natural and social, and the operations and effects of this in society. It develops an appreciation of materials beyond surface intervention towards an analysis of the ideas of materials, questioning the intentionalities of selection and transformation and their effects in the social world (Coupaye 2013; Lemonnier 2012). In the context of Melanesia, these intentionalities are expressed through acts of scaling, through addition and subtraction of elements to generate forms. To refocus on the properties of materials and their work is to focus on design thinking and to appreciate the opportunities certain materials offer over others.

In order to understand the way makers engage intimately with materials, I turn briefly to the craftsman David Pye's analysis of workmanship (Pye 1968). Pye situates the material of the workman as an active ingredient in the material-maker relation: materials demand empathy, a knowledgeable approach and a skillset – certain tools and a particular praxis – if good workmanship is to be achieved. Thus, a piece of timber can only be planed along the grain. Other types of wood are prone to splitting. Workmanship also encompasses a knowledge of other factors that relate to the material to be worked: for instance, the cost of the timber has also to be taken into account; and this determines the design and finish, its quality and value. In other words, materials are laden with potentials and possibilities – they respond to certain environments as conditions change, both natural and social, much like as I show in relation to the emergence of the kapiak basket to fill a niche (see Chapter 2).

In this chapter, I take inspiration from Pye's deep engagement with material knowledge to rekindle a privileging of materials in anthropological analysis in order to appreciate the opportunities they present as they are expressed through calculated acts of scaling. Melanesian society is an ideal location to situate such an analysis because while it could be argued that material knowledge in Melanesia is at risk of loss – given that many communities have abandoned, to some extent, traditional craft-making activities – there are, on the other hand, widespread revival movements supporting the sustainability of crafting knowledge. In Vanuatu, for example, Bolton (1997) has demonstrated how the work of the Vanuatu Culture Centre has helped ni-Vanuatu women reclaim material knowledge required for the production of mats from particular islands. Similarly, in my own work in New Ireland, Papua New Guinea, I have discussed how the work of the Baha'i movement in the Nalik-speaking area has created a public space for a revival of traditional crafting activities that has helped sustain material knowledge through elaborate performances and that in turn endorse a person's commitment to faith (Were 2010). So to consider the untapped potential of museum collections, located in almost every Western provincial town or city, as repositories of material knowledge from across Melanesia is to harness the return of technical knowledge to the communities of origin, through programmes of access, learning and return (a point I come back to in Part III of this book). In effect, the material knowledge condensed into the design of ethnographic collections from Melanesia could be reference points for supporting the transmission of specialist knowledge of crafting activities.

Indeed, in this chapter, I engage the rich collections of ethnographic objects in museum storage as a resource to explore the way in which scale is articulated through design in ways to manage social relations. Coupling this with ethnographic notes documenting the historical and contemporary context will allow me to reveal the computational thinking at play in the selection and application of certain materials in design activities and why Melanesian makers place such a trust in materials to maintain relations vital to the sustainability of society. Drawing on the Solomon Islands ethnographic collections located in the storage facilities of the British Museum, I demonstrate how materials, after their transformation and display, condense a model of social relations in ways that can be understood by those who are adept at thinking through materials. In this way, materials do all the work; they create social worlds and shape the social environment and the natural world.

Materials Computation and Ethnographic Collections

This story of materials computation begins many thousands of miles away from the archipelagos of the Pacific Islands in a cold brick warehouse in London, England, the off-site storage facilities of the

British Museum and the repository of thousands of ethnographic objects collected from the Pacific since the colonial period. Amongst the floors of shelving teeming with artefacts from around the world reside two wooden objects that will form the focus of this chapter. Amongst a flotilla of assorted and different sized canoes from the Solomon Islands and supported by an assemblage of aluminium framework and covered in conservation wrap stands the hull of a large plank canoe, covering a significant area of the storage floor space. Adjacent, decorated with anthropomorphic motifs and a large carved wooden crocodile head at its prow, is what appears to be a dugout canoe, but after closer inspection it reveals itself to be a massive food trough as its attached paper label describes. Both were collected from New Georgia in the Western Solomon Islands over one hundred years ago.

These vessels caught my attention not simply because of the impressive workmanship invested in their production but also because of their sheer scale. The plank canoe hull measures some eleven metres in length, dwarfing all of the other canoes in the storeroom. Similarly, the trough measures over seven metres in length and conjures an idea of ceremonial feasting on a grand scale. Moreover, my interest in these artefacts lies in the fact that the canoe and the trough appear to be linked in another important way: their long sleek form resembles maritime objects. The trough is stored with the canoes and is often mistaken by Westerners as a type of dugout canoe (Davenport 1997: 318). It is easy to see why it is assumed to be a canoe: both the dugout and trough are created through the hollowing out of wood from a single tree trunk, and its storage alongside other canoes suggests that this classification still provides a logical answer to its storage location today. Indeed, James Hornell (1939) postulates how the origins of the plank canoe derive directly from the dugout: he argues how by lashing together planks to the dugout design of the canoe the sides of the canoe could be raised into a plank design.

Both the plank canoe and the food trough provide a fitting comparative case study in this analysis of materials computation because the design of these vessels raises germane questions about the nature of scaling within Melanesian society. My aim is to explore how an intimate engagement with plant and timber materials on the part of Melanesian makers offers a potential for fulfilling key actions through the execution of techniques of scaling. I propose that an outcome of these technical actions is they give substance to the social world and help manage relations with the living and the dead; and the land and sea. In selecting two classic designs in ethnographic museums, my concern is to highlight how two contrasting types of techniques –

additive (plank canoe) and subtractive (trough or pudding bowl[1]) – exist simultaneously in order to dynamically model social relations within opposing economies of scale and spatial domains. This, I assert, develops a deeper understanding of technical relations beyond what art historian Deborah Waite calls 'metaphorically, one and the same'; an assertion made in her comparative analysis of the Solomon Islands plank canoe and the food trough in the collections of the British Museum (Waite 2000). I want to go one step further by arguing that these objects, while productive of metaphoric relations and so situated in the social imaginary, are a product of materials computation that is capable of translating between different domains of life, of the social and the technical. In turn, adopting such an approach brings to light how specific materials and the techniques applied to them carry a logical capacity to map out the nature of actions for the future. As objects related through technical acts of addition and subtraction, I explore the ethnographic contexts of the production of the plank canoe and the food trough from the Western Solomon Islands to delve into how modalities of computation capture the relational nature of action in the process of scaling.

The Plank Canoe

The large single-hulled plank canoes of the Pacific have captured the imagination of archaeologists and anthropologists keen to explore their development and model migration and trade networks over maritime expanses. Citing Woodford (1909) in their classic study of canoes from Oceania, Haddon and Hornell (1936) draw attention to European admiration of the Solomon Islands plank canoe for its sheer beauty.

Haddon and Hornell (1936) state how the plank canoes – or *mon* – were found across the central region of the island region, built using the same techniques, though with differences in their form and decoration. Despite this early survey and observations, analysis of the Western Solomon Islands war canoe has, according to Hviding (2014: 103–4), been thematically restrictive. Hviding (2014) states how existing approaches have been limited to assessing the uses of the craft in warfare and on analysing the decorative elements of their design. Hviding's (2014, n.d.) own contribution adds an important dimension to studies of the war canoe by focusing on the oral traditions from the New Georgian community together with written documents to provide a richer account of its significance in the region.

The plank canoe was manufactured across the Solomon Islands and is testament to the importance of inter-island warfare of the maritime cultures of the region. In the Western Solomon Islands, the canoe was distinguished by its tall sweeping prow and stern, adorned with shiny mother-of-pearl inlay that contrasted with the darkened timber hull. The single-hulled plank canoe was one of several types of canoes used for specific purposes. In Marovo, New Georgia, for instance, Russell (1948) documents three types of canoes used by local people: the plank canoe, the dugout and the war canoe. Published no doubt when headhunting practices had ceased, Russell makes note of how the war canoe 'had all but disappeared from Marovo' (1948: 313) though observes how scaled replicas were still being manufactured in some villages. Sadly, he produces little documentation of the construction of the war canoe and its relation in construction to the plank canoe, but he does provide important details of the prevalence of the dugout canoe, its manufacture using adzes and its length measuring anything from two metres (the smallest) to ten metres in length. He observes how

Figure 4.1 Western Solomon Islands war canoe in the British Museum storage facilities. Photograph by the author.

the larger canoes carry triangular sails with the apex of the triangle pointing towards the bottom of the mast.

Written accounts by colonial officials capture the admiration shown by Europeans towards the plank canoe. The colonial administrator, Charles M. Woodford, posted to the Solomon Islands in the late nineteenth century, provides one of the fullest descriptions of the war canoe of New Georgia.[2] His colourful description depicts how the canoe was once used to take human heads and capture slaves from neighbouring islands. He documents how the war canoes would sometimes set out to visit adjacent islands in parties of between twenty and thirty warriors, attacking coastal populations so effectively that many groups moved inland to escape them.

> Starting out in parties consisting sometimes of only one large canoe, but occasionally in fleets, they would visit the Russell Island group and the western portion of the large island of Guadalcanar, or would sweep down the coasts of Choiseul and Ysabel, and have even been known to extend their raids to the island of Malaita. The consequences have been that the native population of the Russell Island Group has been almost wiped out, and that on Ysabel the remnants of the coast people have had to desert the sea-board and to take refuge in the mountains. (Woodford 1909: 510)

Woodford also recalls a particular event during his visit in 1886 (1909: 510), when about forty heads were brought back to New Georgia during his two-week stay, a practice that continued up until pacification under British colonial rule.

Woodford (1909) was so impressed by the plank canoe that he tried to collect one for the British Museum. Failing to secure the funds to transport a large war canoe captured by the British, the canoe – measuring some 44 feet from bow to stern – was bought by a German museum. He goes on to state how he acquired a smaller canoe a few years later – 'a faithful model' – having taken 18 months to complete the 24 foot canoe, which was deposited in the Bethnal Green Museum (London) – now part of the Victoria and Albert Museum (Woodford 1909: 511) – and whose whereabouts remains unknown today.[3]

Canoe Construction

The New Georgia single-hulled war canoe could have taken five or six years to complete, according to Hviding (2014: 105), using only the stone and shell technology available prior to European contact and involving a body of other people for the ritual activities performed during its construction. The war canoe was constructed using various types of trees of different sizes, which served both a functional role to endure the rigours of seafaring and also a symbolic purpose for their association to the land and the spiritual world. Much as Munn (1977) has argued in relation to canoes of Gawa in Papua New Guinea, the New Georgia canoe captures relations between land and sea through the transformation of wood into an ocean-going vessel.

The 'potential for making something else out of what is given' (Munn 1977) is apparent in the way in which wood taken from the forests of New Georgia is transformed into an ocean-going vessel. This process of transformation is documented by the naval surveyor H.B. Somerville, who detailed a technical description of the canoe's complex construction (Somerville 1897). He states how the planks are planed down into a thickness of half an inch, sometimes less, with a strengthening rib left in the middle that runs the length of the plank. The planks are bent between two posts stuck in the ground, and corresponding planks from the left and right side of the canoe are bent together. The whole canoe is stitched together using a three-ply cordage of coconut fibre before 'puttynut' is applied to the joints to make the vessel watertight. Somerville adds that the canoe was kept under shelter away from the rain for about a week to ten days to allow for the sealant to harden. Midribs constructed inside the canoe were used to maintain the shape of the canoe. Somerville goes on to add that while there was no decking inside, he says that in the war canoes: 'there is in the centre a sort of platform of sticks, similar to those in the houses, on which to place the heads of the slain, or to carry food or other things upon; and there are also wooden crutches at intervals along the length of the boat, to carry spears, fishing rods, etc.' (Somerville 1897: 370). Not only did the canoe's lightweight and stable construction allow for significant voyaging and size and speed; but its design also allowed for the deployment of formidable manpower, which stood in contrast to the design of the heavier dugout.

If the design of the single-hulled plank canoe is geared towards speed and lightness, then the heavier dugout is characterized by its slowness. I also argue that the plank canoe and dugout rely on other important distinctions in technique. The former employs an additive technology: the stitching together of planks sourced from large trees to form a planar surface. The dugout, in contrast, is constructed through a technique of subtraction: wood from a singular tree trunk is felled and the inside removed using an adze. Woodford observes how the planks of the New Georgia canoe are lashed to the timbers with strips of fibre that pass through holes drilled in the projecting bosses

(Woodford 1909: 508–9). The timbers are shaped and lashed tightly together before being allowed to season in canoe houses until their use in assemblage. When the canoe hull is completed, a thick layer of black puttynut is applied to the joints to make the vessel watertight. Thus, the single hull is a composite of many parts intricately aligned and tied together to form one singular entity.

The material construction of the canoe – made from the raw materials of the land – links elements of the land with those of the sea; as well as the living with the dead. This is demonstrated in Hviding's (n.d.: 17) analysis of the plank canoe, where he describes how the tall bow and stern prows of the canoe were built of a particular kind of lightweight wood known as the *tangovo*. Tangovo is significant because it is a very tall tree that may be spotted on land whilst out at sea as it reaches above the forest canopy. Hviding goes on to say that the dead were often placed at the base of this tree, supported in a seated position by the protruding roots. It was believed that a deceased person's spirit would alight and move up the tree towards the canopy and subsequently move across the sea towards the west, the ancestral domain where the sun sets. Thus, the lightweight qualities and strength of the tangovo wood not only served to heighten the seaworthiness and speed of the canoe, but it had a symbolic association to spiritual powers, movement and ancestors.

Hviding (2014: 106–7) also documents some other types of wood used for the war canoe, drawing on the knowledge of a canoe builder from Marovo Lagoon in the New Georgia island group. For example, he states how a pliable though brittle wood called *tobo* – a tree that grows in the coastal forested fringes of the island – was used for the planks. Interestingly, he also states how in the past, divination was used to locate suitable trees in the forest for canoe construction. This practice now abandoned, he states how today canoe builders simply locate suitable trees of sufficient height and strength.

The plank canoe's complex design reflects its computational properties. For example, Frederick Damon (2004) presents a compelling case of how different types of plant materials used in an outrigger canoe design encapsulate different types of relationships in the social world. The type of timber used in the construction of the hull relates to the dead and to seafaring. The land on which the timber is harvested also attaches genealogical ties and asserts historical relations to tracts of land and ancestors. Damon's work clearly demonstrates how the selection of different plant materials condenses social relations in ways that can be understood in Muyuw Island society, though to the untrained eye they would perhaps go unnoticed as simply functional materials.

The war canoe is designed to be fast and light (in contrast to the trough, which I later demonstrate is, by comparison, land-based and heavy and is thus similar to the dugout), and a key design feature that aids its mobility are the decorative elements incised on the prow and hull. Like other canoes in the Solomon Islands outlined by Haddon and Hornell (1936), the New Georgia war canoe features an array of decorative motifs that straddle its hull. The exterior surface of the canoe's hull, especially around the prow and stern, is covered in decorative motifs depicting frigate birds and other symbolic entities using mother-of-pearl shell inlay to create a figure-ground effect. The design of the motifs are said to have played a protective role, warding off malevolent spirits located in the sea and making the canoe swifter at it travels in the sea (Hviding n.d. 18). The motifs – both in their style and technique – resemble motifs found on a number of media including facial tattoos and carvings throughout the islands.[4]

The Economy of *Mana*

The plank canoes were designed for inter-island mobility – enabling New Georgians to travel from their coastal villages to make raids on other communities. Headhunting raids served as an important mechanism in the political economy of mana, an invisible power or lifeforce responsible for replenishing the social and political environment. In New Georgia, mana was concentrated on the skull of dead chiefs and relatives, acting as a source of spiritual power; it was also applied to those heads and skulls of strangers taken in warfare and imported into religious practices on one's own land (Hviding n.d.: 6). By carrying out raids, warriors aimed to return with heads and sometimes captive humans, who would be enslaved and forced into labour to produce shell wealth such as clamshell rings (Hviding n.d.: 7). The taking of heads carried home mana from overseas and also diminished mana of enemies overseas, weakening their spiritual economy and political resolve, whilst in addition plaguing them with the ghosts of the dead, who could no longer be buried on their ancestral land. The planning and organization of raids to overseas islands thus fed into a thriving ritual economy in which the disruption of mana secured success in the exploitation of the land and the sea.

It is thus evident how the effort invested in the overall design of the war canoe enhances its capacity to perform: both the selection of materials and their technical execution in the production of seafaring canoes becomes an instrumental vehicle in the political economy of mana and the reproduction of social relations in the region. In turn, we could say that the scale of the canoe becomes an index of the power wielded by organizing clans, firstly in their capacity to build larger canoes but most importantly in their ability to mount attacks on rivals, allowing for the imagining of an expansive system of external social relations through warfare and the accumulation of mana (see Harrison 1993). It is through the planning, orchestration and deployment of natural resources and suitable manpower on land involved in the calculated building of plank canoes (directed towards external social relations and events, an inter-island spatial-temporal domain) that large-scale canoes can be deployed spatially on a larger scale and thus import mana to regenerate lifeforces at home. Thus, the plank canoe is an index of this expansive system, whereby the technical construction of the canoe indexes the scope of social relations through acts of violence and conquest. The calculations at play in the transformation of wood into canoe therefore totalizes this system – it captures these movements between land and sea and through the choice of materials replenishes the land through the taking of heads (mana), thus serving to link the world of the living with that of the dead. It is through the calculation of addition that this economy of scale takes shape.

Troughs and Bowls

While the first half of my analysis has focused on the incremental scale (additive) of the plank canoe design in relation to extensive maritime relations and ritualized violence in New Georgia (and by their similar construction we could consider extending this model of computation to other plank canoes of the Solomons), the techniques of subtraction associated to the food trough from the Western Solomon Islands offers a contrasting but complementary set of ideas rooted in a logic of scaling operations.

Here I present the food bowl and trough as analogues to the plank canoe. I make this assertion because of their visual form – they are both canoe-like in structure and also have decorative designs on their 'hulls' – and also in terms of their emphasis on scale: bowls come in different sized versions of themselves and exhibit a form of self-similarity.

The Carved Wooden Bowls of the Eastern Solomon Islands

Carved wooden bowls are well represented in museum collections (no doubt due to their portability) though like the war canoe from New

Georgia there is little substantive ethnographic material that provides detailed insights into their use in the Western Solomon Islands. For this reason, I want to begin with a diversion into bowls from the Eastern Solomon Islands as a means to frame my argument here. I turn to museum curator and anthropologist William H. Davenport from the University of Pennsylvania, who has conducted extensive research on collections of carved wooden bowls from the Eastern Solomon Islands. His insights into the design and function of the bowls provide useful comparison to the relative lack of ethnographic material documenting the bowls from the Western Solomon Islands.

Davenport explains how bowls from the Eastern Solomon Islands – as well as the types of animal motifs carved into them – appear in a dream or vision of the carver channelled through tutelary spirits prior to carving (Davenport 1997: 319). The bowls were used for serving food, sometimes consisting of taro and almond mixture pounded into porridge. He documents many classes of bowls from the region: some of which are kept in the canoe house, where ritual feasting takes place. Some are related to spirits of the dead, those slain violently, while others serve more functional purposes. According to Davenport, those bowls with a wooden carved base are related to tutelary spirits.

Davenport also demonstrates how the bowl captures relations between land and sea. He describes (1997: 318) their canoe-like attributes, stating how these bowls may be dragged into the sea by children and played with as though they are dugout canoes. He states how bowls may be stored near the opening of houses, under the rafters, which allows the smoke from the hearth to circulate. This location is thought to be inviting to spirits to visit their own food bowl (Davenport 1997: 320). Before feasting, the bowl is washed off in the sea before it is taken to a canoe house, where the feasting takes place. Davenport states how food in the bowl may be offered to spirits before human consumption. The bowls contain special puddings, made up of cooked yams or taro, sometimes garnished with fish or pork. Like canoes, the wooden bowls also feature decorative inlay designs using mother-of-pearl. The two handles of the bowls are often carved to resemble frigate birds or other sea-based creatures, evoking relations between land and sea and totemic spirits.

Davenport suggests that a notion of lifecycle emerges in the making and unmaking of bowls. Bowls may be retired – left in a special enclosure to rot away (Davenport 1997: 324). He also observes how the bowls are used in lifecycle events, demonstrating their relation to domains of the living and the dead and the transference of clan-based power, which is located in the land. There were different types of bowls for feeding groups of men, both in group size and in terms of status. He describes how a bowl nearly one metre long was used during initiation events. Other types of bowls range from about one to four metres in length and are known as 'large vessels' (Davenport 1997: 318). Some may be used only once during an exchange feast with partners from other communities. During the bonito fishing season, the catch may be cooked in the canoe house and eaten with puddings prepared in bowls (Davenport 1981). Other ritual feasts take place in the canoe house, in particular male initiations, which involve the preparation of puddings in the wooden bowls. The class and size of the bowl therefore appears to frame the type of activity organized and the number of men who eat from the bowl. It also emphasizes the relation between the food trough and the canoe as analogues for one another, as I argue in the Western Solomon Islands.

There are other factors of the bowls that reveal their canoe-like qualities. In the process of making bowls, scaling comes to the fore much like in the construction of the plank canoe. The carver cuts the wood into a series of rectangles, which are related through a system of scaling relations (1997: 322). Davenport notes that 'all details gradually emerge out of intermediate rectangular masses' (1997: 322). For instance, four rectangles emerge of varying scale: a large rectangle from which the bowl will be carved; two smaller rectangles as the handles; and another rectangle at the base for the plinth.

As a technical process combining the material and conceptual, the process of scaling is redolent of the logic of enumeration through its articulation in transforming quantities into evaluative, relative and relational statements about the nature of ritual activities. In a similar fashion to canoe construction, once the basic rectangular form has been carved from the wood block, the bowl is left to season before more intricate carving takes place. Shallow channels are cut for the shell inlay of nautilus and conus shells, held in place using puttynut. The final process involves the sanding down of the bowl. It therefore emerges that the wooden bowl creates an incremental but inward system of scale through the technique of subtraction – the removal of wood from a block of softwood.

The Food Trough of the Western Solomon Islands

While my analysis so far has drawn on Davenport's illuminating survey of bowls from the eastern half of the Solomons, how does this extend to an understanding of the food trough from New Georgia that is housed in the storage facilities of the British Museum?

As stated, the food trough from the Western Solomons thrives on a notion of scale, a property that no doubt led to its acquisition by colonial collectors because it conjured images of exotic practices that conformed to European stereotypes of Melanesians. This is demonstrated in a note filed under British Museum correspondence 1904. A British Navy admiral appears to describe this bowl:

> Kiki dish - taken from the Head Quarters of the Rubiana Head hunters in the Rubiana Lagoon Solomon Islands when those villages were destroyed by HMS Royalist in September 1891 – after a raid on neighbouring villages the cooked captives were eaten from this bowl by the captors.[5]

Russell (1948) describes a large trough bowl in Marovo (New Georgia) that resembles the one in the British Museum storage facilities. Known locally as *koqomo*, this is a long rectangular wooden trough up to six metres in length. Inside these vessels, puddings – a staple item of native diet in Marovo – were prepared.

Edge-Partington (1903: 161) provides some important ethnographic context of the use of the food trough. He mentions how Woodford describes such a food trough for preparing and pounding food. He goes on to describe how Woodford saw twenty-two men seated – including the notorious Roviana chief Ingova – at each side of the trough and an

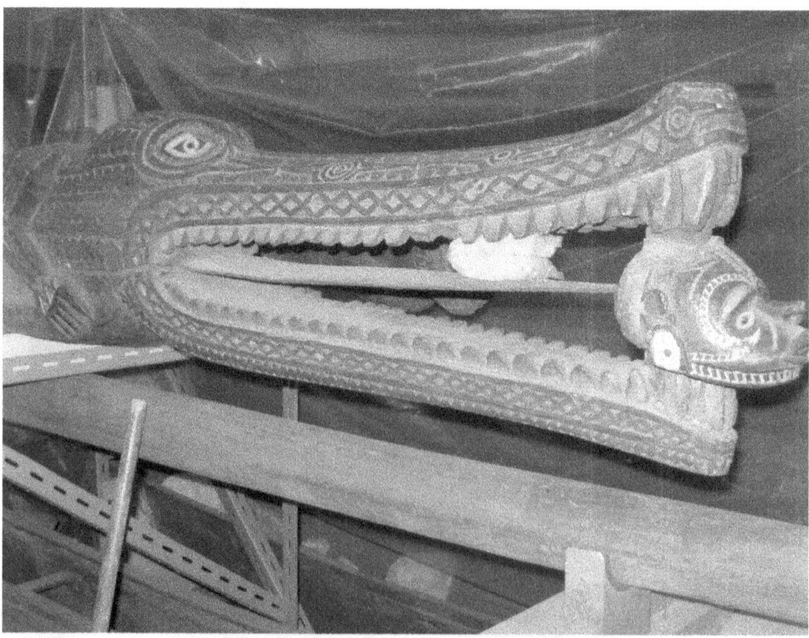

Figure 4.2 Food trough from Roviana, Western Solomon Islands, in the British Museum storage facilities. Photograph by the author.

old man at either end. The food – taro, yams and nuts – were placed in the trough. 'On one occasion,' he says,

> I saw the inauguration of a large trough for preparing and pounding food; the ceremony taking place in the chief canoe house of the town (Sisieta). I was assigned a seat next to Ingova (one of the two chiefs of Sisieta), while above my head were eight heads lately taken in a head-hunting expedition. The trough was about 30 feet long and carved to represent a crocodile; twenty-two men were seated on each side of the trough, and an old man at either end. They had all their ornaments on and wore their shields over their shoulders, while their spears and tomahawks were close behind them. The food, consisting of taro, yams, and nuts, was placed in the trough, and the men sat ready. An old man in full fighting rig was then seen advancing towards the house. Walking up to the entrance he suddenly started back and raised his spear, exclaiming, Basioto (a crocodile) and standing on the defensive. Ingova then advanced from the interior of the house, and placing one hand on the crocodile's head, began a speech which lasted about ten minutes. At a given signal the men began pounding the food, all of them keeping excellent time. When they got tired or hot they were relieved by others, and the pounding was continued for over half an hour. I was then asked to go, and not wishing to offend them I did so.

In a publication three years later, Edge-Partington clarifies what Woodford had witnessed.

> This very ceremony at which Mr. Woodford was present happens to be very interesting, as it was really the ceremony of crowning Ingova king! His brother, who was king before, had died, but the coronation ceremony could not have been held earlier because Ingova had not taken any heads, but just before the ceremony he had been to Choiseul and had taken eight heads, so that he was then able to be crowned. These heads were those that Mr. Woodford saw. The speech that Mr. Woodford heard was not really anything very wonderful, it was simply Ingova telling them how he had taken the heads, and where he found the men, and at what part of Choiseul he had taken them. He ended up by saying what wonderful people the Rubiana people were, and what small and useless people the Choiseuls were. (1906: 121)

The association between the canoe and the trough is apparent through the feasting ritual taking place in the canoe house. According to Waite (2000), the food troughs from which men ate at war-related festivals were kept in Roviana canoe houses through the turn of the century. The canoe houses, according to Hviding (2014: 108), were built in sheltered locations in the coastal forest near the beach and provided protection and storage for canoes and for the display of heads. Frank Burnett, a traveller in the region, stated that in every village he visited he saw:

> … usually in the large canoe house, a huge trough, between thirty and forty feet long, carved out of a solid log, and fashioned to represent either a shark or a crocodile. These are used as receptacles for food, and in them are mashed, the immense quantity of food, consisting of sweet potatoes, rice, and taro, that is required when one village is entertaining another to a feast … (Burnett 1911: 93–94, cited in Waite 2000: 120)

The feasting ritual – in which the trough feeds groups of men – clearly appears related to headhunting and ceremonies to inaugurate chiefs (and so reproduces clan-based power).

The pummelling of land-based root vegetables and nuts into a pudding substance that is then distributed and ingested symbolizes the transformation of land-based products into edible foodstuffs on an intra-island spatial-temporal domain. It also symbolizes the relation of the trough to headhunting expeditions and the articulation of male power and leadership through the enacting of key ceremonies in the canoe house. The canoe, on the other hand, is the vessel to carry heads captured in warfare, and then returned to the point of origin, to raise the status of men and to replenish mana. It articulates how male power is related to mobility and capacity to enact violence through raids on neighbouring communities. This is symbolized in the prominent role of the crocodile as a symbol of aggression and consumption. Just as it functions metaphorically when depicted along the prow of a war canoe, so it serves on an eating trough, which was the focus of war and prestige-related feasts (Waite 2000: 122).

Much like the carved wooden food bowls produced elsewhere in the Solomon Islands, the food trough is an amplified version of this, scaled up par excellence with specific links to canoes, headhunting and ceremonial prestige. The trough is dependent on the successful growth of land-based products – root vegetables – in order to reproduce clan power through the inauguration of new chiefly men in society. The ritual appointment of chiefly men takes place in the canoe house, the site of male power, where the heads of enemies from headhunting missions are displayed. The transfer of power to senior men, as depicting by the colonial records, suggests that taking heads is a requisite to taking up this position. Whereas with the war canoe men are contained within the vessel, the depictions of feasting by colonial officers demonstrate how men are seated outside of the trough, an inversion of the seating arrangement of the canoe.

Thus, in contrast to the plank canoe, which encapsulates temporal and spatial ideas based on expansion and conquest on an inter-island scale, the trough encompasses a known and locatable spatial domain in which power is tethered to land and place. The notion of scale is based on the already known, reproducing a sense of time through the evoking of ancestors and reproducing this through ceremony and performance.

Economies of Scale

This analysis of design shows how the canoe and the trough play on contrasting but complementary economies of scale. The canoe – through the binding together of seasoned planks of wood – emphasizes an expansive system of scaling. This expansive system of design, additive in structure through the addition of planks to the hull, is an index of the use and application of the canoe for long-distance voyaging – headhunting raids to islands across open sea. It is the active taking of heads and captives and bringing them back to the ancestral land that is instrumental in rites of succession in New Georgian society and economies of mana, which enhance the exploitation of land and resources for which the design of the canoe is so well equipped.

The food trough, on the other hand, is a complement to this, and plays on a notion of scaling that is internal to itself, a recursion inwards. The trough is always constrained by the size of the tree felled from which it is made. The bowl's scale is immediately knowable from the raw material that grows on land, the tree trunk. While the taking of heads and captives from abroad sustains mana at home through a movement outwards, the bowl plays on a notion of feeding and replenishment from within to those outside. As Davenport states in his ethnographic analysis of the Eastern Solomon Islands material culture, the filling of the bowl with pudding is about not only feeding your relatives and communities but giving sustenance to the ancestors, the tutelary spirits through which some bowls are constructed (Davenport 1981, 1997). From the ethnographic evidence presented, I argue the same idea holds true in New Georgia; that is, the wooden trough is productive of new clan relations.

The bowl thus thrives on a notion of the already known, imagined and realizable in managing relations to the living and the dead. Scaling is made explicit in the size of the bowl. The larger the bowl, the higher the status of the ancestor for which the bowl is made. But in turn, we find that the larger the bowl the more men can then be fed. This therefore denotes a notion of encompassment that complements that of the canoe. While the canoe is filled with men who paddle the vessel, the aim of the expedition is to encompass external relations yet to be realized; in contrast, the bowl sustains social relations already known –

those already established – such as local villages as described by Burnett (1911).

Materials Computation

This dynamic of scaling, an expansive system based on unknown relations, and an internal system, based on known relations, echo Roy Wagner's theoretical framing of Melanesian personhood as fractal (Wagner 1991). Wagner uses the term fractal to apply and compare the big men societies of Highlands New Guinea with those quasi-chiefly hierarchies in island Melanesia. His focus is on systems of leadership where, in the Highlands, big men seek to influence greater and greater spheres of men in order to increase their status and renown. This involves negotiating and influencing others through barter and exchange as well as ritualized warfare in their pursuit of power and status, aggrandizing relations on wider scales through dialogue and coercion amongst those unknown. In island Melanesia, the big man system operates in a slightly different though related manner. For example, in northern New Ireland, big men known as *maimai* orchestrate influence by performing mortuary feasts. They acquire higher status as they perform increasingly in ancestral activities, using their kin connections (determined through the matrilineal and affinal links) to wield influence and power in larger social and spatial domains. According to Wagner, these two systems have been viewed by anthropologists as opposing, as exemplified in the work of Strathern and Godelier (1991) on big men and great men – personifications of two models of power in New Guinea.

Wagner introduces his own alternative model of Melanesian personhood, a fractal system that contains instantiations of both great men and big men. Wagner's fractal person is squarely focused on the social dimensions of Melanesian society, and certainly within island Melanesia there are both elements of great men and big men styles of leadership at play.

Wagner (1991: 163) states how 'a fractal person is never a unit standing in relation to an aggregate standing in relation to a unit, but always an entity with relationship integrally implied.' His analysis focuses principally on notions of personhood in which he states: 'People exist reproductively by being "carried" as part of another, and "carry" or engender others by making themselves genealogical or reproductive "factors" of these others. A genealogy is thus an enchainment of people, as indeed persons would be seen to "bud" out of one another in a speeded-up cinematic depiction of human life' (Wagner 1991: 163).

I want to extend Wagner's fractal personification of power to its articulation in materials, specifically the canoe and the trough, as material instantiations of these fractal relations. Forms are not simply products of the social imagination, as I have argued; rather they emerge through recognition of a material's performance and natural compliance – its potential to operate within social environments after transformation – and so in this way 'bud out' as technical acts of transformation through calculative processes of addition or subtraction. Seen in this light, materials condense these fractal relations, and it is through technical acts that they enchain and project this fractality as an expression of sociopolitical power relations. As Wagner suggests – though never actually identifies – fractality is projected in different ways in Melanesian society as a form of integral relationships.

Both the canoe and the trough of the Western Solomon Islands reveal how computational techniques of scale come to the fore in the selection and technical handling of materials. The calculus at work in the process of making and thinking through artefactual relations underlies the dispersed and relational nature of the material and technical world in Melanesia as a system of parts and wholes (Strathern 1991). As a logical sequence of actions grounded in the potentiality of materials to meet certain expectations and to perform specific acts, we can begin to see how vital it is to draw attention to the deep-rooted nature of material knowledge in Melanesia as a highly abstract and conceptual understanding of the concrete social world.

Notes

1. Museum catalogues generally refer to these artefacts as pudding bowls.
2. In their survey of canoes of the Pacific, Haddon and Hornell (1936) document several types coming from the Solomon Islands, including plank canoes from the Eastern islands. Their construction is similar to those of the Western Solomons, but what is distinctive is the difference in prow and stern, together with the types of motifs applied to the external surface of the canoe's hull. Davenport describes how large plank canoes were used in the Eastern Solomon Islands for bonito cult activities intricately tied into male initiation and rites of passage (Davenport 1981). He suggests a direct analogy between the killing of bonito and headhunting; bonito blood has a symbolic resonance to that of human blood, both warm and crimson coloured.

3. See Lawrence (2014) for an in-depth study of Woodford and the British Solomon Islands Protectorate.
4. For comparison elsewhere in Melanesia, see Campbell's (2002) work on the famous Trobriand Island *kula* canoe and its highly decorated prow. Campbell (2002) describes how the canoe possesses the capacity to magically transport seafarers across archipelagos; the application of decorative features to the canoe's hull had a similar effect to those in the Solomon Islands, in which their application was believed to reduce the risk of disaster and therefore enhance the success of seafaring expeditions.
5. This record was taken from the British Museum object catalogue. See Bennett (1987) for a comprehensive historical analysis of the Solomon Islands from the colonial period through towards independence.

 5

Enclosures and Disclosures

Materials and Difference

In his science editorial *Material Witness*, the science writer Philip Ball pertinently asks: 'How do the people who want to use new materials on a modest scale even begin to survey the vast and daily-expanding array of choices to find the one that meets their needs?' (Ball 2008: 522). Ball's question, aimed at discussing the haphazard process in which new materials are matched to products in the design industry, reveals how a latent conservatism comes into play in the way materials are selected for use in design projects. Ball blames this attitude on the way designers are wary of supplying a material for uses different from that for which it was originally conceived. He goes on to offer some advice for overcoming conservatism. According to Ball, often the best way forward is to offer designers direct, experiential contact with materials. This involves engaging with materials through touching, feeling and testing and learning about their properties and performance in a hands-on way. Often the best way to learn about materials is by attending special materials trade fairs or by visiting a materials library or archive where samples of materials can be handled and tested.

I begin this chapter with the story of materials matching and conservatism because, as Philip Ball has demonstrated in the context of materials innovation in Western product design, the same types of attitudes prevail in design thinking in the Pacific. With an ever-increasing availability of materials in the region, imported into the region since colonial times, I explore the contestations and debates through which materials are integrated into existing classificatory regimes of performance and aesthetics and the different attitudes towards and perceptions of their perceived social effect.

Focusing on plant materials used in the built environment, this chapter delves into design thinking by exploring the local discourses generated in response to design projects and how these inform an anthropological understanding of the complex classificatory fields in which materials are placed alongside other types of allied materials. I investigate how materials 'make themselves known' as a particular strategy of design thinking through the selective use of 'old' plant materials (DeLanda 2006) in architectural projects– in contrast to ready-made, imported materials – the effects of which mediate and amplify new spheres of male power in the region. I argue how the incorporation of select materials 'of the past' into the built environment – public spaces used for the performance of ancestral ceremonies – are brought into relation with other materials and so used as a vehicle to make tangible connections to the ancestral domain as well as to new sources of power, such as centres of government that reside on a translocal scale. This chapter thus demonstrates how male power is constructed and expressed through the interlinked processes of heritagization of plant materials and projects of scale-making that seek to draw in new financial assets and resources through processes of articulation and performance. This leads towards my main argument; that is, to develop an understanding of plant materials as complex informational systems that make themselves known in ways that provide tangible visual and material expressions for managing social relations in Pacific society.

Materials and Performance

Anthropologists have long understood the performative nature of certain types of materials. As Strathern has noted in her seminal essay 'The Self in Self-Decoration' (1979), in acts of self-decoration, certain paints, feathers and grease are selected in order to be seen in Hagen society. The application of materials renders the inner self visible and thus publicly knowable. Her work has heavily influenced anthropological understandings of Melanesian personhood as one that is neither essentialized nor homogeneous but fluid and polyphonic (Strathern 1988). Thus, Melanesian persons are 'relational entities', composed and decomposed of social relations through the application of material substance (e.g. paint and grease), foodstuff (e.g. cooked taro) and nurture (e.g. caring).

While anthropological debate has specifically addressed the fluid nature of Melanesian personhood as expressed through acts of display and bodily transformation, much less has been said about the dynamic nature of plant materials themselves and their conceptual relation to power in acts of bodily transformation and public display. Much in the way Holbraad (2007) asserts in his analysis of the ontological distinction between dust and power amongst Cuban diviners in which 'dust *is* power', the same can be said of Melanesian society; that is, certain plants – transformed into materials in processes of design – are significant for their technical abilities as they are for conjuring images of social power. In so far as we learn that Hagen men use a normative range of natural and synthetic materials to adorn their skins in acts of display (Strathern 1979), focusing on the performative nature of plant materials reveals how processes of selection and display cannot be understood as a singular activity. Instead, plant materials exist within a relational schema in which materials are brought into analogical relationship with other types of materials. The relational scheme in which materials are situated is always in a state of becoming (Ingold 2012) because new materials are always emerging in New Ireland society through discovery, revival or reinvention. As new materials emerge, so then are the objects that can be designed from materials. Thus, materials are performative in the sense that they capture shifting social and power relations and are indicative of the changing nature of personhood in Melanesian society.

Of significance in this chapter is the fluid nature of material identities in New Ireland society. Much like in Western societies, where new materials are constantly being invented in the laboratory in ways that appeal to consumer tastes and sensibilities (Ball 2008), I am concerned to engage with similar processes of materials innovation in New Ireland society. What is profound is the way in which 'old' or 'traditional' materials of the past have suddenly emerged as materials for the future in New Ireland. Even though Melanesia in general has seen an influx of materials like metal, plastics, cotton and so forth (new materials in their day), what is significant is how today, in Nalik society, people now show a desire to reclaim the technical skills and knowledge in processing plant materials of the past for use in design. Like Melanesian selves who are not stable categories (Strathern 1979, 1988), my ethnographic case study demonstrates how materials continually shift as the environments in which they are embedded also change (Ingold 2012). To be specific, I describe how Nalik men strategically select certain types of materials for use in public events and building projects, such as cemeteries, garden enclosures and men's houses. Their choice of materials makes visible claims to spiritual power and so acts as a means to assert their political authority. These claims, moreover, are understood through a complex set of relational schema and political environments in which they are articulated.

These claims are performed through activities known as kastom to conjure an image of connectedness to political and economic sources of power on different scales – both temporal and spatial – and allow for a flow of resources on a translocal basis. I draw on Anna Tsing's concept of projects of scale-making because her work is particularly useful for analysing frames of scale that are fabricated through performances in the Melanesian context. It can be applied to demonstrate how scale is not simply a neutral frame for viewing the world. As Tsing argues (2005: 58), scale must be brought into being and made visible in order for it to become operative, much in the same way that Strathern (1979) describes the process of articulating male power through performance. Moreover, she states that to focus on the making of scale is to draw attention to key interests and alliances that this process mobilizes, as scale-making provides the space for asserting claims and contestations. A crucial part of scale-making, Tsing argues, is to make visible projects in distinctive ways, and these projects never exist independently but are connected in some way.[1]

Eric Hirsch has fruitfully drawn on Tsing's work in his analysis of the connections between national scale-making projects of the Papua New Guinea nation state and the local projects of Fuyuge speakers of the Papuan highlands (Hirsch 2007). Framed within a discussion of forms of epochal thinking, his analysis focuses on the different perceptions of time involved in unique scale-making projects and the links between such projects. These projects are expressed in the form of connections between state development projects in the 1980s (e.g. roads, cash cropping, urban development) and the flow of Fuyuge resources (the appropriation of law and the flow of betel nuts). These connections, Hirsch states, are influenced by Fuyuge speakers and disclosed in various mythical narratives and ritual events, which also highlight how the Fuyuge speakers perceive time as epochal (Hirsch 2007: 136). Projects of scale-making, in this context, rely on the Fuyuge orchestrating ritual events in order to magnify themselves and create a translocal presence.

Amongst the Nalik people of northern New Ireland, the channels of connection between local and global forms differ to that of the Fuyuge. The visibility of the nation state is weak compared to that of the overseas missionaries, who have exerted a huge and highly visible influence on people's lives on the island and continue to do so up until the present day. Government (*gavman*) is understood in terms of distant relations in which Naliks refer to the remote location of New Ireland in relation to Port Moresby by evoking the term '*las peles*' or 'last place', denoting that Kavieng is the furthest domestic flight from the country's capital on the domestic carrier Air Niugini and also that the province is often overlooked in receiving development (see also West 2017). Naliks have attempted to hold the national government accountable for a lack of development and resources through the establishment of translocal connections between peles and capital. In particular, kastom is utilized as a powerful frame for mobilizing political obligations based on kinship and moral personhood. In contrast to Chapter 2, in which new products were reinvented outside the domain of kastom, kastom is deployed as a material and visual resource, a tool for enacting change in the community. Henceforth, kastom mobilizes a social and political presence on different scales focused on the use of particular materials. These materials evoke a sense of ancestrality, an authentic understanding of the past. At the same time, materials provide a powerful image of what it is to be a Nalik person and a Papua New Guinean through affirming difference (of materials). Much like the search for finance capital in the events of the Bre-X scandal as described by Tsing (2005), the use of select materials are dramatized through performances by Naliks to attract exclusive rights to resources on a local, regional and global scale; and thus can be seen as a project of scale-making. Thus, materials can be seen to be selected on the basis that visibly connects Nalik men to sources of potency and power; that is, the politicians and capital that lie beyond the immediate locality.

The Category of Kastom in New Ireland

The term kastom has been widely discussed by anthropologists working in Melanesia from the 1980s onwards (Foster 1992; Jolly 1992; Keesing 1982, 1993; Lindstrom 1993b; Otto 1992; White 1993 and others). In general, the term refers in a quite abstract way to traditional practices that are understood to derive from the precolonial past, whether invented, idealized, imagined or revised. Kastom activities are often politically orchestrated, a response to processes of mission Christianity, colonialism and modernity. People may live their lives according to kastom, but they may also reflect upon, evaluate, discuss, modify and dispute it, and this takes increasingly politicized forms (Harrison 2000: 663).

In terms of the origins of the usage of kastom, in New Ireland, the term most probably emerged in the post-war era as it did elsewhere in Melanesia as a response to the changing world vision held by Melanesians. A major factor in this change was black American military personnel stationed in the Pacific, especially in centres of conflict such as Guadalcanal in the Solomon Islands and across New Britain and New Ireland (Lindstrom 1993a; Lindstrom and White 1990). Another major contributing factor, however, were the feelings of disenfranchisement felt by local people towards the missionaries. This feeling was manifested in divisions between rights of access to resources, such as Western goods, food, medicines and education. In effect, an apartheid situation existed in which a privileged white people were separated from the local Melanesian population. In addition to this were the enforced missionary proscriptions of the production of ritual carvings, malangan, as well as other ancestral performances deemed 'unseemly' in an often overzealous manner. This situation generated antipathy towards the Catholic and Methodist missionaries in the region in the post-war era.

Amongst the Nalik people, kastom is not used in any abstract sense but is applied, instead, much like as White (1993: 478) describes in the context of Santa Isabel in the Solomon Islands, to specific contexts to refer to pragmatically defined forms of customary knowledge and practice. In particular, amongst the Nalik, kastom is often deployed in a way that is antithetical to mission though this itself has many complexities (Were 2005b, 2010). However, there have been many changes to the religious landscape in New Ireland over the last fifty or sixty years that have altered the oppositional relation between mission and kastom. For instance, while narratives of missionary activities on the part of Naliks were once clearly framed within an oppositional language to that of kastom, as they were saturated in a political rhetoric of enforced cultural loss and prohibition, the period of the 1950s and 1960s appeared to be a watershed moment that has led to a process of liberalism, which sparked new religious movements based on kastom and led to the strengthening of the Catholic and Methodist missions through the implementation of Vatican II liberal reforms.

In Nalik society, the major change to the religious landscape was the emergence of the Baha'i faith in the aftermath in the 1950s. The Baha'i faith – a Middle Eastern world religion espousing a unifying message of religious and cultural harmony (see Smith 2008) – established a foothold in the Nalik area and led to the conversion of several key senior Nalik men and women in the community to the faith. In Were (2005b), I describe how the faith established with its epicentre in the

Nalik village of Madina, where I undertook fieldwork. The faith then spread out to other villages in the Nalik region, primarily to villages where close kinship connections existed. The faith was bolstered by the support of senior men and women in the community. It espoused a unifying message – mission and kastom – and put this into practice by integrating kastom as a form of worship alongside the teachings of Baha'u'allah, the principal Baha'i prophet. As the Baha'i missionary[2] Hancock (2002) states, religious transformation came about during a period when the Methodist mission in Madina – the epicentre for these religious transformations – had a particularly weak grip on community life and when 'drunkenness, lawlessness and anarchy' were pervasive aspects of community life.

With the establishment of an administering body, the local spiritual assembly and elected representatives from the local community, who were also senior men and women, the Baha'i faith held the largest body of adherents in the Madina community. Permissive of traditional beliefs and practices, which included the acceptance of the carving of malangan sculptures, the faith became synonymous with kastom in northern New Ireland, and this liberal attitude led to further conversions throughout the region. As a consequence, Nalik Baha'is became recognized as the wielders of kastom, and many of their activities – including the New Year celebrations on 21–22 March (New day or '*naw ruz*' is a syncretic term that connects the Baha'i holy day to its homonym '*niu rus*', which coincides with the event in the Nalik calendar when fresh water springs emerge on the sandy beaches due to the low tides during the day) – conspicuously featured masked performances (*amaru*), the display of malangan, ceremonial feasting and other events that were deemed by Naliks as authentic of the ancestral past.

The capacity of the Nalik Baha'is to harness the ancestral domain in public events and ceremonies has evidently been a major factor in their success in terms of persuading other Naliks to convert. It has also, in addition, helped them cement their reputation as the true or authentic arbiters of kastom. However, in recent years, their influence in the production of kastom has waned somewhat, especially since the relaxing of missionary practices in the 1960s under the Vatican II changes, which witnessed an altogether different attitude towards Nalik carving practices and performances. More recently, the faith experienced disunity and lacked direction because in 2012 many of the key advocates became politically active in the Papua New Guinea national elections. Their affiliation to political parties was looked on by the faith as compromising the integrity of the spiritual assembly and so the Nalik members were forced to step down. This has meant that the faith, formerly led by knowledgeable senior men and women, is run by more junior community members, who express their belief through rote recital of Baha'u'allah's teachings, rather than through the orchestration of kastom.

These transformations in leadership have had a profound effect on the religious landscape of northern New Ireland. Now, there is considerable competition between the various religious groups as to who can harness kastom most effectively. The Methodist and Catholic missions are now competing against the Baha'i faithful over performing kastom, as this brings status and converts. This reveals, as Harrison (2000) has claimed, the competitive and contested nature that lies at the heart of Melanesian sociality and how practices such as kastom are often the focus for dispute, contestation and resolution. Indeed, this contestation and competition operates at various levels in Nalik society. For instance, a person's religious denomination and their village of birth and upbringing help shape a person's access and knowledge of kastom, which can be hotly disputed and is a continual topic for discussion in community life. This highlights the competitive nature of kastom and how successful performance leads to recognition and status.

Indeed, the competitive claims to kastom have produced a new public culture of spectacle in which church gatherings, openings, anniversaries, political gatherings and many other events evidently take place with lavish ceremony, focused on performances, dances, masking ceremonies and many other activities that are deemed to be kastom. These performances are considered to be indexical to the success of the mission or faith in transmitting their message of unity or togetherness and act as a powerful smoke screen for the schisms that once divided the New Ireland landscape along sectarian lines (Were 2010).

Central to understanding these kastom activities and performances is an analysis of the attention to detail on the part of the men who orchestrate, produce and instruct young men to collect and process materials used in ancestral performances and objects; not to mention those adherents, spectators and onlookers who scrutinize each performance, image and dance for signs of authenticity or inauthenticity, as the case may be.

The competition and rivalry in which kastom is situated has meant that special attention to the detailed elements of ritual practice has emerged. This means that the selection of plant materials has come to the fore in thinking about the efficacy of kastom and the production of the ancestral past. Plant materials selectively used in the design of public culture elevate objects and installations beyond mere 'mundane objects' as Lemonnier (2012) has argued. Rather, enclosures, lashings, thatch and architecture embody complex thoughts and practices that interconnect the social with the technical within a matrix of relational schema. Furthermore, the selection of certain plant materials over others has the effect of amplifying kastom in localities beyond the Nalik-speaking area. Instead, the status accorded to kastom and generating images that are deemed to embody ancestral power operate on magnified spatial and temporal scales, reaching into the past but also beyond the shores of New Ireland to centres of governance such as Port Moresby, where economic capital is believed to be located. Thus, the performance of kastom becomes a form of scale-making in which decisions about types of plant materials and their public presentation are crucial for presenting a form of connectedness, for attracting resources on a translocal scale and an amplification of male power.

I attempt to engage with this question through an analysis of the materials that structure and organize the cemetery in New Ireland society. The cemetery is the single most important space in Nalik society, as it is the area in which ancestral performances take place and articulations of ritual power.[3] The space can be understood as a site for the public display of different types of plant materials, each of which has their performances, such as their visible aging process and rates of decay, longevity and resistance. This complex assemblage of material components brings to the fore ritual assertions of power and personhood through the relational schema and complex environments in which materials are situated. I now focus on an analysis of the cemetery enclosure together with the men's house, which is built inside. Coupled with this is the garden enclosure, which I also analyse in terms of its materials and design, and compare these structures as forms of complex informational systems (Damon 2004).

Cemetery Enclosure

As Kuechler (2002) powerfully points out, it is death that signals the onset of ritual activities in northern New Ireland, which is marked by the transformation of the hamlet space to the focal point of communal activity. Naliks put significant effort into transforming the hamlet space for funerary ceremonies. The hamlet space is organized as a cluster of several residential houses, mostly constructed from local timber and thatch, arranged around an open public space that is adjacent to a clan cemetery. The cemetery is an enclosure inside which is constructed a men's house adjacent to which is the burial site for the deceased. The enclosure is made from fossilized coral (*karanas*), cordylines (*tanget*) and lengths of bamboo (*mambu*) laid horizontally between upright sticks to create a fence (*banis*). A small entrance exists in the cemetery enclosure in which men may pass by stepping over a V-shaped tree bough on which are hung the jaws of pigs that have been slaughtered during mortuary feasts in the past in the same hamlet space.

Each cemetery is owned and cared for by the resident clan of the hamlet. The cemetery is understood by Naliks to be a powerful place in which – in the past – the men's house was located, a focal point for ritual activities in the community. Naliks generally comment how respect for kastom has diminished in comparison to attitudes of the past. Naliks recalled to me how women were once prohibited from entering these areas, though today this protocol appears to have lapsed somewhat, though the sites are regularly tidied and respected. Indeed, I witnessed an example of this respect on one occasion when a senior man scolded some young men for their lack of respect as they fired slingshot from catapults at birds over the cemetery area.

While Naliks may cite a diminished lack of respect towards traditional attitudes of respect and decorum in and around the cemetery, the onset of mortuary feasts sees special emphasis placed on the public presentation of the cemetery enclosure. A key aspect of the enclosure is the type of design used in its construction. The design indexes clan power and the capacity of the clan to orchestrate kastom, and as I show, it is a public demonstration of material knowledge.

A range of plant materials, each with their own biophysical properties and their own habitats in the forest, are gathered to make the enclosure. The plant materials are collected by young men from deep inside the forest interior in locations already known to them. A senior man or maimai directs the young men to areas in the forest where he wants them to harvest the materials from, describing the names and details of the types of plants required in the construction of the fence.

According to some senior Nalik men, each clan has its own style of fence construction. The design of the enclosure communicates the land-holding clan. As Kuechler notes amongst the Kara of west coast New Ireland (2002: 83), the bamboo fence design is considered to be part of malangan. Hence, particular attention is paid to the design of the enclosure, as its successful completion is recognized as an index of the land-holding clan's capacity to orchestrate kastom. The design – transmitted through generations through the process of observation and reproduction – is powerful because of its association to the ancestral past, which itself is considered potent. Thus, the transmission of ancestral designs is important to the continuity of clan-based resources in Nalik society and their continued stability and wellbeing.

In 2009, I attended a series of funerary rites that took place in the hamlet of Kosinai ('the place where rubbish washes up') in the Nalik village of Madina. These rites took place to honour some of the dead of the Moxomaaf clan, the resident landowners, who had passed away over the last five years. Directed by a senior man, Kambarenges, himself an initiated Moxomaaf man and weaver of a special woven malangan known as *wawara,* the cemetery enclosure was constructed over a number of days prior to the feasting ceremony. It involved almost a dozen young men resident in the village, who were orchestrated by Kambarenges. Central to the construction of the enclosure was a bamboo structure on one of the cemetery fences, which was called '*bikmaus*' – literally 'big mouth', a term used to refer to a type of fish found in the waters off the reef. The bikmaus is also carved in malangan sculptures, and this particular fish is a totem for the Moxomaarf clan.

Bikmaus took a day to construct. The activities involved several young men chopping down poles of bamboo and carrying them to the Kosinai hamlet. Kuechler (2002) describes how young men often sing

Figure 5.1 Bikmaus cemetery enclosure, Kosinai, Madina village, New Ireland. Photograph by the author.

songs associated to malangan as they carry bamboo back to the hamlet, reinforcing their relationship to the malangan carvings. In Kosinai, there were no songs but constant talk and excitement over building the fish design. On returning to the cemetery space, the bamboo poles were split open with bush knives and then hit with hammers to flatten them into a plane. Sections of flattened bamboo were then battened together with nails. A mouth shape was cut from the bamboo and batons placed along the edge. Once completed, the fish mouth was secured to the edge of the enclosure so that the mouth opened out towards the hamlet space where the participants would later gather.

Each side of the cemetery enclosure was constructed by different clansmen. Groups of young men gathered materials from areas within the forest known for the cultivation of the materials used in the enclosure. The bamboo poles used in the construction of the cemetery enclosure were secured to upright posts using liana collected from plants in the forest interior. Careful attention was paid to the type of rope (*rop*) fastenings in the design. In Nalik society, all sorts of lianas are used for a variety of purposes. Young men and women have an intimate knowledge of their use and application in a variety of construction contexts. For example, a type of liana called *minis* is used as a lashing for securing sago-leaf thatch to a house's timber frame. Minis is a creeper with green leaves and a thick stem. It is processed by removing the leaves from the stem and then scraping off the outer bark. Naliks separate the inner green bark – which is peeled back using a knife – for use in building. Although minis is not as strong as other types of lianas that Naliks source from the forest, it is known to have water-resistant properties and, according to Naliks, grows stronger when exposed to wood smoke. It is thus considered an ideal material for using inside thatch houses, as fires are usually lit inside for cooking purposes.

In the construction of the cemetery enclosure, a special type of liana is used called *gasin*. Gasin differs from minis in that it requires no processing. This is because it is simply cut down from large trees in the forest from which it hangs. Gasin is a very elastic vine measuring around eight millimetres in diameter and is naturally available in long lengths (unlike minis, which has short strips). It is strong in tension and when pulled stretches longitudinally several centimetres. Due to its elasticity, it is employed by Naliks to fasten the legs and mouths of pigs and secure leaf wraps that surround food for the stone oven. In the construction of the cemetery enclosure, gasin is tied around the horizontal bamboo poles and wood uprights.

During mortuary feasts, the cemetery enclosure is on public display. Naliks – especially those from outside the hamlet, who have an obligation to attend mortuary feasts – congregate in the hamlet for days, weeks and sometimes even months. They will inspect the enclosure as well as observe the ritual proceedings to make sure the activities follow kastom. The fastenings are scrutinized by participants as they walk around the perimeter of the enclosure and enter the cemetery space. Their observations on the authenticity of the event will be communicated privately to clanspersons. The correct use and application of plant materials is vital for achieving a sense of ancestrality. Sometimes criticism of incorrect use of materials will be levied at senior men such as Kambarenges as a way to diminish their standing and capacity to orchestrate kastom. A lack of material knowledge denotes a lack of leadership and kastom. It follows, therefore, that in creating a desired sense of ancestrality – through the authentic use of plant materials – Naliks deem the proceedings as successfully running 'according to kastom'. The selection of specific plant materials in the enclosure's construction therefore serves to make a visible connection between the temporal identity of the burial space (i.e. of the past and associated to ancestral times) and the technical knowledge of the senior man or maimai that is organizing the design of the enclosure. This technical knowledge is thus made public through the construction process and acts as an index of the power of the clan, since the senior man or maimai encompasses this corporate identity through his organization of clan members in its corporate construction. I have therefore demonstrated how the public display of material knowledge is vital to the efficacy of the built environment in ways in which articulations of male power are adjudicated and performed.

Garden Enclosure Design

As I have outlined in the above section, the cemetery space is a highly complex design with special attention spent on the selection and display of certain types of materials. In contrast to the highly stylized and selective use of plant materials used in the design of the clan cemetery during mortuary feasting, the garden enclosures were made from a mix of discarded and found objects located in the New Ireland landscape as well as plant materials. Nalik informants told me that this was not always the case, however. Rather, in the past, the garden enclosure – necessary to prevent wild pigs from destroying crops – resembled the design of the clan cemetery, and therefore suggests a connection to the evocation of ancestral power.

In Lewis's (1969) ethnography of the Notsi of northern New Ireland (just south of the Nalik-speaking area), he observes the following about gardens.

> Most feasts for traditional purposes were considered to be complete only if they served taro, pig, and bananas. The garden plots were within close range, within one hour's walk of the village. The men cleared and burned over the plots and constructed bamboo fences around them against the inroads of domestic and feral pigs. The women then planted, cultivated, and harvested the crops. Useful trees, nut trees, fruit trees, etc. were left standing in the garden plots. One crop was taken from one plot and the land allowed to go to bush. The fences rotted and by the time the plot was grown over again they had to be rebuilt. There was no storage of foodstuffs so that each day they harvested enough for the day's needs. Each family maintained several plots in various stages of cultivation, some were being cleared, some were just beginning to grow, others were ready to be harvested, and some were almost finished. In 1954 there seemed to be plenty of land in spite of much land having been alienated in long leaseholds to European-run plantations. There seemed to be plenty of available garden plots, usually near the village, with additional unused land lying ready also. (Lewis 1969: 39)

Much in the way that the cemetery enclosure witnessed ancestral performances, the garden enclosure was also a site where ritual events took place, such as garden magic. For example, W.C. Groves (1898–1967) – an anthropologist and educationist who taught in New Guinea in the 1930s – notes in his diaries (2–3 August 1932) how a special offering took place in a freshly cleared and planted taro garden with the cutting up of a turtle. The connection of the turtle to crop growth can be understood through the timing of the arrival of the turtle to the shores of the east coast to lay its eggs. I have already described how this event ties to critical points of alignment in the Nalik life cycle when the arrival of life-giving forces to the land coincides with the timing of mortuary feasting and the cultivation of taro crops (Were 2010).

Naliks described how enclosures were once built of bamboo poles placed horizontally on top of each other and secured in place using vertical posts. Lewis (1969: 53) describes how the garden fence 'consisted of a four-foot-high lower section made of horizontal rows of bamboo lashed between upright saplings, in the manner of construction of the ordinary garden fences, and an upper section made of coconut leaves lashed vertically atop the horizontal bamboo lower fence, resulting in a fence about ten feet high'.

Like the cemetery enclosures, thought and effort went into the construction and design of them. This appears to be at odds with garden enclosure design today: only a few people put the technical effort into constructing these enclosures in the way that ancestors did in the past. Indeed, many garden enclosures are today made from a combination of wood posts and found or waste materials. For example, in the village of Madina, in the land that stretches towards the inland mountain range between the coast and the high school, several gardens are observable from the potholed road and forest paths that criss-cross the interior. Many of the gardens use rusted corrugated tin roofing sections as fencing held in place with upright poles. The tin roofing is no longer functional for house roofing so it is used as walling in its afterlife.

How do we account for this diminished attention to the design of garden enclosures in Nalik society? One way to approach this question is to examine how Naliks attach particular associations to the landscape in order to understand the articulation of material knowledge. As I mentioned in Chapter 1, the coastal fringes are open, public spaces where people may congregate during the day and night. It is a space where the majority of housing is located into clan-based hamlets. Tracts of land are owned by clans, and this land may be associated to land- or sea-based masalei, or clan spirits, whose stories provide an ontological reference point for ownership of land. The forest interior, which stretches high up to the limestone peaked mountainous interior, is considered to be the place of spirits, especially after dark. Inside the forest, freshwater springs emerge from rocky crevices. Naliks believe that at night malevolent spirits congregate around fresh water.

Groves (1936: 234) observes how masalei in the forest

> ... are known upon occasions to leave their location and wander about in places frequented by natives. Every one has seen one or more of them at various times. They frequently make their appearance along lonely tracks, or are seen by lone wanderers at unfrequented parts of the beach. It is because of their fear of them that few natives like to go about alone at night.

In the precolonial past, the interior landscape was the place where Naliks lived. Stone settlements still mark out the old burial grounds of clans and leave traces on the landscape of settlements. In a period in which inter-clan warfare was endemic to the region, Naliks lived in the mountains in temporary settlements. Under German administration, Naliks were brought down to the coast and lived in hamlets and villages (Kuechler 2002; Were 2010).

This demarcation of the land and its biographical relation to the past helps explain why there are different approaches to the presentation of enclosures. The interior space rarely hosts mortuary events and so is no longer on show for public scrutiny. The hamlet space, however, is continually a site for public gathering and contestation. Naliks continually make judgements and assertions about the 'ancestrality' of the hamlet space, as it is on public view, especially during mortuary feasts, when people travel from surrounding villages to partake in ceremonial exchange. Unkempt hamlet spaces or litter and waste on the beaches are a sign of poor moral fortitude and reflect a lack of leadership in the hamlet. Mondays are typically called community days. These are known as *lain* or 'line', which denote colonial inspections, when people lined up for the patrols. Other days are spent travelling to Kavieng to buy trade store goods such as tinned meats and rice. While the hamlet space is transformed into a productive area where temporary housing, enclosures and piles of root crops, sago, pigs and firewood are stored, the forest space remains out of sight.

The garden is productive of ancestral power (since root crops are harvested from them) and yet it remains unseen. The garden enclosure is not open to scrutiny in the way that the products of the garden are. Thus, the garden enclosure is purely functional in nature, as it protects root crops and vegetables from marauding pigs. But since time spent gardening is limited, as people are involved in other activities and events in Kavieng or earning cash, people are generally distracted from garden activities. This has led to a de-emphasizing of the importance of material knowledge in the construction of the garden enclosure. What matters are the results of gardening – the harvesting of taro – and many Naliks will buy root crops for mortuary feasts at market rather than rely on their own garden produce.

This demonstrates how the cash economy has impacted on material and ritual knowledge by unsettling links to the ancestral domain. In a contemporary era where Naliks '*sot kut kastom*' (short cut kastom) so as to find time for both maintaining traditional rites and obligations alongside engaging in the cash economy, emphasis is placed heavily on the public spaces where ancestral performances take place, which can be scrutinized by large numbers of people. In this way, the articulation of power is geared towards mass audiences and therefore is intended to amplify status and renown over the course of ritual proceedings. In contrast, gardens and their enclosures are marginalized and not open to the same scrutiny (as they remain out of sight).

Tamun's Men's House

The feeling of cultural dissipation is perhaps felt most strongly in the demise of the men's house in Nalik society, and this is an activity in which the public display of material knowledge comes to the fore. The men's house is one of the largest and most imposing structures that Naliks construct and is commonly referred to as *'haus boi'* in tok pisin. Men's houses are rectangular buildings constructed from a timber frame, thatched sago palm roof and flattened bamboo walling. Men take many weeks to complete them, starting with the erection of a timber frame and ending with the thatch, sewn and threaded onto a series of horizontal poles (the most laborious process in the task).

Men's houses are built under direction of a senior clansman along the coast in village hamlets and inside the walled cemeteries (*rabaarau*) belonging to individual clans. In Nalik society, the men's house housed young men under the tutelage of a chiefly man (maimai) or senior man (*piranabina*) from the hamlet. Within the men's house, clan knowledge would be transacted, and collaborative projects in the community would be delegated and planned. The location of the men's house – inside the clan's enclosed burial site – is seen by Naliks as a generative space where clan power can be passed on and thus renewed. Many Naliks recount stories of how, in the past, the men's house was so powerful that it could protect the clansmen that resided within. The men's house would be built in a special location so that the entrance faced a special rock that could regenerate the strength of the clan. Naliks claimed that human remains of their enemies attained from headhunting raids were stored at these sites and a strict set of ritual protocols was once enforced when men stepped inside the enclosure.

In contemporary Nalik society, few men's houses now exist.[4] Married men tend to live with their wives, and unmarried men may have their own room or outhouse in the hamlet. Museum curator Phillip Lewis noted the decline of the men's house as early as 1954 in the Notsi-speaking area, about thirty minutes' drive south of the Nalik area (Lewis 1969). He relates how an older man from the community had lamented the demise of the men's house, saying that 'all married men prefer to live in their wives' houses' and thus were not present to plan fishing expeditions (Lewis 1969: 30). He describes how missionaries and local leaders coerced others to abandon the men's houses and how in the Notsi village of Lesu the men's house functioned as a second residence, cook house and dining room for both men and women (Lewis 1979).

Lewis's observations on the Notsi men's house apply equally to the Nalik situation. In my last few visits to New Ireland there were numerous conversations about the loss of the men's house. Such discussions tended to arise when conversations centred on cultural transmission and revitalization. One response to this has been to re-establish the men's house as a means to reinvigorate kastom. In the

Nalik village of Fatmilak, local men built a men's house as a resource centre, in which they placed a computer, a generator and health information. The house was built using traditional thatch and timbers, the posts secured with shop-bought nails. In Madina, a men's house was built in 2012 under the direction of maimai Sioti Lupai in the hamlet of Panabuk, but when I left in March 2013, there were plans to demolish it, as residents thought that the building was being used by young men to consume alcohol. Naliks argued that because no maimai was present there was no authority to guide the young men in kastom.

Hence, the story of these two men's houses reveals current issues in Nalik society about their use. First, the men's house can only be operative if there exists a mentorship relationship between the young clansmen and a senior man in the community. The reality is that there are few senior men in the community who wield this respect or have the time to invest in this. Second, as is the case of the Fatmilak men's house, Naliks are rethinking the function and use of the institution. This means it has to appeal to young men in new ways in order to command respect. The outcome of this is that the mentorship relation between senior men and young clansmen is being transformed. Rather than senior men in the community taking the lead, a new elite – such as politicians and businessmen – are increasingly taking on these leadership roles in the community and so the knowledge transmitted in these spaces equips young men for life in different ways to the traditional knowledge once taught before in men's houses.

So how do men's houses in northern New Ireland lead to a discussion of material knowledge and difference? In 2007, senior men in the Nalik community of Madina embarked on building a men's house. Their motive was that Sir Michael Somare, the then Prime Minister of Papua New Guinea and *big tambu* to the Nalik people (one of his sons was married to a woman from the village) would be invited to open the building.[5] Tamun Kossep, a Nalik chiefly man (maimai) responsible for orchestrating dealings in the ancestral domain, oversaw the building of the men's house, employing his expert technical knowledge of the traditional techniques of rafter binding, sago-palm thatching and bamboo-wall weaving in its construction. Within the community, Tamun was considered one of a last generation of knowledgeable men to know how to construct an authentic men's house 'according to kastom'. As a maimai and piranabina, he was regarded in the wider community as particularly knowledgeable of the ancestral past. Tamun instructed young clansmen to collect special creepers from inside the forest. The plant fibre lashings (*axalawa*) extracted from the outer bark of a type of creeper that grows in the interior forest had been used instead to secure the beams to the upright house posts.[6] As a consequence, the design of the men's house was talked about throughout the Nalik villages for resembling one that came from the ancestral past. It was deemed as 'kastom' and referred to as 'Tamun's men's house' even though the house (and its design) belonged to one of the matriclans in the community. Although its form resembled other men's houses in the area, it was classified as an achievement because it had been built without the use of metal nails (a 'white man's invention' according to Naliks).

Much like the discussions held by Hageners about self-decoration and success in conspicuous acts of display, the conversations held by Naliks on the design of the men's house concentrated on the materials selected and their perceived sense of ancestrality (*axulmul*). It was for these reasons that the men's house was constructed and publicly presented to form the centrepiece for the arrival of the Prime Minister to the village – who would officially open it – and was to demonstrate publicly how the Nalik people had retained strong links to their ancestral past. On the one hand, the men's house was foregrounded as a powerful reminder of the persistence of Nalik cultural knowledge and a potent symbol of their struggle for political recognition by the

Figure 5.2 Tamun's men's house, Madina village, New Ireland, after the tidal surge. Photograph by the author.

nation state. Indeed, over the last decade at least, New Ireland has continually campaigned for the payment of mining royalties from the industrial gold mine on the outlying island of Lihir (Bainton 2010).

Plans for the opening event revealed a complex interplay of power relations between political and traditional structures neither of which functioned independently of the other. The acknowledgement of the Prime Minister as the big tambu was a means to express an affinal connection to a 'big shot' politician and an attempt by Naliks to reach out to urban elites for support (Martin 2013). The opening of the men's house was intended to create a space and context for traditional obligations to be affirmed and publicly recognized, especially in the form of financial aid and development packages from the national government, which Naliks thought were long overdue.

On the other hand, the men's house – built from traditional materials – shows how the selection of certain types of plant materials added value to the design of the house. The use of plant fibre lashings differentiated the design of the men's house from others made with conventional nails. As 'Tamun's men's house', it also expressed his knowledge of kastom and his expertise in dealing with the ancestral domain. Many of the young men who helped construct the men's

Figure 5.3 Details of rafter lashings inside Tamun's men's house, Madina village, New Ireland. Photograph by the author.

house talked about how the lashings were smoke and heat resistant and took a long time to decay. In rivalling the strength of nails, fibre lashings symbolized Nalik self-sufficiency and resilience (also, the fact that lashings were free whereas imported nails cost a significant amount of money and therefore require engagement in the cash economy). Holding on to this technical knowledge and making it visible through the use of special fibres (in preference over other materials) was pivotal to Tamun and the efforts of some of the Nalik people to make tangible their authority in the eyes of the audience. This signifies a positioning of plant fibres as 'of the past', a process of heritagization in which a plant's identity becomes transformed into an ideological or invented notion of the 'authentic' past, whereby the identity of the lashings was placed in the past when compared to the metal nails. Naliks were thus able to measure the performance of the men's house in relation to others (constructed from other materials or 'white man's materials') and so stake their claim as the true arbiters of the ancestral past in northern New Ireland. This act of display, brought to bear through the relational schema in which materials are situated and the public construction of the men's house, demonstrates how the selection and display of certain types of materials are crucial for the desired effect to be created.

The men's house, although acquiring an elevated sense of fame, became the focal point for a calamitous sequence of events. First, Somare failed to arrive for the men's house opening, and then a year later Tamun sadly passed away. The final episode took place in December 2008, when his men's house was partially destroyed by a catastrophic tidal surge that swept through villages along the east coast of New Ireland. Built for the arrival of politicians and the possibility of a better future, the men's house was never used as a functional space or as a traditional space for transmitting ritual knowledge and traditional values for which it was intended and was eventually left to decay on the beach. By 2013, no traces of the men's house were left in the hamlet, and a new cycle of house building took place in the hamlet. Much like the 'dead canoes' of the Murik people of the Sepik region of Papua New Guinea (Lipset 2005), for which Lipset argues that the contemporary construction of canoes takes place due to the demand of tourist markets and the global art trade, the men's house was constructed primarily to enable Naliks to generate economic wealth and to lever political obligations. Once this project had failed to attract the bigshots of Port Moresby, there was little motivation to train young men inside under the mentorship of a senior man, especially after the chief architect had passed away.

Despite this sequence of events, the story of the men's house in northern New Ireland serves to emphasize the co-productive relationship between material substances and objects in design. Materials, on the one hand, are associated with perceptions that influence their selection, help shape objects and give value to their design. Equally, it is through the design of objects that the identities of materials can be made transparent and their performance understood (Shove et al. 2007). Indeed, it was the selection of the plant fibre lashings over the metal nails that made Tamun's individualized agency operative. And it was the realization of the potential of certain materials – through their transformation – to create events, an opening and the possibility of financial return that distinguished Tamun's men's house over others built in the same style. As Strathern (1990) notes in the context of Melanesian revelatory practices, images possess the potential to create events and to carry with them future possibilities as well as to enchain relations of the past. This demonstrates how materials, through their transformation, take on image-like qualities in the dynamic way Strathern (1990) suggests. That is, through the process of design, Naliks are able to think through the possibilities and potential outcomes of selecting one material over another. In other words, materials enable events to take place.

Conclusion: Materials and Social Effect

This chapter has demonstrated how the built environment of the hamlet and the forest is designed through the selective use and application of plant materials. In turn, these design activities are orientated towards engendering particular sorts of social relations, not only on a local basis but, as I have demonstrated, on a translocal scale. Materials are, as Thomas (1999) has claimed in his analysis of the transformative capacity of imported cloth as it was introduced to societies in the eastern Pacific during the nineteenth century, technologies for creating events in which new forms of agency are put into effect. Their integration within design projects – of architecture, installation and so forth – reveals localized ways and strategies to encompass and control different forms of resources, both spiritual and economic in nature. I have demonstrated how, much like Strathern's analysis (1979) of Highlands New Guinea body painting, selves are made visible through the articulation of technical knowledge in public performances. What is expressed in these acts of revelation and articulation is the social power of Nalik men, their capacity to harness clan power and the technical knowledge handed down by the ancestors, and also the ability to organize and control groups of young affiliated clansmen to construct clan-based design.

In the cases of the cemetery, the garden enclosure and the men's house, what is crucial to understanding this relation is the notion of performance and product. As I have argued in previous chapters, we can no longer assume that the operational qualities of certain objects reside simply as a facet of its form. Rather, artefacts should be understood as a conglomeration of complex assemblages involving decisions, ideas and practices. These assemblages involve judgements about performance: the performance of materials, their public presentation and impact, and their context of production. Such an analysis reveals, much like Strathern's work on the Highlands performers, how inner ideas are brought to the surface and revealed. And as I have argued elsewhere, in Nalik society (as is no doubt true for much of Pacific societies) people have an intimate understanding of the social role of plant materials and how their articulation in specific contexts expresses ideas about social and ritual polities.

The operational qualities of plant materials, which I have alluded to, help explain how they play such a central role in processes of scale-making. Their capacity to create value through selection decisions and utilization of technical skills – much like the 'fame' attributed to kula shells (Munn 1992) – situates them within a complex schema that competes against other types of plant materials that Nalik people may or may not select. Their layered understanding of objects and materials points to their deeply embedded role of product and performance in Nalik society and their capacity to elicit connections on temporal and spatial domains. It also asserts how materials make objects operative through processes of design and selection. It brings to light the importance of understanding the workings of 'mundane objects' (Lemonnier 2012); that is, not as linear entities that are constructed from materials to be mechanically transformed into forms. Rather, this chapter has demonstrated how material substances are informed as much by other materials as they are about the products that they aspire to become. In this manner, we can begin to appreciate materials as complex assemblages of thoughts and actions that shape the way objects, environments and persons are understood and perform.

But what is just as clear is how the revival of 'old' plant materials such as the cordage lashings in the construction of the Nalik men's house ties into wider issues about the nature of the materials and environments. How the 'old' can be reframed within a political context that attracts financial reward says something very profound about the positioning of Nalik society and its relation to the Papua New Guinea nation state. The moralizing discourse promoted by the Papua New Guinea national government in articulating the value of kastom as a means to address a breakdown in law and order and youth disenfranchisement from traditional society has meant that plant materials – indicative of the past and traditional society – play an important role of new forms of social being in the region. But it also suggests, in contrast to discourses on kastom as oppositional to colonialism and missionization, that plant materials are placed in relation to imported materials, fibre and steel, as a means to assert the transformational capacity of crafting knowledge over the ready-made.

This form of engagement with plant materials on the part of Naliks testifies to the transformative potential of plant materials in Nalik society. It underlines the importance of plant materials in the creation of value in Melanesian society. As I have argued from the outset, the process of materials innovation provides an important point of comparison. As the history of economic botany testifies, plant specimens brought back to centres of empire in the nineteenth and early twentieth centuries carried transformative potential to better society and improve people's lives. The transformational changes brought about by new materials did not take place by simply mimicking plant uses. Instead it involved observation, innovation and development, which led to a new range of possibilities for product design.

Notes

1. Tsing's argument concerning scale-making is based on an analysis of events that took place in Indonesia in the 1990s. Her analysis describes how vast sums of international investors' money were lost in the Bre-X gold scandal, when people unwittingly invested in non-existent gold reserves that were supposedly discovered in the forest. She demonstrates how scale-making is implicated in this context through the performance of finance capital on a global, national and local scale. This can be seen in the way events were exaggerated through media coverage until the gold strike was portrayed as the largest in the world, drawing in investors worldwide. She says that this kind of spectacle is necessary to attract future investment capital; profit has to be imagined before it can be extracted (Tsing 2005: 57). Tsing states that such projects cannot limit themselves to conjuring at different scales: they must conjure the scales themselves so that we may imagine globality in order to see how it might succeed (Tsing 2005: 57).
2. Baha'is use the term 'pioneer' to refer to the act of journeying to spread the teachings of the faith.

3. There is a rich anthropological literature focused on and around cemeteries as part of discussions of mortuary traditions in Papua New Guinea and across Melanesia (e.g. De Lannoy 2005; Jacka 2016; Lipset and Silverman 2016).
4. For further discussion of shifts in masculinity and ritual activities in Papua New Guinea, see Tuzin (1997), Lipset (2017) and Lipset and Roscoe (2011).
5. *Tambu* is a Papua New Guinean pidgin term to refer to an in-law. The use of the qualifying adjective 'big' is used as a mark of respect.
6. The tok pisin term for the Nalik axalawa is *kanda*.

PART III

Material Futures

6

Returning Cultural Knowledge in a Digital Design Context

Collecting Legacies and Archival Futures

So far in this book, I have introduced a variety of plant materials of the Pacific and examined the different types of forms that emerge through design activities. My primary concern has been to highlight the ways in which people possess an intimate knowledge of materials and how, in particular, specific plant materials are deployed to manage diverse forms of relations. The affordances of plant materials such as their fragility or propensity for decay were central to developing this insight as were material identities, as these framed ways in which materials were perceived and understood in society. As the drivers of social change, I have also demonstrated how plant materials offer possibilities for political and religious transformation, as they are selected for use in innovative design projects in the region.

This chapter and the next turn attention to a discussion of the way material knowledge is transformed and transacted in Melanesian society in response to the encroachment of digital technologies in the region. In particular, the chapters examine how new knowledge networks, set up between museums in the West and rural communities in Melanesia, are making material knowledge highly mobile and accessible to people without the need for people or things to travel long distances, either permanently or as loans.

I consider the impact of these changes on the communities of origin in Melanesia and use anthropological fieldwork to gauge the types of understandings and perceptions held by local people towards the codification of materials and objects in digital formats. At first glance, digital return looks entirely problematic (Bell, Christen and Turin 2013). Newly codified material knowledge threatens to destabilize crafting knowledge, liberating knowledge resources from museum storage facilities around the world. In what follows, the chapters explore the politics of a recently introduced digital means of access to ancestral images – and the transformations of materials and design brought about by such technologies – and critically assess the implications for local stakeholders in Papua New Guinea and the Solomon Islands. Rather than simply replace or challenge existing orders, I consider ways in which material knowledge is augmented, animated and brought to life by digital technologies as it is presented in rural contexts and the values, connotations and challenges that this poses for local people.

Acknowledging the global connections between Melanesian museum collections and source communities, I also reflect on how stakeholder collaborations with museums have obvious implications for the future role of ethnographic collections in supporting the restitution of material knowledge, and these chapters raise important questions of the role of ethnographic museums. In asking 'what is the future of ethnographic museums?', this chapter outlines the values involved in digital return and how museums – as warehouses of material knowledge – offer the potential means for the emancipation of crafting knowledge from traditional hierarchies through digital design projects that support intergenerational transmission. Thus, given their newfound impetus to embrace digital technologies, museums offer possibilities to become the materials libraries of the future for the technologically savvy younger generation, where revived forms of object-making and crafting knowledge could be supported through an expanded knowledge network. How this transpires in practice is a focus of these chapters.

Digital technologies have revolutionized our engagement with the material past. Rapid advances in imaging technologies have significantly reshaped museum and heritage experience. Digital graphics and virtual environments are now everyday media used for interpreting artefacts, sites and documents. The 'recoding' of the museum, as Parry (2007) calls it, promotes new knowledge of museum collections, objects and dispersed assemblages and also fosters new ways of sharing material histories (Were 2008). These advances in the museum have been met with a proliferation of scholarly literature examining the philosophical and moral questions that arise through the use and application of digital technologies in collecting institutions. In particular, a key area of concern has focused on how digital technologies unsettle one of the core expectations of museum visitor experiences, which is to see authentic and original objects. While this body of research questions the future fabric of the museum experience and the status of material histories produced in museums (e.g. Brown 2007; McTavish 2005; Simpson 2005; Tallon and Walker 2008 and others) – the most recent of which is tackled by Conn's (2010) provocatively titled *Do Museums Still Need Objects?* – fewer studies have examined how digital technologies have influenced the production of material histories and promoted new economies of knowledge through digitally mediated access to museum collections.

In this chapter, I counter this shortfall by examining the ways in which material histories are produced, mediated and transformed by digital technologies. By material histories, I mean an object-driven approach to history in which objects instantiate relationships to complex social, political and historical environments (Labrum 2010). I am especially interested in the way digital technologies enfranchise the production of history on the part of museum stakeholders; in particular, those who are typically excluded from the museum and yet for whom, ironically, digital technologies are especially deployed to engage. In particular, I extend material history to invoke not just the relation of object forms to historical narratives but also how the materials themselves generate debates about the past, the land, changing environments and traditional crafting knowledge. I take as my focus a digital heritage project in which I have played a key role since 2012. The project – centred on the Nalik community – set out to establish a participatory museology in order to understand the issues and effects of remote access to culturally significant artefacts physically located in Australia.

My key concern is to explore how digital technologies mediate acts of remembering and help reconstruct material knowledge; and how the introduction of such technologies also mediate the organization of social relations (Van Dijck 2007). Mediation involves a separation that requires bridging and derives from the Latin *mediare*, 'to be placed in the middle'. It also implies an intervention, an active process in which two sides are brought together. Mediation is as much a vehicle as it is a strategy and it therefore invokes political, social and moral frameworks.

The nature of the political, social and moral frameworks in which digital technologies are mobilized in order to secure access to heritage is a key issue I explore. This is important to analyse because, as Mirzoeff (2011) reminds us, technologies such as digital imaging tools are now used by those whom the technology originally set out to control. The assumed democratization of the museum, aided through the development of digital technologies, opens an active space from which to investigate how communities assert 'the right to look' (Mirzoeff 2011). In considering these matters, my discussion brings into focus for the first time the perspective of those stakeholders excluded from the museum and their histories and who reside on the other side of the digital divide. I show how a remote community is engaging with digital imaging technologies to participate in political and religious groups and affirm identities, experiences and rights to rekindle and ultimately take control of their material past.

Digital Objects = Immaterial Lives?

Mobile phones, digital photography, film and the internet mediate new cultures of participation, new forms of memory and foster new ways to manage social relations through the sharing of digital images (Hills 2008; Horst and Miller 2006; Jenkins 2006; Van Dijck 2007; Van Doorn 2011). However, the notion that digital images are somehow separate from the material conditions of everyday reality continues to persist in much scholarly literature. As art historian David Freedberg (1989) explains, even images are generally understood within a separate ontological realm to reality itself.

Following Freedberg's comments, my concern in this chapter is to question the assumed immaterial nature of digital images, especially in light of the growth of affordable 3D digital imaging technologies for use in scanning museum objects. The advancement of these technologies has radically altered conceptions of digital images as secondary or derivative to the real object, resulting in the blurring of boundaries between real and virtual worlds. For instance, Deidre Brown (2007) has demonstrated how detailed 3D digital facsimiles of Maori artefacts are perceived by some Maori people in the same way as the actual physical objects themselves. She states how both are said to be imbued with ancestral power and are thus considered potent. As a consequence, she describes how these newly created digital *taonga* (Maori treasures) require management, involving the establishment of ritual protocols in order to deal with their powerful presence. I follow Brown's approach and investigate the potency and presence of (digital) images and, as Belting (1994) asserts, recognize a physicality or likeness that makes digital objects inseparable from the actual entity that the technology seeks to depict.

Brown's work is important because it challenges the prevailing tendency to confine digital images to the realm of 'simulacra' (Baudrillard 1994). Her work underlines how digital objects could be considered animate and alive, as they make present the ancestral past much like saintly relics or remains. And yet the massive boom in production of digital images – due to the widespread availability of image editing software for private publishing and liberal access to millions of stock photographs on internet websites such as Flickr – has drawn into question their reliability and their relation to reality. As binary code, digital images are easily manipulated and, of course, this has led to claims that digital images lack the status to testify or provide evidence for authenticity, and thus they are open to scrutiny.

While digital technologies intend to generate lifelike reproductions of museum artefacts (especially in relation to 3D digital objects) in ways to mimic real-life experience, for Naliks – the focus of this discussion – the 3D digital objects produced for the digital project reanimated their material histories in ways that separate the physical from the digital. I argue that this demonstrates how digital objects display the various modalities of 'imageness' (Rancière 2008) – a multi-sensorial capacity that can be experienced in different ways – which provide an authoritative and potent version of the ancestral past as well as harbour the potential to be remade and re-enacted. Since these digital objects offer a new form of materiality, or as Favero (2013) claims (in relation to interactive documentary film) they offer a way of 'getting our hands dirty', the technology provides a platform for Naliks to retrieve material knowledge as well as participate socially in ways that did not exist previously. As Ross Gibson (2013) points out in his creative engagement with the forensic photographs archive at the Justice and Police Museum in Sydney, digital experimentation allows for the layering of sounds and voices over crime scene photographs in ways that add sensorial depth to the archive and to scenes of violence and death, ascribing voices to victims and to the archive and so retrieving a material history that was considered silenced or lost.

The implications of pointing to the varying modalities of 'digital imageness' demonstrate how the experiential qualities of digital images give sense and meaning to understandings of history, of place and of people.[1] They underline the specific strategies of representation and qualify the 'authentic' and 'true' lives of people, events and places that are mediated. It is such qualities of digital images that I apply to my case study of the digital heritage project in the Nalik community. The aim of this project was to examine how, amongst the Nalik of northern New Ireland, digitally mediated access to museum collections influenced social memory and social relations. Such approaches offer opportunities to layer images with text and meaning and so reformat knowledge through connecting and sharing information about the past. Therefore, I wanted to explore how 3D digital objects and their associated technologies transform image-based economies of the region in ways that may bring to the fore the challenges, issues and potentials for sustaining material knowledge in the region for future generations.

Mobile Museum Project

The Mobile Museum was set up in January 2012 as a pilot project to facilitate remote access to Queensland collections of historical ethnographic artefacts for Nalik people living in New Ireland, Papua New Guinea. It was initiated after Naliks in the community expressed a strong desire for access to museum collections and asked me to work with them to develop a digital project. Access was mediated digitally by generating ten high resolution 3D digital objects of Nalik artefacts in the Queensland Museum and the University of Queensland Anthropology Museum. Funded by seed money from the University of Queensland's Collaboration and Industry Engagement Fund, the project was a formal collaboration between the University of Queensland, the Queensland Museum and the Nalik community and involved the expert services of Ortelia, a digital design company based in Brisbane who specialize in producing 3D virtual environments quickly and cost-effectively. I was one of the core team members of this collaborative project. Two senior members of the Nalik community led the collaboration in New Ireland – Martin Kombeng, a maimai (chiefly person), and Adam Kaminiel, an *aitek* (a traditional carver of malangan) – both of whom I had worked with extensively since 2000, when I first started research in New Ireland. Lazaros Kastanis was the project manager for Ortelia – he had expertise in digital heritage design and worked closely with the University of Queensland on a number of projects.

As a pilot project, our aims were to provide access to the ten digital objects for people living in the Nalik community. Few, if any, Nalik people have the opportunity to visit collections, let alone Australia. What made the project so timely was the introduction of mobile telecommunications in New Ireland. In the past, the only phones available on the island were landlines in provincial centres such as Kavieng. This has changed over the last few years since Digicel, an

Irish telecommunications company, erected mobile phone masts throughout the rural areas. The result is fledgling mobile and internet coverage along the coastal villages, although the reception is at present patchy.[2]

An important aspect of the project was its significance to the community. Within the Nalik community, cultural preservation and revivalism are important issues, as traditional beliefs and practices are perceived to have declined over the last century. In particular, a focal point of debate has been the sustaining of the malangan tradition, of which northern New Ireland is famous. Malangan carvings objectify the material histories of the Nalik people and they play a central role in funerary rites. According to Kuechler's authoritative study of the Kara people of northern New Ireland (Kuechler 2002), malangan carvings make visible relations to land and to history through the incorporation of clan totem designs. However, unlike those carvings that are placed on display in glass cases for public consumption in Western museums, malangan carvings are not on show or on display in everyday life; they are significant because they are displayed fleetingly during events leading up to the culmination of mortuary feasting in communities. While clan members can inspect the carvings, it also ensures that the image is transacted from one generation to another because at the end of the ceremony the carvings are removed and destroyed (either by burning on a fire or through decay when left in a special place in the forest). Kuechler's insights also apply to the Nalik community, who place high value on the image and the right to reproduce it, rather than the physical form itself.

The Mobile Museum project thus offered a chance to reconnect Naliks with museum collections that were inaccessible to them. It provided them with the opportunity to access historical collections dating to the late nineteenth century that exhibited diverse styles of carving and compare them with objects that are currently made in Nalik society, which were seen as less sophisticated. Crucially, the project opened the door for Naliks to learn about past carving practices through visual analysis of museum collections and so create a new way in which people could learn about the past using laptop computers and 3D imaging.

One of the challenges of the project was that knowledge of malangan is controlled and their display is ephemeral. Malangan carvings are made by specially sanctioned men called aitek in the community. Carvers produce the malangan figures in ritual seclusion, out of sight from the public, after undergoing a short period of fasting. The carver builds a special leaf shelter and inside sets to work on a seasoned piece of softwood, *azabaf*. The carver, for whom the image of the carving is said to appear in a dream, performs a series of ritual offerings during the production process. Each malangan is carved using a template design so they are recognizable as a particular class of carving and includes clan totems and designs that are known to the carver and knowledgeable people in the community.

Young men learn how to become a carver through a mentor relationship with a master carver in the community. Apprentices take many years of study and practice before they attain the credentials to practise carving and receive commissions from land-holding clans. Those carvers who attain renown in New Ireland are known as master carvers, which generally infers that their work is also known by art dealers in the West.

As is true in many parts of Melanesia, carving ancestral figures introduces an element of risk to the carver, as each design involves invoking ancestral images, which are considered potent. This is exemplified in the New Ireland case, as the softwood from which malangan are carved is said to be inhabited by a spirit. This spirit can devour humans and so Naliks treat malangan with utmost caution and respect. Many stories circulate in New Ireland society about carvers who have disrespected the malangan spirit and died as a consequence.

Thus, what is important about the Mobile Museum project is that it did not replace the mentor-apprentice relationship in the process of learning to carve. Rather, it reintroduced into the community the types of ancestral images from the Nalik region that were produced in the past and that may or may not have been lost though most certainly may have changed in style. The software provided the opportunity for young people to learn the history of malangan and to study its form and style. It also allowed them to learn about technical and material knowledge – the types of leaves and pigments used in adorning the carving – and to view this in full colour 3D. The technology itself was important, as the community felt that, given young people's interest in computers, the software provided a contemporary solution to the dissipation of traditional knowledge.

The Mobile Museum project attracted considerable attention given its promise of reinvigorating knowledge networks in the region. For Demas Kavavu, a senior Nalik man and cultural activist, the project offered 'a chance for strengthening of traditional culture and will form part of a literacy programme ... the project can be implemented to sustain the understanding of culture through training programmes'. As the project later revealed, museums are repositories of particularly old malangan that have never been seen by Naliks today.

Naliks regarded digital technologies as an appropriate method for providing access to malangan images, particularly so if these were 3D. This is because 3D images – through their manipulation and handling – give some sense of 'total documentation' (Steinbach 2011). 3D digital images are lifelike textured images of spatial complexity, consisting of high levels of surface detail so as to conjure the notion of replica or digital surrogate. They can be distinguished from 2D images or photographs by the fact that they evoke the sensorial capacity of depth perception, which imbues images with a spatial dimension and tangibility that lets one feel round objects. Naliks expressed this in being able to 'see' the object in its entirety rather than rely on photographic formats, which offer only partial views. As Adam Kaminiel, a malangan carver said: 'The software allows me to see the carvings as light in my eyes.' Indeed, Kuechler (1999) has observed how it is not just the totemic emblems and symbols on the malangan that are significant but also the topological surfaces; the interweaving openwork in-between that reveals to Naliks the memory of relations to land. Thus, the potency of the 3D digital objects resides in their potential to be remade again, and it is this future possibility, at present, which gives 3D digital objects their value in the community.

While 3D digital objects may seem attractive solutions to providing access to carvings and material histories, Naliks also considered the possibility of building a museum or cultural centre to help reinvigorate cultural practices. When I first started conducting fieldwork in the Nalik area in 2000, there were several attempts to set up a local museum to house some of the carvings still in the community. The idea was to build a museum in one of the villages and place malangan carvings inside for tourists and local people to view, as a kind of educational resource. During my first visit, timber was felled to construct the vertical posts for the museum. Later, I found out that the posts were used for another house-building project. Another attempt at establishing a provincial museum also failed: a proposal for a Kavieng-based museum was sanctioned by the Provincial Government and apparently land even set aside, but the funding for the project never eventuated. Although there was much talk and many meetings about the proposal, no form of museum ever materialized.

A museum would pose many problems to Naliks. 'Who would look after the objects?' asked Martin Kombeng, a prominent maimai in the community. Martin's words imply complex questions of who would retain control over such an institution in a society where rights to images – both in terms of access and production – are carefully controlled (Kuechler 2002). As Christie and Verran (2013) state in their analysis of an Aboriginal knowledge centre and the role of the digital archivist in northern Australia, caring for powerful knowledge is dangerous work. Malangan carvings and objects from the past are considered potentially harmful, especially if placed in the wrong hands. Who would want to care for them and who would trust another clansperson to care for their own carvings? This is why, as Kingston (2007) has pointed out in relation to a southern New Ireland museum-building project, the expression 'dangerous heritage' can be applied to malangan carvings, especially those ones in museum collections that are from a period of time beyond living memory. Thus, a key aim of the Mobile Museum pilot project was to ascertain the social effects of providing access to 3D digital objects in the community and the impact on the transmission and circulation of material knowledge.

Participatory Methodology and Awareness Project

Too often, museums design websites and digital interfaces facilitate access to collections without any understanding of community needs. In many cases, high-end digitization projects are driven by government agendas to promote tourism and national heritage. Digital assets such as photographs are placed in the public domain with little consideration of cultural protocols. Mindful of these issues, a key aspect of our collaborative project was to oversee the implementation of a participatory methodology in order to establish and define these cultural parameters. We wanted to ensure that the design of the software application had been informed by the Nalik community and their cultural requirements.

Our participatory methodology involved working closely with the two Nalik project members and deciding together the best way in which to engage local people on the project. Working with two senior men who had traditional roles in the community meant we could organize the most culturally appropriate model of engagement. As a result, the project team ran a series of consultations – called 'awareness' by Naliks – in several of the villages along the east coast Nalik area during 2012 and 2013. The awareness campaign involved visiting several communities and meeting with community leaders, senior men and women, women's groups, teachers and school children to ascertain the ways in which the software could be designed to benefit local people and meet their needs. As the Naliks stated, this was a culturally important way to implement the project, or as Kreps (2008) might argue, an example of 'appropriate museology'. Some of the meetings were held with several people and sometimes meetings were held on a one-to-one basis. Many of the villages along the east coast of the Nalik area were consulted several times over the duration of the project, and key reference groups from each village were established to help implement the project. In all cases, Nalik people used the application and were asked to comment on its functionality, how they could use it (if at all) and the potential implementation issues. Such problems of implementation included the number of computers in the community, who had access to the software and questions about digital literacy.

One of the key challenges of the digital toolkit, as Verran and Christie (2007) recognized in relation to their digital project amongst Aboriginal Australians, was to design a digital application that was sensitive to local knowledge systems and practices.[3] In the Nalik community, this meant one that could accommodate the specific ways Naliks viewed carvings. Through the awareness consultation, it became apparent that people were interested in the form of the malangan, the types of materials used (including leaf headpieces), incisions and pigments.

Figure 6.1 Adam Kaminiel demonstrating the Mobile Museum software at awareness meeting, Lugagun village, New Ireland. Photograph by the author.

Being able to see the malangan in its totality was important as was the ability to compare.

The outcome of our awareness consultations was a set of requirements Naliks made for viewing the digital objects. First, local carvers requested 'hotspots' to be placed on certain artefacts. These were small blue spots placed on the surface of carvings on points of special significance to Naliks. On clicking the hotspot, a detailed photograph could be launched in the digital platform. This allowed the carvers to see details of the carving and tool marks. Second, some participants requested that they be able to compare two 3D objects side by side. This would allow them to analyse variation in design and style of artefacts. Third, Naliks were interested to know the size of the artefacts – so a matchbox was inserted into the virtual environment in order to ascertain scale. Fourth, Naliks also wanted museum documentation to be included in the digital platform: this allowed users to learn about the object's collecting history and contextual information. Finally, a notes field was introduced on the request of Naliks so that annotations could be added to the 3D images.

In addition to these design requirements, the workshops also defined the technical limitations of the project. The mobile network in New Ireland lacked bandwidth, which meant that large file sizes were slow to transmit even though the project used relatively small file sizes compared to other 3D imaging projects (i.e. 5 to 10 megabytes). Furthermore, while most Nalik people owned mobile phones, less than 10 per cent of these phones had the capacity to access the internet. Even among this small number of owners, the cost of purchasing internet data was relatively quite high, which was a deterrent. As a result, it was decided to provide access to the digital platform, in the first instance, using a CD-ROM (rather than a website providing access to the 3D images), which would be distributed widely in the Nalik communities. This meant that people could study the malangan without internet access and without the burden of having to find money to buy internet data to download the images. It also allowed people to study privately rather than view the images in front of the community, which had many implications for the way the application was perceived in the community.

A key stage of the consultation process involved a ten-day visit by Martin Kombeng and Adam Kaminiel to Brisbane in late 2012, the two Nalik partners in the project. The aim of their visit was to access the New Ireland collections in the museum storage at the Queensland Museum and the Anthropology Museum at the University of Queensland – institutional project partners. Together, both institutions housed around two hundred artefacts of New Ireland provenance in total. The two Nalik men were able to view all of the objects and spent time identifying which of the artefacts came from the Nalik area. For the two Nalik men, the New Ireland objects were seen as very potent, as they were made in the past when ancestral power was most potent (compared with ancestral power today). Belief in their potency was demonstrated when they asked many questions about who from the community had accessed the collections before as they believed misuse of the collections could cause harm to the community.

Over the duration of their visit, their goal was to narrow the New Ireland collection to an identifiable corpus of objects from the Nalik region. They were able to recognize various designs, styles and motifs that made the collections recognizable from their community. They also analysed the different types of materials used in constructing the objects, some of which had dried or decayed, making them hard to recognize. They then selected ten objects for 3D scanning. Nine of these were malangan carvings and the other was a fish trap. The two men chose the carvings because they were ritually important and recognizable (from totemic symbols and motifs) from the Nalik area; while they argued that the fish trap was typical of New Ireland as a

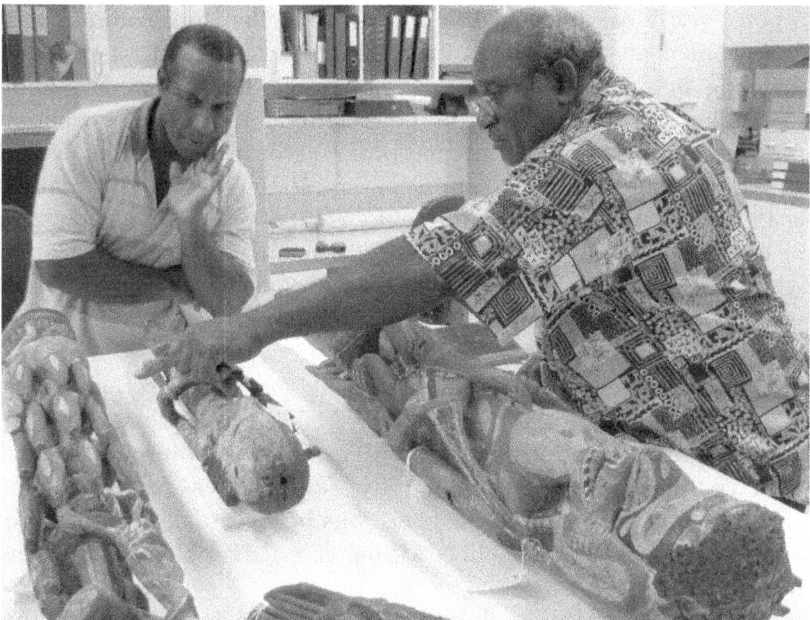

Figure 6.2 Martin Kombeng and Adam Kaminiel select malangan carvings at the Queensland Museum, Australia. Photograph by the author.

region (and they were somewhat reluctant to include this everyday object in the scanning process, a point I return to later).

Implementation

The completed project was implemented in 2013 when we travelled up and down the Boluminski Highway with a group of other senior Nalik men distributing the CD-ROM to key community members and school teachers. The distribution was described in terms of the Nalik term '*poxai*', which means 'obligation' or 'reciprocity'. The thinking behind this form of distribution was that for any unforeseen technical problems related to the software the Nalik could seek Martin or Adam for help. As Martin Kombeng exclaimed: 'People will come to Adam for help with the software; they know where to find him. They know he is knowledgeable about computers!'

The software and its content met with much discussion about how old objects – and the material knowledge these images carried with them – could revitalize Nalik society and restore a sense of traditional order. There are many reasons for Naliks to want to reinstate the traditional order and strong leadership in the communities. There was a perceived breakdown in law and order in the rural communities. Young men in particular were notorious for rowdy behaviour, drinking homebrew and petty theft. Strong leadership, according to Naliks, would regulate this behaviour and instil a new moral personhood. Restoring traditional order, according to Naliks, would strengthen their society by supporting the reintegration of the maimai leadership system into community life, as this was widely perceived to be of declining influence. In the past, the maimai was a chiefly figure who had authority to speak and make decisions for clans. In times of warfare prior to pacification, a senior maimai – *xalxaal* – presided over decisions in communities with total impunity. He adjudicated life and death situations, symbolized today in the wearing of certain leaves by maimai at initiation ceremonies. For Naliks this leadership system garnered respect and established order within communities. Digital heritage therefore took on a redemptive role, as it was perceived to be able to restore an idealized past and thus help regulate social control and order, and so promised to tackle major social problems in the New Ireland society.

But there was also another important reason for supporting this project. Due to social fragmentation over the last century as a result of disruption by mission Christianity, the influx of workers from other provinces of Papua New Guinea, and the introduction of a cash economy (to name just some of the factors), many clans were unsure of their malangan carvings. The museum, and thus the software application, provided a resource to potentially retrieve this material knowledge for their use and application in contemporary society.

Figure 6.3 Distributing the Mobile Museum CD-ROMs amongst the Nalik community, New Ireland. Photograph by the author.

For many Naliks, however, there was an obvious reluctance to admit to having lost their own malangan. The Mobile Museum project revealed the dynamics of how this loss was expressed during several episodes. For instance, during a consultation workshop in one village along the east coast, about twenty men and women gathered around the laptop computer and the software was demonstrated. Each of the ten artefacts was exhibited to the crowd, who were especially eager to see the malangan. As the crowd dissipated after about thirty minutes, a senior man came to me and informed how people were so pleased to see the malangan. He then explained how he thought that each person was interested in spotting their own clan's malangan. Once they discovered that their own clan's malangan was not captured in the software, he claimed that they were no longer interested.[4]

This episode is important for appreciating how Nalik people relate to their material histories through the production of images. Malangan are transacted as images. It is through the recall of images that new carvings are made. Senior men may describe malangan to their close male relatives in terms of whether it comes in the form of a pig, a clamshell or fish, for example. So there are ways in which individuals are able to recognize their malangan without physically having seen the actual carving. In this way, the software becomes a conduit to remembering the carving – a material trace of a verbal exchange between two persons in the past. In this sense, the digital technologies mediate memories by reproducing in digital formats an archive or collection of physical artefacts. Even though personal memory fades, the software aids recall and provide a point of reference for future re-making.

The digital project also raised the spectre of the competitive nature of access and transacting knowledge relating to malangan. This was exemplified in 2013 at a meeting in the Nalik village of Kafkaf. During the meeting, a senior man from the Tabar Islands, a group of islands visible from the east coast of the Nalik region, started talking about one of the malangan carvings he had seen in the software application. In front of a group of Nalik men, the Tabar man confidently recounted the story of a carved malangan depicting two men standing inside a clamshell from the University of Queensland Anthropology Museum collection.

After the Tabar man departed, the Nalik men told me how surprised they were by his story because he had been so forthright about eliciting this knowledge. Malangan stories were not generally given in such contexts and instead passed on in private situations between mentor and apprentice. The Tabar man's stories, as a result, were dismissed as arrogant. But their negative reaction was also based on the Tabar man's attitude to their use of the software to recall material histories. When pressed on his opinion about the Mobile Museum, the Tabar man's response was 'that's for Naliks'. In Tabar he claimed 'we remember our malangan.' 'We don't need these technologies – it's in our blood.' This reveals how difference and status are tied into material histories and cultural authenticity. In effect, the digital technologies – although trying to build into a wider project of cultural revitalization and community strengthening – were understood by some as an instrument that was entirely separate from that domain. Thus, the medium through which new knowledge networks were mediated took on an altogether authentic/non-traditional framework and value.

Even though knowledge of malangan is considered by most Naliks to have dissipated, how this knowledge is appropriately transacted is still open to contestation. In particular, tensions existed over who has the right to produce malangan. This can be explained by narrating another event that occurred in 2011, just before the Mobile Museum project was established. The event involved an ethnographic museum in Europe that houses a malangan carving in the form of a fish dating back to the late nineteenth century. Most Nalik people, however, were unaware of this carving until recently (which demonstrates the significance of museum collections to the community). Known as '*nuf*', the fish belonged to a clan from the Notsi-speaking area, just south of the Nalik-speaking area. During September 2011, a museum consultant travelled through northern New Ireland collecting stories about the carving in the museum's collections as a means to demonstrate the museum's commitment to engaging community views for its possible re-display. During the trip, the consultant also travelled with an art dealer, who had a particular interest in collecting New Ireland malangan, the commercial value of which was in the thousands. While many Nalik people came forward to tell the story of the nuf malangan, a carver from Notsi – known for selling his artworks to international art dealers – reputedly offered a contemporary nuf carving for sale to the Western collector. As a consequence, stories abounded about how they purchased the carving, paying 'a car full of cash' for the nuf.

Sensational stories such as these are rife in Nalik society. They highlight the heightened concern about applying appropriate rights to existing images and foreground the tensions that arise with renewed access to collections. Indeed, a senior man, after hearing about these events, claimed that the Notsi carver had no right to carve his clan's malangan. He explained that carvers could not carve malangan 'for nothing' (*kat natin*) – but had to be commissioned by a senior man in an organizing clan for a malangan ceremony. He accused the Notsi carver of infringing his clan's rights, especially because he was selling the carving for his own individual gain, and so threatened to take him to court.

Events like this are increasingly common in Nalik society. Due to a lack of leadership and the lure of cash payments due to the demands of an expanding international art market, it has become harder to control the production of malangan and sanction offenders. While on the one hand the Notsi carver probably thought that his carving practice helped reinvigorate the identity of the region by generating cultural tourism and commodifying malangan carvings (and there was a quiet acknowledgement of the positive benefits of this), others claimed it had the effect of disrespecting the protocols that apply to image production (and was therefore considered dangerous).

These events give an indication of the way in which knowledge and control over material histories are articulated in Nalik society. On the one hand, clans risk the problem of losing their malangan, their material history, if the carvings are not reproduced from memory. Because there are fewer carvers and fewer new carvings made in contemporary society, specialist knowledge of carvings is at risk of dissipation. On the other hand, attempts to liberalize the economy of image production are met with sanctions or trepidation.

The Right to Look

A language of return and recovery developed amongst Naliks during the project. Community members used the expressions '*bringim bek*' (returning) or '*putim bek*' (putting back) to describe how the software application was providing access to the material histories carried by the museum artefacts. In some instances, this process of recovering the past drew an emotional response. In the village of Lugagun, a senior man, Momos, exclaimed passionately: 'It makes me cry, it makes me worried … that the young generation are no longer interested in malangan.' He described how young Naliks no longer respected traditional culture and its values and how the software application could restore the past in a modern way, using digital technologies. Momos's words, echoing many of the thoughts of other Nalik people involved in the project workshops and consultations, demonstrate how digital heritage generates the potential for a form of recovery and cultural completeness. Using digital images to mediate material histories, these new technologies offer the potential to bring back what is considered to be lost. In gaining remote access to museum objects from the late nineteenth and early twentieth century in Queensland, Naliks placed value on the integrity of the 3D digital objects, as they were deemed to transmit an authentic and powerful version of the past, since they referenced a time that Naliks had only heard about and not directly experienced.

The awareness consultations generated much reflection in the Nalik villages about cultural loss and revitalization, which demonstrates how access to digital resources catalyses community reflection and subsequent affirmative action (Srinivasan 2012). Martin Kombeng, later interviewed on Australian SBS World News, reflected on the problems of returning malangan carvings to the Nalik people.[5] He said: 'most of the originating clans who own those (*malangan*) masks, maybe they cannot remember. Now you might as well leave them where they are.' Given that most museum documentation lacks exact village provenance, Martin claimed that it would be problematic to return carvings to villagers without knowing the rightful clan owners. Digital return, on the other hand, could be seen as a form of 'first level' repatriation (Phillips 2013) in which the digital object supports the opportunity to gain new knowledge and understanding of Nalik culture through community-based research but without the issue of dealing with the physical object.

Attempts by senior Naliks to take control of their own history then took another turn of events. In 2013, the senior men showcased the Mobile Museum project to the Kavieng District Council and received funding to formalize the integration of a Council of Chiefs (maimai) within the Tikana region (Tigak-, Kara- and Nalik-speaking areas). Their discussions were the culmination of a series of meetings held over the previous five years in which the Provincial Government had workshopped the idea of establishing a formal organization to administer a traditional leadership system in the region. They were alarmed about the declining moral and social fabric of New Ireland society.

The senior men's success was built on the claim that because these images were 'out there', they therefore required some management, and so the maimais had the ritual authority to take control of them. Thus, the proposed Council of Chiefs needed the finances and resources to administer the digital objects with the purchase of computers and phones. Yet, what also appears to have happened is that the technology fell under the auspices of local power structures. With their ritual authority, the maimais seized control of it.

This is a reminder, given the emergence of digital technologies and digital assets within an image-based economy, of how this material knowledge becomes an important resource to which individuals make claims and contestations. It is the maimai who hold control over the ancestral past and who have made great strides in using the technology for reinvigorating their position. Since malangan and their production are so carefully controlled, their access and administration of the Mobile Museum project upholds their authority on traditional matters to the exclusion of others. Thus, even though there are increasing numbers of Naliks with access to laptop computers and the internet, access to the means of production is clearly, even on the other side of the digital divide, centred on the 'right to look', as Mirzoeff (2011) claims. That is why, in returning to the selection of the everyday fish trap from the museum in Queensland, the two Naliks could have been reluctant for its reproduction. They knew that the rights of reproduction with regards to reproducing an everyday object such as a trap are harder to control within the community, as the trap is a functional rather than a ritual object, and knowledge of its production is not owned by specific clans or individuals. As is the case of the fashion basket produced by Nalik women (Chapter 2), the classification of objects within domains of ritual and the everyday offers different kinds of opportunities, whether for commodification, as with the basket, or for strengthening the articulation of male or clan-based power (see also Chapter 5).

Conclusion

The Nalik Mobile Museum project shows the ways that digital heritage technologies and material histories intersect in one locality. In focusing on the social context of technological use and application, this account demonstrates the dynamics between digital objects (images), museum collections and historical narratives. This case study also contributes to an emerging anthropology of digital communication, which by and large has until recently ignored digital images in favour of text-based mediation (e.g. Miller and Slater 2000). Redressing this underdevelopment through exploring how people are utilizing digital images to initiate and foster social relationships and representations in new creative forms helps us to rethink taken for granted assumptions regarding the meaning of ethnographic collections and forces us to reconsider the very nature of material histories themselves.[6] As I have emphasized, digital objects offer a form of tangibility – something to grasp and hold on to – animating objects and knowledge. My analysis of digital objects serves to reveal the complex intersection of materiality, virtuality and histories from the perspective of a remote community considered marginalized from the museum.

Yet, perhaps importantly for museum curators, anthropologists and historians, as well as those working in the humanities and social sciences, is the question of how the digital recoding of museum collections is impacting on ethnographic artefacts. Museum spaces have always been used as repositories for the past and still many ethnographic artefacts languish in storage, never to be researched or displayed. Yet, these newly produced digital assets resonate with the sea change in museum productions over the last two decades towards a participatory museology (Golding and Modest 2013; Karp, Kratz, Szwaja, and Ybarra-Frausto 2006; Peers and Brown 2003; Silverman 2015; Sully 2007). What the emergence of digital technologies in the museum and heritage sector allows is a way for ethnographic collections to perform and become participants again, beyond the physical realm of the museum. If museums still cling on to ideological notions of the object rooted in terms of its originality and authenticity, as Conn's (2010) work purports, and institutions still continue to hold on to ethnographic artefacts in their collections, then perhaps it is time to acknowledge that digital objects take on a more real and significant presence than those locked away in museum stores all over the world.

Notes

1. See Wright's work on Solomon Islands historical photography as an example of how images are indexical of ancestral power (Wright 2013).
2. There is now an emerging anthropological literature focused on mobile phone usage in Papua New Guinea. See Andersen (2013), Lipset (2013) and Foster and Horst (2018).
3. See also Christen's discussion of open and free information in the context of indigenous Australia and cultural preservation (Christen 2012).
4. While Naliks saw malangan as intrinsic to the 'sacrificial economy' (Kuechler 1997), they also blamed loss on senior men and women (who lived in the past and are now deceased) who sold carvings to Westerners.
5. See http://www.youtube.com/watch?v=ZQ_gdA0dNcE for SBS journalist Stefan Armbruster's full interview with Martin Kombeng. Stefan is the Pacific correspondent for SBS News and was covering a number of stories on New Ireland at the time.
6. The social outcomes of 'digital return' have been examined by a number of anthropologists working in difference cultural contexts. See in particular: Bell, Christen and Turin (2013), Isaac (2015) and Hennessy et al. (2013).

7

Material Histories and the Changing Nature of Museum Collections

In the previous chapter, I argued that the uptake and use of digital heritage technologies in rural communities in the Pacific was transforming ritual and political structures by reinforcing hierarchies and elevating social status because the technology (as an object and as a process) provided access to material histories that were themselves understood as authoritative of the past. The discussion focused primarily on the end users of digital media and the new forms of engagement with material knowledge that have emerged through the mobility of objects and images from museum storage facilities over the course of a consultation process between the museum and community of origin.

This chapter builds on this discussion by exploring further the new knowledge networks that digital technologies create. It examines another digital heritage project that intended to support a Melanesian community to address issues of dissipating material knowledge, much like the New Ireland example described in Chapter 6. This chapter focuses on the technical production of new types of digital objects and examines how this process was guided by the value placed on making material knowledge visible and knowable. It focuses attention on how museums – as repositories of material knowledge – unmoor new mobile forms of objects and material knowledge from storage facilities and how these are transmitted and received in faraway places like the Solomon Islands for cultural restitution purposes. I explore how such digital projects raise important questions about the future role of museums and collections in sustaining knowledge networks, and consider how the legacies of colonial collecting can become the new material archives of the future. In the context of the rise and use of digital media within cultural institutions, then, what does this transformation into binary code have on the nature of materials and making? And how is material knowledge itself then constituted, particularly so for Pacific peoples, who may actively be seeking out this knowledge for revival purposes?

In this chapter, I return to the Western Solomon Islands war canoe, which was an earlier focus for an analysis of the calculative nature of material knowledge (Chapter 4). Here, I examine how the return of material knowledge relating to the construction of the plank canoe – expressed in the form of a colour digital 3D scale model of the original canoe currently housed in a museum storage facility in London, England – offers potential in its mobile and immaterial form to the community of origin. I focus on the process of reconfiguring the canoe into a 3D digital model and the implication of this imagistic and binary form for understandings of materials. I demonstrate how this knowledge transfer relies on aspects of dematerialization and scaling, as well as manipulation, display and reconstruction. Through its transfer and viewing via a CD-ROM, I argue how material knowledge takes on a performative role in its articulation, encoding and transmission in order to bring to life the physical object. It affirms, importantly, how this knowledge is not simply brought back to the Solomon Islands; rather it undergoes a transformation in value, much like the case of the New Ireland digital project, in which the form of this knowledge is transformed through the media in which it is situated. The context of this return is equally significant: the canoe and canoe-building knowledge is a politically and socially potent symbol of place and history of a region as the canoe plays an important part in the resurgence of interest in culture and identity. As Hviding (n.d.) has aptly noted, the canoe's image features on regional flags and stamps, and the canoe is often remade as a replica for use in political ceremonies in the region.

Digital Return of Traditional Knowledge

Digital community engagement projects – which intend to 'respectfully' return traditional knowledge to communities through consultation and dialogue (Christen 2011; see also Basu 2011; Bell, Christen and Turin 2013; Isaac 2015) on the premise that it has the effect of restoring knowledge that may have been dissipated or lost due to social and political upheavals in the past – are becoming increasingly fashionable in ethnographic museums around the world. Such digital projects apply community-based protocols such as gatekeeper permission to control access to restricted imagery to senior or initiated people in the community. Software is now designed using participatory design methodologies as has been demonstrated in the Mobile Museum project in New Ireland, Papua New Guinea (Chapter 6), which employs local sensitivities, symbols or categories in order to make the application conducive to local knowledge systems. As Christie and Verran (2013) have cogently demonstrated, digital technologies can be adapted to mimic the structures and aesthetics of indigenous knowledge through collaborative design and application.

While these projects intend to empower indigenous people through the transfer of material histories, they rely on local access to the technology, both in terms of infrastructure but also computer literacy. Many digital projects claim to bridge digital divides by supporting local people's aims in reinstating traditional imagery into the ritual and social economy, thus making the assertion that these technologies are emancipatory.[1] Yet, there are many other factors that point to the contrary; that the installation of digital technologies in communities actually fuels social inequalities and reinforces divisions over access and use of culturally relevant material. Indeed, as the Mobile Museum project emphasized (Chapter 6), the appropriation of digital heritage technology by a chiefly organization in the community was a means for them to reassert their own custodianship over the use of ritual images and did little in the way to widen participation in ancestral and threatened images housed in museum storage facilities. It simply rehoused them on the hard drives of their computers and into the minds of those who seek to control them, reasserting through transformation the institutional frame that governs their dissemination from the controlled environment of the museum to the restrictions of access to traditional imagery in New Ireland society.

This chapter thus extends discussion on new forms of material networks linking the Solomon Islands by tracing out the operations and effects of digital heritage technologies in the region. It will ask: in what ways are new forms of material knowledge perceived through such digital projects between museums and communities of origin? How are new forms of material knowledge transforming the way knowledge about plants and their affordances is constructed in Pacific society? These are important questions for anthropology and material culture because they require informed responses to the new virtual materials that digital technologies circulate and the types of restorative practices that access to these entities invites.

In terms of the former question, Verran et al. (2007) raise this in terms of digital archives of Aboriginal traditional knowledge in northern Australia. Their insightful work – whilst advocating for more bottom-up practices to engage Aboriginal communities in Australia using digital technologies – also warns of the pitfalls and dangers inherent in creating repositories of knowledge. They point to the case of the digital archive and the role of the archivist, stating how the archivist's role is potentially dangerous, as he has to care for traditional knowledge that is housed in a digital archive. Caring for the archive, in this sense, means maintaining the database and providing access to it and bringing archivists into contact with this knowledge. This knowledge, encoded in binary form, is still considered to be potent and therefore debilitating. So, Verran et al. (2007) conclude that new forms of knowledge do not liberate access or desensitize it; rather, this knowledge remains problematic and requires appropriate modes of engagement.

The second question raises important points about how knowledge is constructed in Western Solomon Islands society. It requires an understanding of the social context of learning that takes place in craft-producing activities; how crafting practices are transmitted from generation to generation (Lave 2011; Marchand 2010). This is a process that has been approached in anthropology. In his groundbreaking ethnography on the Polynesian atoll Pukapuka, Robert Borofsky (1987) explores the way in which traditional knowledge is constructed and transmitted in social situations. He describes a particular situation where two young men learn to repair a canoe under the mentorship of a recognized senior man and technical expert in the community. Observing the learning environment, Borofsky observes how little direct advice took place; rather learning involved observing and experimenting. The young men never asked their mentor for help; the novices experimented with their tools and materials, sometimes hesitantly, building confidence as they proceeded. Borofsky summarizes that traditional education in Pukapuka is less explicit and formal than in Western schools. Children and adults learn through observation and mimicry and rarely through direct instruction or question and answer. Learning involves a process of internalization, which I have also shown in the context of pattern learning in New Ireland, Papua New Guinea (Were 2010). Knowledge is acquired in practice, during the performance of certain activities, where it has relevance and a purpose.

Indeed, this digital project was initiated on the premise that traditional canoe-building knowledge was at risk of loss. While the plank canoe plays a significant and enduring role in the vitality of

Western Solomon Islands regional identity, there are local concerns about the sustainability of material knowledge required to construct and recreate the plank canoes. For example, Hviding notes (2014) how canoe builders in the Western Solomon Islands search for suitable materials for constructing canoes rather than the specific materials that were used in the past.

This dissipation of traditional knowledge required to build canoes – brought about by habitat loss, lower frequency of craft production and the fragility of specialist knowledge – has created a space for museums, who can support communities and give their collections new relevance through access and learning.

The Digital War Canoe Project

The digital project was initiated by a community in Vella Lavella, a small island in the Western Solomon Islands that in the past was known for its war canoes and inter-island warfare (Chapter 4). The community wanted to rebuild the war canoe following an early twentieth century design, particular so as the local Christian missions in the region had been reviving canoe-building for race events. The Vella Lavella community were especially interested in regaining access to the complete design of the war canoe, as no living person was thought to know the specifications of the entire design. Living canoe builders were confident about the canoe's hull construction – made by using seasoned planks of wood lashed together. However, they were less certain about how the hull was sealed using puttynut. In addition, they were interested in learning about the technical application of a shell inlay patina, which covered the bow and stern of the canoe, as well as the type of cordage lashings inside the canoe, which secured the ribbing. Canoe builders had worked from black-and-white colonial photographs to help revive their skills; however, this was considered limited because the inside of canoes remained unknown. The shift from 2D to 3D, moreover, presented an opportunity for canoe builders to revive their understanding of the hull interior and the shell patina too, which may otherwise have remained forgotten.

As part of the Norwegian research funded project 'Pacific Alternatives' led by Professor Edvard Hviding of the University of Bergen, a small project team with expertise in the Western Solomon Islands and 3D digital imaging was assembled to undertake the scanning. The aim was to document entirely – interior and exterior – the Western Solomon Islands war canoe in the British Museum, which had been collected in the 1920s and had stood for several years in a dusty London museum storehouse. The project team included anthropologists, geomatic engineers and technicians, museum curators and collections staff from three institutions: the British Museum, University of Bergen (Norway) and University College London. Two Solomon Islanders living in London were also able to take part in the scanning process.

Digital return, in this instance, was considered to be a particularly appropriate means of return for the Solomon Islands because, according to Professor Hviding, rural communities already had access to laptop computers through a UNESCO-sponsored scheme. An extensive VSAT internet broadband network existed that was also accessible in rural areas. This meant that people had the potential to gain access to their own cultural heritage online simply by using a networked computer provided by local educational and governmental institutions. While this also meant that access to online heritage resources was dictated by access to digital telecommunications, much like the Mobile Museum project, the project also developed a CD-ROM set with software drivers for people without reliable connections or those interested in working offline.

Figure 7.1 Technician Mona Hess scanning the war canoe in the storage facilities of the British Museum. Photograph by the author.

Digital Production Process

The digitizing required two major stages of development before the 3D model was returned to Vella Lavella. Stage one of the process began in 2009 in the storage facilities of the British Museum inside a large warehouse room filled with oversized canoes and water craft from all over world (see Chapter 4). This was the location for the capture of the digital image required to create the actual canoe.

3D scanning was selected as a method to capture the canoe because it provided both a detailed metric survey and digital documentation of the canoe. The scanning team used a highly portable Metris K-Scan handheld laser scanner designed for recording the high accuracy measurement of manufactured components. Set up in the cramped storage facilities of the British Museum, the system was ideal for on-site 3D digitizing, as it was highly portable and usable. Using the handheld device, the scanning team were able to capture the geometry of the canoe at sub-millimetre resolution. This meant that the 3D digital image contained detailed documentation of the canoe's technical construction, such as the hull design, the joints of the planks and interior configurations in full colour resolution. It was hoped that the 3D scan would enable Vella Lavella people to learn about the technical construction of the canoe and visually recognize the types of materials used.

The system consisted of a handheld scan head (resembling a paint gun) and a mobile Coordinate Measuring Machine (a computer console on wheels) with three synchronized linear camera units (a horizontal boom). A number of infrared LEDs built into the handheld scan head were imaged and accurately tracked by the measuring machine using a method called triangulation, delivering scan head position and orientation in real time, enabling the operator to freely walk around and efficiently acquire surface scans of the measurement object. Triangulation is a process that involves transforming planar surfaces, such as the canoe hull, into a system of triangles to form a net of triangles giving the appearance of a surface.

The scanning process meant clearing space in this storage space so that the eleven metre canoe could be accessed and scanned in its entirety. Surface scanning entailed physically walking around the plank canoe and capturing its surface details, both inside and outside, in minute detail. This involved the complex task of visualizing the hull's topology as the technician walked around the hull. The scan head was held at a constant distance of about five millimetres from the canoe's surface and moved across in a sweeping movement. Crafting the canoe digitally meant engaging with the canoe's slightly uneven surface and imagining the parts that had been scanned and those yet to be scanned.

Production of the digital model also involved reconstructing the canoe, both in the real world and in the digital/virtual world. This is because the actual canoe had had its two tall sweeping prows cut off to allow for its transportation and storage. Moreover, the canoe's shell decorations had also been removed and stored in separate parts of the museum store. Scanning each component separately thus allowed the canoe to be digitally reconstructed in its totality using specialist software – with prows and decorations attached seamlessly – thus making the object complete for the first time since its acquisition by the British Museum.

The process took two weeks of intensive scanning, using the handheld scanner to move across the surface of the canoe to capture its structure.

Following the first stage of model development was a second stage that involved a two-month period of post-processing. A specialist technician cleaned and calibrated the 3D model and pieced together the canoe's various components in a 3D digital environment so it

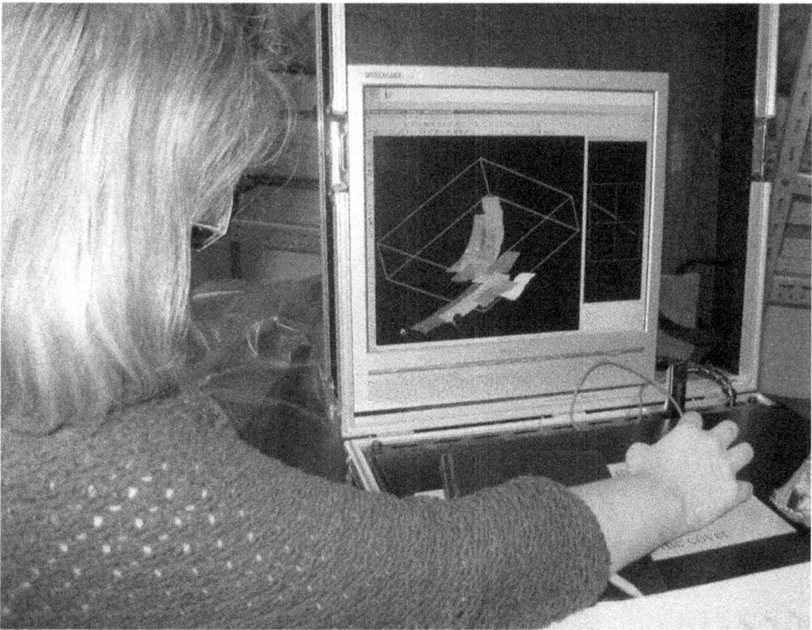

Figure 7.2 Detail of the scanned canoe hull appearing as a model on computer screen in the British Museum storage facilities. Photograph by the author.

could become readable by end users. This process involved crafting the surface of the canoe hull and accessories by adding textured points to the overall scan that the initial scan had not picked up. Therefore, empty or void spaces in the scan were imagined by the technician and rendered over by points to form a surface.

This process of digital crafting – involving specific hand movements to digitally plane surfaces to make them appear seamless, is what McCullough (1996) singles out as convergence of digital work with traditional craft. This process was akin to conserving the object in the museum. The 3D reconstruction or 'conservation process' involved adding missing pieces such as the uncaptured underside of the canoe. Constructive elements like ribs and planks were modelled. Not only were the prow and stern put back to their original positions on the canoe but their decorative details were also completed virtually – so presenting the canoe in its complete state. Missing shells in the prow's white cowries grid were replaced, and the now faded colours of the twill decoration were recoloured dark red again and flanked by white cockatoo feathers using digital techniques.

Figure 7.3 Detail of shell inlay on the hull of the war canoe. Photograph by the author.

The high-resolution 3D scanning method produced a dense greyscale point cloud. A point cloud is a three-dimensional coordinate system representing a series of points on a computer screen indicating the surface of an object. In this instance, the object was the large and complex canoe structure from the Solomon Islands. The collected point cloud data were imported into a specialist software program, and the point clouds were filtered and algorithmically aligned to form a complete model of the current condition of the war canoe in storage facilities consisting of around eight million points.

Much like the discussion on scaling in Chapter 4, in which the form of the canoe emerged through adding planks to the hull, the technique of building the 3D digital image of the canoe relied on an additive technology. More and more points were added to the image to create a visible and recognizable form, a mass of points that could be distinguished as the surface of the canoe and its accessories. The resulting point cloud was a dense surface consisting of millions of points, colourless and without texture.

Once this 3D point cloud had been created, the next stage of model construction commenced, which involved adding colour and texture to the surface. The colour surface of the canoe was captured using a high-resolution photogrammetrically calibrated Nikon camera to image the complete canoe hull. The photographs provided a detailed documentation of the canoe and were used for texture mapping to produce a coloured point cloud. Digitally authentic reconstruction relied on the expertise of the University of Bergen team, who had worked with canoe builders in the Western Solomon Islands, as well as the two London-based Solomon Islanders (see Hviding 2014).

The Digital Return of the Plank Canoe

In 2010, the first high-resolution 3D digital image of the war canoe was returned to the Solomon Islands by the Norwegian anthropological team during a ceremony in Honiara. While the political elite in Honiara heralded the success of the project – captured on Solomon Islands media broadcasts – the Vella Lavella community's responses to the 3D digital model of the plank canoe were, in contrast, somewhat mixed. The initial repatriated scan – although enthusiastically received by local people – still lacked colour in its digital reconstruction. One of the Norwegian anthropologists working on the canoe project in Vella Lavella, and who collected first hand the ethnographic data, reported that some people were unable to identify the canoe as 'one of their own'. Indeed, they explained to him that this was because the canoe was undecorated: there were no cowry shells, red twill and feathers (these had not been added to the scan at this stage); so they did not recognize the digital canoe as a particular class of war canoe from Vella Lavella. They were unable to relate the 3D digital image of the canoe to what they imagined the canoe to be in the past or in the present. Moreover, they claimed the digital image represented a canoe that was dead or lifeless and that may also be broken.

Their perceptions of the digital image changed subsequently when the Norwegian anthropologist returned with a full colour 3D model with details of decorations, which was subsequently presented to the Vella Lavella community. The community were able to view the canoe in full 3D on their laptop computers. This enabled local people to explore the interior of the canoe, its hull and the shell inlay, mediated through the computer keyboard, mouse and screen. Interestingly, a range of local idioms were used to describe the physical manipulation of the canoe image by hand and computer mouse. The practice of moving across the surface of the image and examining specific features was termed 'torching' (relating to the battery-operated flashlight) by the local people.

In the Solomon Islands, there are similar set of issues relating to the return of physical objects in terms of what to do with them. Objects, now in Western museums, are still considered powerful, 'lost cultural corpora' (Pellizzi 1995: 5), as they presence the ancestral past much like saintly relics or remains. The ancestral past is understood to be a powerful realm, one which needs to be controlled. Art historian Francesco Pellizzi describes similar stories about wooden saint relics by the Highland Maya of southern Mexico. The relics were found 'living' in caves and were brought to Catholic churches where they are said to roam around at night, thus potentially causing harm because of their inherent powers (Pellizzi 1995: 9).

Images also harbour potentially dangerous forces. Visual anthropologist Chris Wright has shown how photographs of early twentieth century Solomon Islanders are today received with trepidation (Wright 2008). Portraits of ancestors wearing an assortment of shell decorations have to be locked away at night in case they roam and cause harm. For Wright, photographs can be understood in terms of likeness and presence. Each photograph has a potency indexed through their content: images of ancestors, shrines and shell valuables are considered particularly potent. Fingermarks on the photographic print in areas where such potent images are depicted suggest how the object can be accessed through sight and touch in a bid to sense the power such images are thought to contain. It indicates how ideas of proximity exist in relation to photographs.

This idea of proximity is useful when we consider the Vella Lavella community's description of their handling of the 3D canoe as 'torching'. 'Torching' implies a distancing of the image from the viewer, holding it at arm's length rather than necessarily an idea of proximity. This distancing is also related to the fact that the canoe appears to float on the screen, abstracted from any social landscape, much like a scientific specimen. In other words, while museums are trying to make objects more real and immersive through 3D imaging and digital repatriation, the paradox is that for Solomon Islanders, or so it seems, the 3D image is perceived in a distant and less threatening manner. Torching allows the nature of an object to be revealed through the shining of light on its surface. It is the ultimate process of transformation, from one of concealment to revelation. In contrast to the photographs of ancestral shrines and ornaments, which thrive on touch and sight, the notion of torching allows for the image to be internalized by holding it at a safe distance and looking.

Remaking the Future

This study of digital return demonstrates the ways in which new forms of collaboration between communities of origin and ethnographic museums are mediated by 3D digital images/objects. Working in consultation with communities of origin helps museums understand the political, cultural and technical needs of individual communities and the types of frameworks in which material knowledge participates. Until recently, digital resources had often been uploaded onto institution servers with little understanding of the impact – social, cultural and religious – of the unfettered access to material and technical knowledge (in the form of images) brought to communities.

In the Solomon Islands, the 3D digital image, as a scaled representation of the original canoe that exists in the British Museum and in the minds of Solomon Islanders, can now be imagined in its entirety. The 3D digital image creates an indexical link to the Solomon Islands landscape, as it reveals different timbers, shells, pigments and plant fibres used to make the canoe. Seeing detailed profiles of the canoe means that the interior design of the hull and the types of materials used in the complex construction can be studied and potentially reconstructed. Rather than acquire knowledge via an apprentice/master relationship as Borofsky (1987) has described in Pukapuka, learning involves lighting surfaces as both a performative act in the movement of hand, eye and computer mouse and also a process of observation and internalization between computer and individual.

This chapter has therefore demonstrated that in terms of returning material knowledge to communities, digital images are the conduits for innovative forms of material expression. This is because, as Alpers has argued in relation to pictorial knowledge (Alpers 1983), the image is not simply read: rather its visual presence exists as a form of knowledge for recording and internalizing. The image therefore carries with it the capacity to rekindle known and unknown knowledge of the landscape in which materials are part. As is the case with the Mobile Museum project in New Ireland (Chapter 6), digital return of the canoe did not necessarily precipitate new acts of production but rather access to this knowledge to hold on to created value. In this sense, the potency of digital return resides in its virtuality and the future potential to objectify this knowledge through specialist crafting skills in particular moments of the life cycle.

The potency of the virtual world in Melanesia – expanded and enhanced through the onset of digital projects – relies on an understanding of how images can be utilized or deployed politically – through the use of computers privately, digital archiving and formatting – or more formally via activities in classrooms, in which the transmission of technical skills occurs. The virtual evidently raises issues of property and ownership: (re)possessing the image is to (re)possess the material and technical means of reproduction. The implication of this is significant for museums and debates about ethnographic objects and repatriation. Even though objects remain behind lock and key in institutions, digital technologies carry the potential to unmoor images from their material forms through their reproduction and circulation as photographs and models.

Yet, given the transformations in technologies and the spatial trajectories of objects as they traverse the globe in often uncontrolled ways, it is surprising how some museum curators still cling to ideological notions of the object rooted in terms of its originality and authenticity (e.g. Conn 2010), in which the virtual is downplayed or of lesser value. And yet moving beyond these notions of authenticity and originality, the crucial issue for ethnographic museums seems to be one of legitimation: in order to continue to hold on to ethnographic objects in their collections, new forms of relations have to be established with communities of origin that embrace new forms of curatorship and access (Harris and O'Hanlon 2013). For people of the Pacific, like those I have described in the Western Solomon Islands and northern New

Ireland, the adoption of new digital technologies heralds a new phase in object relations and new forms of museum engagement that may not have been possible before. And importantly, it signals a return of material knowledge through localized forms of digital archiving and dissemination – a potent virtuality that is both real and vibrant – and perhaps negates the framing of digital return as a first step towards full physical repatriation towards a new narrative of completeness and materials expressivity (DeLanda 2006; Phillips 2013; Rowlands 2002).

Note

1. See Rowley's (2013) overview of the opportunities, challenges and tensions of the Reciprocal Research Network project established between ethnographic museums and First Nations organizations in Canada.

Conclusion

Towards a New Understanding of Materiality

Considering new approaches to materials is not only about searching for the novel and the innovative; many techniques and practices associated to fibres, timbers, barks and cloth are centuries old and are unlikely to change. Rather, to consider materials and innovation is to focus on the social context of design; the way in which design itself is orientated towards building a better future for society (Forty 1986; Norman 1988). This raises questions not only about the nature of design and its significance but also warrants further investigation as to why design takes on such an important role in society as a set of creative actions or projects. In the twenty-first century, materials and design have become more important than ever. Design is not simply about aesthetics and 'looking good', it also intersects with technical worlds and society itself. Materials and design create new possibilities in the world, bringing together disparate ideas and people in projects of collaboration and creativity. Design not only reinvigorates the use of materials, old and new, but it expands and enhances the value of materials and their relation to people's lives. Moreover, the values, uses and identities of materials are constantly shifting as I have demonstrated in this book: materials can make and break relationships and their overuse and availability can contribute to waste and environmental problems (Hawkins 2011; Norris 2010; Sheller 2014). In this case, materials never really depart from the social domain but undergo a continual cycle of transformation, reuse and reinvention.

Materials lie at the heart of human experience as we move through a world of concrete, plastic, fabric, fibre, paper and pulp. They give us pleasure; they keep us warm at night; and they alert us to danger. Our own cultural memory is shaped through our sensory experience of materials: often the smell of an old pair of jeans or the feel of black nylon jogs back fleeting memories of youth or childhood or a particular moment in the past. Materials give form to stories and memories through the twisting, weaving and stitching of fibres and strips and are a means of making sense in the world. Their deeply sensory qualities – evoking tactile and visual experiences – means that they act as a tangible medium for managing relations to the past and present.

Using materials requires specialist skills, an intellectual activity that requires concepts, planning and predictions that all involve a process of 'working it out' and know-how. Materials are a form of thinking because thought emerges with making; and so the process of making is productive of thought and of action. The material is the medium that produces this; it is for the mind to inhabit. As making proceeds in steps, materials are transformed and tested; objects emerge and give rise to events, a feast, a hunt or a gathering. Materials, as Shove et al. (2007) rightly state, are co-productive of relations – they hold potential for objecthood – and in their state as objects materials can be understood through observation of their performance. The way in which materials condense social relations is elaborated by Gell (1996), writing on the Zande hunting net from Central Africa. The making of the Zande hunting net, Gell argues, is more than just collecting materials in order to make the net: it involves planning the hunt, deploying specialist skills in trapping prey and also preparing a feast.

If materials ensnare minds as people gain knowledge and experience of their potential for technical actions, then any analysis of materials requires paying attention to the qualities of materials and the potentials of these qualities – their affordance (Gibson 1979) – and understanding the reasons people make such informed choices of material selection in the process of designing objects. As I have demonstrated in this book, small differences in the technical and aesthetic qualities of plant leaves, such as those of the pandanus, raise profoundly different types of social action. It also raises issues not just about the production of objects, which anthropological approaches to making so readily emphasize. It also points to an understanding of emergence through the observed decay of materials as an operational logic and how this leads to the making and remaking of relationships in society.

So, I have argued that materials mark out time as they age; their surfaces whither or dry much like human bodies. Their fragility or longevity in the environment maps out seasons and ingrains natural events through erosion, saturation and fading. Their presence anchors connections to place, a garden or a forest, and they act on the world as carriers of knowledge and experience. Materials require a frame of analysis that pays attention to their transformative states, not their stable states, which does not just disturb their presence but also animates it (Gregson, Watkins and Calestani 2010). This recognition of the performative properties of materials, how their presence is made known (DeLanda 2006), demonstrates how material properties are not fixed but processual, relational and distributed.

In Melanesia and across the Pacific, these conceptions of renewal through observed decay are crucial to understanding rights of succession and kinship. My argument, therefore, has been to prioritize the role of materials as constituent elements in the formation of people's lifeworlds in the Pacific. It has emphasized how diverse materials such as plant leaves, lianas, timbers, stems and sap are understood as transformative, not just in terms of creating form and function but also as 'enabling' forms of sociality through their transformation and the responses these elicit. Through the display, wearing or gifting of particular kinds of objects, forms of kinship are made visible and understood. In this way, materials are the machines that create, manage and connect. This kind of analysis can no longer be confined to Western technoscience and laboratory discourse as demonstrated by Bensaude-Vincent (2011), Ball (1997), Barry (2013), Hawkins (2011) and others; there should be recognition of the operational qualities of Pacific plant materials evidenced in the way people there use materials to manage informational environments.

The implication of these ethnographic insights that I have presented in this book are important for anthropological debates on materiality because they stress the significance of the relation between the technical and social domains, areas that traditionally have been seen as distinct and separate in anthropology. My argument has put forward the notion that materials condense social relations in ways that can be understood through their transformation, use and reinvention. Thus, the ideas materials communicate are built into the material itself, manifest in its biophysical structure, its natural compliance and its outward aesthetic. This informational approach seeks to reclaim an analytical focus on materials as socially co-productive; a model that appreciates how social relations are condensed in matter and made manifest in processes of making. This approach extends Ingold's phenomenological approach in which he explores how forms emerge through making towards an understanding of materials that takes account of their properties in design that influence their selection. In other words, my approach has followed that of Pye (1968), who emphasizes how materials matter, and they matter much in approach, as they demand knowledge and action. As a craftsman himself, Pye knew that craft-makers must have know-how about the performance of certain materials, not just in their physical sense, such as their capacity to withstand forces or remain waterproof, but also in the sense of their workability, their cost and their finish. This approach to materials is also identified in Ashby and Johnson's (2002) analysis of product design, which suggests how acts of making, both in traditional craft practices and contemporary product design, follow basic approaches to materials – that is, there is a mapping of different types of attributes to select the best material for the job. The success of design is dependent on materials, the performance as well as the look.

In order to develop my approach to materials and materiality, I have foregrounded the complex nature of material knowledge not simply as a set of ideas about applying forces to mould, shape and contort but also an intergenerational way of knowing and acting on the environment. Design involves empathy: knowing how to select the appropriate type of leaf or fibre, a consideration of its performance, its colour and sensory attributes, its spatial and place location and balancing these attributes to contexts and intended outcomes. I have shown throughout this book how the environments of materials are equally important factors that influence the uptake of materials in the Pacific, whether these are products sold in marketplaces or shops, or presented at important life-cycle ceremonies. As I have demonstrated in Chapter 3, the story of harakeke, New Zealand flax, provides interesting insights into how the natural fibre, after decades of declining use, suddenly found a new foothold with its branding as a green fibre, linking the material into a wider network of nation-branding and New Zealand consumer identity. It has been the fibre's propensity to decay that has shaped its positive future, whereas in the recent past its material identity was shaped by its strength under tension. Similarly, in Chapter 1, I argued how a type of pandanus known in Nalik society as amotmot, protects people, especially the most vulnerable such as newborn infants, in ways that other varieties of pandanus do not. Its resilience to rain water and invisible forces (such as sorcery and malevolent spirits) manages relations between the visible and invisible, and ensures that certain forms of gifting take place between kin, an important factor in the Pacific.

Enabling Materials – Materials as Enablers

Materials enable thought and action. This agentic capacity of materials to manage social relations sets itself apart from three dominant approaches in the humanities and social sciences: approaches that have either focused on linking the surface qualities of materials (their shininess, their colour, etc.) as metaphors for a larger external world outside; approaches that situate materials within emergent lifeworlds; or those that examine the social-political networks in which materials themselves enter the world, often as a consequence of laboratory life.

There are many limits to these approaches, and I hope this book has introduced an alternative perspective that restores an analysis of materials within a sociotechnical framework. My argument has been influenced by these various perspectives – rather than discounting them altogether – and places them within a framework that places importance on their social effects. Materiality, I argue, demands an acknowledgement of the potency of materials to ensnare human imagination and create social action. By situating the technical properties of materials in direct conversation with their social outcomes and employing an ethnographic methodology to tease out the nuanced interactions between materials and persons – material biographies, networks of knowledge and so forth – what is important to developing my approach to materiality are the ways in which materials are constitutive of materiality. That is, there is a social dimension to materials that impregnates the substance of materials beyond their surface interventions, and people act on this.

The idea that materials are enabling – much like technology – is expressed most clearly in the way materials are creatively selected in design projects in the Pacific in order to carve out a niche. In Chapter 4, my focus on the revival of barkcloth amongst Nalik women in Papua New Guinea highlights the way in which material knowledge is claimed by some and used in gendered domains to transform fibres through commodification into wealth. In earning small amounts of cash through the sale of these baskets in a competitive marketplace enables women to enter new markets and scale up earnings through trips to urban centres to bulk-buy products. This process of converting fibre wealth into capital not only sees a categorical division between male and female gendered spheres but also enables women to trade up by using newly found wealth to set up small food stalls in village hamlets. It enables female makers to take control of cash income – helping sustain their families and pay school fees – but also strengthens their own kin ties and rights to land in a society where men may be absent, working on the industrial mines on offshore islands or even unemployed for long periods of time. Cash, in its physical form, offers more than access to store-purchased goods; it can also be traded up through bulk purchase and reselling. Seen this way, materials enable relations: as natural resources, they can be transformed into wealth by creating desirable products that fill niche markets in order to make small though significant amounts of money.

In this sense, materials create contexts anew, which animates and mobilizes women to enter into new social domains and networks. Through the transformation of baskets into marketable commodities, women are occupying a niche in society by utilizing a material's natural connection to place and identity. The material therefore is an agent for empowering women in New Ireland society, transforming their world. Yet this study reaches further in its analysis: my analysis of the materiality of the barkcloth basket also demonstrates how the market drives further searches for better materials. The rise of barkcloth and its replacement by a superior material (mulai) that is more workable, more aesthetic and more valuable underlines the rapidly shifting economy of material knowledge in parts of the Pacific and the demand for something new as a hallmark of difference and identity. The basket is an excellent example of the resourcefulness of Nalik women to market a product in terms of its place identity, using locally sourced materials, and commodify a traditional object outside the domain of kastom, and thereby operate in a realm without causing conflict inside communities. It is precisely the everydayness of the basket together with its novel incorporation of barkcloth and its style of wearing that makes the basket an attractive accessory for New Ireland women to purchase.

The Constituents of Environments

Materials are relational, never to be understood in isolation. Enchained in assemblages, as Bennett (2010) has cogently argued, materials are connected to networks of actors and other materials that shape the way materials emerge in society. Thus, materials can be seen as overtly political as they negotiate complex environments in which they are developed and used in design: their mere selection can signal an allegiance, a boundary or even a dispute. As I described in Chapter 5, the absence of the metal nail (with cordage lashings preferred in the construction of a Nalik male meeting house in Papua New Guinea) raised crucial questions of motivations and informed selection of materials as well as the political aspirations such a design elicits to the community and a wider audience. The lashings, sourced from the coastal forests and conspicuously woven into the architecture frame, speak volumes about social change, identity and male power. Their presence ties into political manoeuvres that seek to restore the past, a golden age, for the future prosperity of all. It is these modes of material expressivity – materials that make themselves known – that point to the importance of materials in creating new social worlds through their incorporation into design in public spaces, as well as the new forms of moral personhood that emerge through such actions.

The environments of materials are constantly shifting and so are the types of materials available in society. The revival of old materials in the Pacific for innovative 'new' fashion accessories clearly articulates how the past can be reframed to give meanings. As shifting symbols of life, the integration of old materials into new forms empowers women or men and creates new classifications and typologies through which ritual and political activities are channelled.

And yet perhaps some seventy years or more ago it was the materials of colonial officers and missionaries that spoke volumes about the political and social environment. As I have argued elsewhere (Were 2005a), cloth – as a new material – was seen as innocent by Europeans when worn by Pacific peoples, even though its transformation and display was far from this. Its incorporation into existing regimes of dressing the body, as well as integration into pattern systems (such as chequered cloth), had the double effect of reinforcing ritual polities whilst at the same time making a visual statement about new forms of sociality with the stationing of colonial forms of government in the region.

The shifting identities of materials and environments have been a major focus of this book. An analysis of these shifts points to the dynamic materialities of the Pacific. I have described how the story of harakeke, New Zealand flax, is inseparable from an analysis of the global fibre market and the shifting identity of New Zealand as a tourist destination, a must-see destination branded as a clean, green country. Up until recently, harakeke had a rather indifferent story of boom and bust as a hard fibre in the international market. Its success was not dependent on its natural properties: rather its social history reveals how warfare, trade agreements, crop management and extraction technologies shaped its fortune on the international market. In other words, it was not the fibre that could be blamed; it was its relation to other hard fibres on the market that constrained its success. In this way, like the story of barkcloth in New Ireland, harakeke has been contingent on the social, political and historical environments in which it is embedded, all of which shape the way that the plant itself is transformed, either by stripping its leaves or extracting gum or resin. Thinking about these materials as they are processed involves thinking about their performance in these competitive environments. Thus, materials are never thought of alone. We could say, therefore, materials conjure an assemblage of relationships through which they can possibly emerge and come to prominence.

Materials in Mind

The chapters in this book demonstrate how makers in the Pacific have an empathy for materials rooted in a spirit of working them out; thinking through the biophysical structures, their compliance under certain conditions and the types of opportunities this presents in a region that places a strong emphasis on the status of kin relations through exchange. This empathy requires an understanding of the affordances of materials, knowledge about material constraints and product specifications. The story of the pandanus mats, which I described in Chapter 1, demonstrates how affordances and know-how is made operative, manifest in the selection of pandanus leaves and their connection to varying types of kin relations for which each mat is designed. The rate of natural decay ensures renewal and return obligations as well as fulfilling a functional role of protection against visible and invisible elements in the environment. These types of relations are condensed into the structure of the leaves and recognized within communities as tacitly understood. Thus, plant materials create and manage connections and play a vital role for future wellbeing in fragile environments such as the Pacific.

As with all skilled craft-makers, people have a good understanding of the performance of certain materials and the Pacific is no exception to this rule. Knowledge is internalized so that the landscape for the women and men who inhabit island communities becomes a map of particular plants and trees that potentially could be sourced for various purposes. Plants, timbers and other materials afford many potentials, and it is through their transformation into crafted objects that their performance can be measured. We could say that in thinking about a material, one thinks about its objecthood; but equally in thinking about its objecthood, one is also keen to work out its very physical nature, the elements of its design and how to reproduce this. In this way, objects as much as materials enchain ideas and offer potential and opportunities for social action.

The strategic engagement with the environment through observation and analysis of the various fibres, leaves and barks demonstrates how material selection involves a complex set of skills and practices. This book has applied an understanding of material computation to the world of materials in the Pacific in order to account for how people empathize with materials. This notion of empathy that has been introduced derives not just from the role of maker as bricoleur, as Levi-Strauss (1966) has famously argued; rather, I have demonstrated how the process of making is a complex intellectual activity that combines an intimate knowledge of biophysical structure and material affordances, and how this performance finds expression in the social world. In design thinking, I showed that what was important was how computational techniques – the mind writ large – were expressed through the operations of scale, both as an incremental calculation as well as a reduction. I have argued that a mathematical logic, manifest in scaling design, provides a logical framework for thinking about the way materials can be transformed, either through stripping and shredding – as is the case in New Ireland, where leaves are often reduced before they are woven – to the notorious plank canoes of the Western Solomon Islands, which were used for headhunting. Even with the introduction of Western imaging technologies, I have described how analogical operations of addition contribute to new understandings of objecthood and form.

Reconfiguring Materials

This book has examined how the exposure of materials to sunlight, humidity, saltwater and smoke initiates their gradual erosion and breakdown. I have explored how 'observed decay' can lead to the recovery of memory (DeSilvey 2006) and allows materials to participate in social actions from exchange and storytelling. This movement towards an ultimate immaterial state (though some see materials as inextinguishable, e.g. Gregson, Watkins and Calestani 2010) often signals preparations for the cyclical processes of remaking and renewal; the collecting of palm leaves, their sun bleaching, restitching of mats and gifting presentations and ceremonies. This economy of materials and making reflects the transition from material to immaterial, the externalization and internationalization of material knowledge and its transmission from one generation to another. It maps out genealogical pathways between generations as well as tracts of land where the materials are cultivated, and punctuates social history through ceremonial presentations.

One of the questions addressed in this book regards the impact of new materials and how the different structures of new materials – such as their permanence, their resistance to decay and their perceived performance – has impacted on a traditional economy of materials, which was generally (though not solely) located locally or in the vicinity through exchange networks. What makes this contribution so significant is that it provides an anthropologically informed approach to perceptions and use of new types of materials. On the one hand, this has been covered through a body of literature that examines the introduction of metals, cloth and other materials; however, this book is innovative in the way that it explores the effects of the almost ubiquitous digital domain and how material knowledge is transformed through the forms of digital media now accessible in the Pacific. Digital renditions of actual physical objects, displaying different types of woods, pigments and leaf fibres, became instrumental in rekindling material knowledge, as the case of the political groups in New Ireland (Chapter 6) and the Solomon Islands (Chapter 7) testifies.

An important argument made throughout this book has been the call to recognize the performative nature of materials – how they make thought and action operative through their selection, transformation and display. This is particularly true in the context of the emergence of new technologies in the Pacific region that have transformed the nature of materials and the forms through which these materials move. Here, as Hawkins (2011) has argued in the context of plastic water bottles and the marketing and packaging of water as healthy, a similar process has taken place in terms of the use of digital heritage technologies as a means to recover the past and material practices and so herald a new 'healthier' future in which communities prosper from the rewards attached to this new economy of knowledge. Like bottled water, technology and the materials accessed are entirely potent and political. Whereas the software application allowed Nalik men and women to observe and analyse physical objects housed in remote locations (the Australian state of Queensland) – the new forms of objects allowed for new imaginings of political and ritual power expressed through the activities of the chiefly organization and their commitment to safeguarding the objects in a localized archive. The materials of the archive thus presented local chiefly men with the capacity to manage social relations in new ways by making claims to the technology and an expanded virtual world of 'old' images through which the new materials could be accessed. In this way, the new digital forms became more than just 'signs of recognition' (Keane 1997) – expressions of the tensions that exist in the community about the distant past and the rewards this harbours through access to ancestral power – but about their manifestation within a new order through which power relations could be restored and normalized. The fact that these digital objects seemingly appeared as imagistic did not detract the local people from these political aspirations; rather, it was the visible use of the technology and their aesthetics (the community's engagement in the handling of the 3D objects) that presented a potent symbol of the new materials to transform social movements in the region. These transformations were articulated as promises of a better future and as assets that could be deployed for the benefit of communities, as empowering the local people and redemptive in the face of social fragmentation.

And yet the archive in its new and decentralized form now heralds a new and potent force for the rekindling of material knowledge worldwide. While these immaterial forms of archival apparatus form the spearhead for new forms of religious and political activism in the Pacific, as my research in New Ireland and the Solomon Islands demonstrates, there are also other potentials of the archive that are revealed through public access. Throughout the Western world, in urban centres, in architects' buildings and in universities, there has been a growth of materials libraries – shopfronts for designers, architects and engineers, who use these resources as one-stop shops to learn about the latest materials that have been developed. Such tactile spaces, where swatches of new textiles can be tested, witness a renewed emphasis on sensory knowledge and aesthetic judgement in terms of material selection. Whereas materials libraries and archives form nodal points for the dissemination of material knowledge in industrialized societies, it is the advent of digital technologies that cultivates a possible new era in the return of material knowledge in its digital form. These new forms of knowledge transmission literally make museum collections mobile, unmooring ancestral images and material knowledge from storage facilities in urban centres in Brisbane, London and Berlin to faraway places in the Pacific where they are incorporated into new crafting practices. Thus, while virtual environments offer new forms of observation and looking, they also sow the seeds for new forms of knowing and making. As Deger (2013: 369) notes, it is not the newness of new media that brings the ancestral to life, value is instead placed on the potential for renewed acts of making through which ancestral power can emerge.

The Future of Materials

While some have traced the social life of materials as they move from development to households or industrial application (e.g. Drazin and Kuechler 2015), this book has asserted how social life itself is created and managed through material substances in the Pacific. Plant materials cultivate sociality, and their transformation makes this real. This book has demonstrated how sociality permeates materials, impregnating substances as matter emerges through the selection of materials in design projects in the Pacific. Rather than simply consisting of surfaces, substances and structures, the matter that constitutes materials is embedded in social relations through their articulation as objects, which in turn are informed through material selection. I have demonstrated how plant materials resonate with complexity: beyond their chemical and physical structure, their potential to be transformed into forms and ideas makes them potent entities as a locus for human thought and action. Their performativity in the social domain and the ways in which technical transformations map onto the diverse dynamics of social life, managing relations in economic ways, enables new ways of thinking about their importance in society.

As new types of materials emerge in Pacific worlds as well as Western consumer culture, what will be the effects of their circulation and use? In a rapidly changing world with increasing sophistication in the materials available in design, the new possibilities shaping society appear endless. I have hoped to demonstrate that in focusing on the Pacific region, debates about the complexity of materials are equally covered in the developing world. Too often, as was the case during the heyday of economic botany in the nineteenth century through to the development of sustainable materials, it is stories of materials scientists, civil engineers or architects that we hear. And yet, significantly, this anthropological study has revealed Pacific sociality is deeply rooted in plant materials, and how engrained these materials are in creating and managing connections. It is the human activity of design – through acts of selection, transformation and display – that gives materials their potency and that this book ultimately draws attention to and celebrates. In doing so, my intention has been to open up a new debate on the co-productive possibilities of materials and designs and reveal the social worlds that emerge through their engaged use in design projects. Like most natural materials that eventual deteriorate and decay, the ideas of materials outlast their forms. This I hope prompts new debates on the intentionalities of materials and their place in shaping our future.

In sum, this book delves into the modalities of human engagement with plants, barks, timbers and other materials on the part of Pacific peoples. It brings together long-term ethnographic fieldwork amongst the Nalik community of New Ireland with short-term projects in a biomaterials laboratory in Rotorua in New Zealand. The storage facilities of the British Museum, University College London Anthropology collections, Queensland Museum and the University of Queensland Anthropology Museum also provided an invaluable resource for a close-hand analysis of museum collections. When combined with archival documents such as missionary and colonial papers, historical ethnographies and economic botany papers, this book provides a rich insight into the world of materials from a Pacific viewpoint. Moreover, presenting materials as 'made to measure' highlights the ways in which Pacific peoples have an intimate understanding of plants, their performance, their aesthetics and qualities, and their social and political effect. In this way, there exists a shared empathy with materials that serves to manage social relations so that to articulate certain materials through transformation and display is to externalize ideas in society.

References

Alpers, Svetlana. 1983. *The Art of Describing: Dutch Art in the Seventeenth Century*. Chicago, IL: University of Chicago Press.

Andersen, Barbara. 2013. 'Tricks, Lies, and Mobile Phones: "Phone Friend" Stories in Papua New Guinea', *Culture, Theory and Critique* 54(3): 318–34.

Appadurai, Arjun. 1996. *Modernity at Large: Cultural Dimensions of Globalization*. London: University of Minnesota Press.

Ascher, Marcia. 2002. *Mathematics Elsewhere: An Exploration of Ideas across Cultures*. Princeton, NJ and Oxford: Princeton University Press.

Ashby, Mike F. and Kara Johnson. 2002. *Materials and Design: The Art and Science of Material Selection in Product Design*. Oxford: Butterworth-Heinemann.

Bainton, Nicholas A. 2010. *The Lihir Destiny: Cultural Responses to Mining in Melanesia*. Canberra: ANU Press.

Ball, Philip. 1997. *Made to Measure: New Materials for the 21st Century*. Princeton, NJ and Chichester: Princeton University Press.

———. 2008. 'Material Witness: Materials Matchmaking', *Nature Materials* 7: 522.

———. 2012. 'Material Witness: Material Computation', *Nature Materials* 11: 362.

Barry, Andrew. 2005. 'Pharmaceutical Matters: The Invention of Informed Materials', *Theory, Culture and Society* 22(1): 51–69.

———. 2013. *Material Politics: Disputes along the Pipeline*. Chichester: John Wiley and Sons.

Basu, Paul. 2011. 'Object Diasporas, Resourcing Communities: Sierra Leonean Collections in the Global Museumscape', *Museum Anthropology* 34(1): 28–42.

Baudrillard, Jean. 1994. *Simulacra and Simulation*, trans. S.F. Glaser. Ann Arbor: University of Michigan Press.

Bell, F. Dillon and Frederick Young. 1842. *Reasons for Promoting the Cultivation of the New Zealand Flax*. London: Smith, Elder and Co.

Bell, Joshua A., Kimberly Christen and Mark Turin. 2013. 'Introduction: After the Return', *Museum Anthropology Review* 7(1–2): 1–21.

Belting, Hans. 1994. *Likeness and Presence: A History of the Image before the Era of Art*, trans. E. Jephcott. Chicago, IL: University of Chicago Press.

Bennett, Jane. 2010. *Vibrant Matter: A Political Ecology of Things*. Durham, NC: Duke University Press.

Bennett, Judith A. 1987. *Wealth of the Solomons: A History of a Pacific Archipelago, 1800-1978*. Honolulu: University of Hawai'i.

Bennett, Tony. 1995. *The Birth of the Museum: History, Theory, Politics*. London: Routledge.

Bensaude-Vincent, Bernadette. 2011. 'Materials as Machines', in M. Carrier and A. Nordmann (eds), *Science in the Context of Application: Boston Studies in the Philosophy of Science*. vol 274. Dordrecht: Springer, 101–111.

———. 2013. 'Plastics, Materials and Dreams of Dematerialization', in J. Gabrys, G. Hawkins and M. Michael (eds), *Accumulation: The Material Politics of Plastic*. London: Routledge, 17–29.

Bijker, Wiebe E. 1995. *Of Bicycles, Bakelites and Bulbs: Toward a Theory of Sociotechnical Change*. Cambridge, MA: MIT Press.

Boivin, Nicole. 2008. *Material Cultures, Material Minds: The Impact of Things on Human Thought, Society, and Evolution*. Cambridge: Cambridge University Press.

Bolton, Lissant. 1997. 'A Place Containing Many Places: Museums and the Use of Objects to Represent Place in Melanesia', *The Australian Journal of Anthropology* 8(1): 18–34.

———. 2003. *Unfolding the Moon: Enacting Women's Kastom in Vanuatu*. Honolulu: University of Hawai'i Press.

Borofsky, Robert. 1987. *Making History: Pukapukan and Anthropological Constructions of Knowledge*. Cambridge: Cambridge University Press.

Brockway, Lucile H. 2002. *Science and Colonial Expansion: The Role of the British Royal Botanic Gardens*. New Haven, CT: Yale University Press.

Brooker, Stanley G., Richard C. Cambie and R.C. Cooper. 1989. 'Economic Native Plants of New Zealand', *Economic Botany* 43(1): 79–106.

Brooking, Tom. 2004. *The History of New Zealand*. London: Greenwood Press.

Brown, Deidre. 2007. 'Te Ahu Hiko: Digital Heritage and Indigenous Objects, People, and Environments', in F. Cameron and S. Kenderdine (eds), *Theorizing Digital Culture Heritage: A Critical Discourse*. Cambridge, MA: The MIT Press, 77–92.

Brunton, Ron. 1981. 'The Origins of the John Frum Movement: A Sociological Explanation', in M.R. Allen (ed.), *Vanuatu: Politics, Economics, and Ritual in Island Melanesia*. London and Sydney: Academic Press, 357–77.

Bulmer, Ralph and Andrew Pawley. 1991. *Man and a Half: Essays in Pacific Anthropology and Ethnobiology in Honour of Ralph Bulmer, Memoir*. Auckland: Polynesian Society.

Burnett, Frank. 1911. *Through Polynesia and Papua: Wanderings with a Camera in Southern Seas*. London: Francis Griffith.

Butler, Beverley. 2006. 'Heritage and the Present Past', in C. Tilley et al. (eds), *Handbook of Material Culture*. London: Sage, 463–79.

Campbell, Shirley F. 2002. *The Art of Kula*. Oxford: Berg.

Christen, Kimberly. 2011. 'Opening Archives: Respectful Repatriation', *The American Archivist* 74(1): 185–210.

———. 2012. 'Does Information Really Want to be Free? Indigenous Knowledge Systems and the Question of Openness', *International Journal of Communication* 6: 2870–93.

Christie, Michael and Helen Verran. 2013. 'Digital Lives in Postcolonial Aboriginal Australia', *Journal of Material Culture* 18(3): 299–317.

Clay, Brenda Johnson. 2005. *Unstable Images: Colonial Discourse on New Ireland, Papua New Guinea, 1875-1935*. Honolulu: University of Hawai'i Press.

Colchester, Chloe. 2003a. 'Introduction', in C. Colchester (ed.), *Clothing the Pacific*. Oxford: Berg, 1–23.

———. 2003b. 'T-shirts, Translation and Humour: On the Nature of Wearer-Perceiver Relationships in South Auckland', in C. Colchester (ed.), *Clothing the Pacific*. Oxford: Berg, 167–91.

Conkey, Margaret W. 2006. 'Style, Design, and Function', in C. Tilley et al. (eds), *Handbook of Material Culture*. London: Sage, 355–72.

Conn, Steven. 2010. *Do Museums Still Need Objects?* Philadelphia, PA: University of Pennsylvania Press.

Coupaye, Ludovic. 2009. 'Ways of Enchanting: Chaînes Opératoires and Yam Cultivation in Nyamikum Village, Maprik, Papua New Guinea', *Journal of Material Culture* 14(4): 433–58.

———. 2013. *Growing Art, Displaying Relationships: Yams, Art and Technology amongst the Nyamikum Abelam of Papua New Guinea*. Oxford: Berghahn.

Critchfield, Howard J. 1951. 'Phormium Tenax – New Zealand's Native Hard Fiber', *Economic Botany* 5(2): 172–84.

Cruthers, N., D. Carr and R. Laing. 2009. 'Research Note: The New Zealand Flax Fibre Industry', *Textile History* 40(1): 103–11.

Damon, Frederick H. 2004. 'On the Ideas of a Boat: From Forest Patches to Cybernetic Structures in the Outrigger Sailing Craft of the Eastern Kula Ring, Papua New Guinea', in C. Sather and T. Kaartinen (eds), *Beyond the Horizon: Essays on Myth, History, Travel and Society*. Helsinki: Finnish Literature Society, 123–44.

———. 2017. *Trees, Knots, and Outriggers: Environmental Knowledge in the Northeast Kula Ring*. New York: Berghahn.

Daston, Lorraine and Peter Galison. 2007. *Objectivity*. New York: Zone Books.

Davenport, William H. 1981. 'Male Initiation in Aoriki: Man and the Spirits in the Eastern Solomon Islands', *Expedition* 23(2): 4–19.

———. 1997. 'Ritual Bowls of the Eastern Solomon Islands', *Baessler-Archiv* Neue Folge 45: 315–31.

DeLanda, Manuel. 2006. 'Material Expressivity', Domus No. 893, 122–23. Lebbeus Woods. January 5, 2009. http://lebbeuswoods.wordpress.com/2009/01/05/manuel-delanda-matters-4/.

De Lannoy, Jean. 2005. 'Graves of Malakula: Anthropological History and Indigenous Christian Historiography', *History and Anthropology* 16(3): 307–20.

Deger, Jennifer. 2013. 'The Jolt of the New: Making Video Art in Arnhem Land', *Culture, Theory and Critique* 54(3): 355–71.

DeSilvey, Caitlin. 2006. 'Observed Decay: Telling Stories with Mutable Things', *Journal of Material Culture* 11(3): 318–38.

Desmond, Ray. 2007. *The History of the Royal Botanical Gardens Kew*. Kew: Royal Botanic Gardens, Kew.

Dodge, Charles R. 1897. *A Descriptive Catalogue of Useful Fibre Plants of the World*. Washington: Government Printing Office.

Drazin, Adam and Susanne Kuechler (eds). 2015. *The Social Life of Materials: Studies in Materials and Society*. London: Bloomsbury.

Duffield, A.J. 1886. 'On the Natives of New Ireland', *The Journal of the Anthropological Institute of Great Britain and Ireland* 15: 114–21.

Edge-Partington, J. 1903. 'Food Trough from Rubiana, New Georgia', *Man* 3: 161–62.

———. 1906. 'Note on the Food Bowl from Rubiana, New Georgia', *Man* 6: 121.

Eglash, Ron. 1999. *African Fractals: Modern Computing and Indigenous Design*. New Brunswick, NJ: Rutgers University Press.

Favero, Paolo. 2013. 'Getting our Hands Dirty (Again): Interactive Documentaries and the Meaning of Images in the Digital Age', *Journal of Material Culture* 18(3): 259–77.

Filer, Colin. 2011. *The New Land Grab in Papua New Guinea: A Case Study from New Ireland Province*. Discussion paper for State, Society & Governance in Melanesia. http://ssgm.bellschool.anu.edu.au/sites/default/files/publications/attachments/2015-12/2011_02_filer%5B1%5D_0.pdf.

Firth, Stewart. 1983. *New Guinea Under the Germans*. Melbourne: Melbourne University Press.

Forty, Adrian. 1986. *Objects of Desire: Design and Society since 1750*. London: Thames and Hudson.

Foster, Robert J. 1992. 'Commoditization and the Emergence of *kastam* as a Cultural Category: A New Ireland Case in Comparative Perspective', *Oceania* 62(4): 284–94.

Foster, Robert J. and Heather Horst. (eds). 2018. *The Moral Economy of Mobile Phones: Pacific Islands Perspectives*. Canberra: ANU Press.

Freedberg, David. 1989. *The Power of Images: Studies in the History and Theory of Response*. Chicago, IL: University of Chicago Press.

Gabriel, Jennifer, Paul Nelson, Colin Filer and Mike Wood. 2017. 'Oil Palm Development and Large-scale Land Acquisitions in Papua New Guinea', in S. McDonnell, M.G. Allen and C. Filer (ed.), *Kastom, Property and Ideology: Land Transformations in Melanesia*. Canberra: ANU Press, 205–50.

Gamage Harshi K., S. Subrata Mondal, Lynley A. Wallis, Paul Memmott, D. Martin, R. Wright Boyd, S. Schmidt. 2012. 'Indigenous and Modern Biomaterials Derived from Triodia ("spinifex") Grasslands in Australia', *Australian Journal of Botany* 60: 114–27.

Gell, Alfred. 1993. *Wrapping in Images: Tattooing in Polynesia*. Oxford: Clarendon Press.

———. 1996. 'Vogel's Net: Traps as Artworks and Artworks as Traps', *Journal of Material Culture* 1(1): 15–38.

———. 1998. *Art and Agency: An Anthropological Theory*. Oxford: Oxford University Press.

Gibson, James J. 1979. *The Ecological Approach to Visual Perception*. Boston: Houghton Mifflin.

Gibson, Ross. 2013. 'On the Senses and Semantic Excess in Photographic Evidence', *Journal of Material Culture* 18(3): 243–57.

Golant, William. 1984. *Image of Empire: The Early History of the Imperial Institute, 1887-1925*. Exeter: University of Exeter Press.

Golding, Viv and Wayne Modest (eds). 2013. *Museums and Communities: Curators, Collections and Collaboration*. London: Bloomsbury.

'Greening New Zealand's Growth', Report of the Green Growth Advisory Group. December 2011.

Gregson, Nicky, Helen Watkins and Melania Calestani. 2010. 'Inextinguishable Fibres: Demolition and the Vital Materialisms of Asbestos', *Environment and Planning A* 42: 1065–83.

Groves, W.C. 1932–4. *Records of Anthropological Research*. PMB 611, Pacific Manuscripts Bureau, Canberra: Australia National University.

———. 1933. 'Report on Field Work in New Ireland', *Oceania* 3(3): 325–61.

———. 1936. 'Secret Beliefs and Practices in New Ireland', *Oceania* 7(2): 220–45.

Gunn, Michael. 2006. 'Kinship, Marriage, and Land', in M. Gunn and P. Peltier (eds), *New Ireland: Art of the South Pacific*. Paris: Musée du Quai Branly, 48–55.

Gunn, Michael and Philippe Peltier (eds), 2006. *New Ireland: Art of the South Pacific*. Milan: Five Continents Editions.

Haddon, Alfred C. and James Hornell. 1936. *Canoes of Oceania* (Special Publication No. 27). Honolulu, Hawaii: Bishop Museum Press.

Hancock, Rodney. 2002. *Longpela Bun Nating: My Life as a Baha'i Pioneer in Papua New Guinea*. Boroko, Papua New Guinea: National Spiritual Assembly.

Harris, Clare and Michael O'Hanlon. 2013. 'The Future of the Ethnographic Museum', *Anthropology Today* 29(1): 8–12.

Harrison, Rodney, Alison Clark, and Sarah Byrne (eds). 2013. *Reassembling the Collection: Indigenous Agency and Ethnographic Collections*. Santa Fe: School of Advanced Research.

Harrison, Simon. 1993. *The Mask of War: Violence, Ritual and the Self in Melanesia*. Manchester: Manchester University Press.

———. 2000. 'From Prestige Goods to Legacies: Property and the Objectification of Culture in Melanesia', *Comparative Studies in Society and History* 42(3): 662–79.

Hau'ofa, Epeli. 1994. 'Our Sea of Islands', *The Contemporary Pacific* 6(1): 148–61.

Hawkins, Gay. 2011. 'The Politics of Bottled Water: Assembling Bottled Water as Brand, Waste and Oil', in T. Bennett and C. Healy (eds), *Assembling Culture*. London: Routledge, 177–89.

Hawkins, Gay, Emily Potter and Kane Race. 2015. *Plastic Water: The Social and Material Life of Bottled Water*. Cambridge, MA: The MIT Press.

Hays, Terence E. 1983. 'Ndumba Folk Biology and General Principles of Ethnobotanical Classification and Nomenclature', *American Anthropologist* 85(3): 592–611.

Haywood, Janine and Nicola Wheen (eds). 2016. *The Waitangi Tribunal: Te Roopu Whakamana i te Tiriti o Waitangi*. Wellington: Bridget William Books.

Hector, J. 1872. *Phormium Tenax as a Fibrous Plant*. Wellington, New Zealand: Colonial Museum and Geological Survey Department.

Hennessy, Kate. et al. 2013. 'The Inuvialuit Living History Project: Digital Return as the Forging of Relationships between Institutions, People, and Data', *Museum Anthropology Review* 7(1–2): 44–73.

Henare, Amiria, Martin Holbraad and Sari Wastell. 2007. 'Introduction: Thinking through Things', in A. Henare, M. Holbraad and S. Wastell (eds), *Thinking through Things: Theorising Artefacts Ethnographically*. London: Routledge, 1–31.

Henare, Amiria, Martin Holbraad and Sari Wastell (eds). 2007. *Thinking through Things: Theorising Artefacts Ethnographically*. London: Routledge.

Hermkens, Anna-Karina. 2005. *Engendering Objects: Barkcloth and the Dynamics of Identity in Papua New Guinea*. Leiden: National Museum of Ethnology.

Hills, Matthew. 2008. 'Participatory Culture: Mobility, Interactivity and Identity', in G. Creeber and M. Royston (eds), *Digital Cultures: Understanding New Media*. Maidenhead: Open University Press, 107–21.

Hirsch, Eric. 2007. 'Epochs of Scale-Making in Papua', in M.E. Lien and M. Melhuus (eds), *Holding Worlds Together: Ethnographies of Knowing and Belonging*. Oxford: Berghahn, 121–41.

Holbraad, Martin. 2007. 'The Power of Powder: Multiplicity and Motion in the Divinatory Cosmology of Cuban Ifa (or Mana, Again)', in A. Henare, M. Holbraad and S. Wastell (eds), *Thinking through Things: Theorising Artefacts Ethnographically*. London: Routledge, 189–225.

Hornell, James. 1939. 'Origins of Plank-Built Boats', *Antiquity* 13(49): 35–44.

Horst, Heather and Daniel Miller. 2006. *The Cell Phone: An Anthropology of Communication*. New York: Berg.

Hviding, Edvard. n.d. 'War Canoes of New Georgia', Unpublished Manuscript.

———. 2014. 'War Canoes of the Western Solomons', in B. Burt and L. Bolton (eds), *The Things We Value: Culture and History in Solomon Islands*. Wantage, UK: Sean Kingston Publishing, 103–15.

Hyndman, David. 1984. *Ethnobotany of Wopkaimin Pandanus: Significant Papua New Guinea Plant Resource*. New York Botanical Garden.

Ingold, Tim. 2000a. *The Perception of the Environment: Essays on Livelihood, Dwelling and Skill*. London: Routledge.

———. 2000b. 'On Weaving a Basket', in T. Ingold (ed.), *The Perception of the Environment: Essays in Livelihood, Dwelling and Skill*. London: Routledge, 339–48.

———. 2007. 'Materials against Materiality', *Archaeological Dialogues* 14(1): 1–16.

———. 2011. *Being Alive: Essays on Movement, Knowledge and Description*. Oxford: Routledge.

———. 2012. 'Towards an Ecology of Materials', *Annual Review of Anthropology* 41: 427–42.

Isaac, Gwyneira. 2015. 'Perclusive Alliances: Digital 3-D, Museums, and the Reconciling of Culturally Diverse Knowledges', *Current Anthropology* 56(S12): S286–S296.

Jacka, Jerry K. 2016. 'Development Conflicts and Changing Mortuary Practices in a New Guinea Mining Area', *The Journal of the Polynesian Society* 125(2): 133–47.

Jebb, Matthew. 1991. *A Field Guide to Pandanus in New Guinea, the Bismarck Archipelago and the Solomon Islands.* Madang, Papua New Guinea: Christensen Research Institute.

Jenkins, Henry. 2006. *Fans, Bloggers, and Gamers: Exploring Participatory Culture.* New York: New York University Press.

Jolly, Margaret. 1992. 'Custom and the Way of the Land: Past and Present in Vanuatu and Fiji', *Oceania* 62(4): 330–54.

Jones, J. 2003. *Harakeke Flax*, Alpha 127. Wellington: The Royal Society of New Zealand.

Kabariu, Luke. 2013. 'Lihir biok or pii masks', *Lihir i Lamel* (July-Aug Issue 7).

Kaeppler, Adrienne. 1999. '*Kie Hingoa*: Mats of Power, Rank, Prestige and History', *Journal of the Polynesian Society* 108(2): 168–232.

Karp, Ivan, Corinne A. Kratz, Lynn Szwaja and Tomas Ybarra-Frausto (eds). 2006. *Museum Frictions: Public Cultures/Global Transformations.* Durham, NC: Duke University Press.

Keane, Webb. 1997. *Signs of Recognition: Powers and Hazards of Representation in an Indonesian Society.* Berkeley, CA: University of California Press.

———. 2005. 'The Hazards of New Clothes: What Signs Make Possible', in S. Kuechler and G. Were (eds), *The Art of Clothing: A Pacific Experience.* London: UCL Press, 1–16.

Keesing, Roger M. 1982. '*Kastom* and Anti-colonialism on Malaita: "Culture" as Political Symbol', *Mankind* 13: 357–73.

———. 1993. '"Kastom" Re-examined', *Anthropological Forum* 6(4): 587–96.

Kingston, Sean. 2007. 'Dangerous Heritage: Southern New Ireland, the Museum and the Display of the Past', in N. Stanley (ed.), *The Future of Indigenous Museums: Perspectives from the Southwest Pacific.* Oxford: Berghahn, 47–69.

Knappett, Carl. 2004. 'The Affordances of Things: A Post-Gibsonian Perspective on the Relationality of Mind and Matter', in E. DeMarrais, C. Gosden and C. Renfrew (eds), *Rethinking Materiality: The Engagement of Mind with the Material World.* Cambridge: McDonald Institute Monographs, 43–51.

———. 2005. *Thinking through Material Culture: An Interdisciplinary Perspective.* Philadelphia, PA: University of Pennsylvania Press.

———. 2007. 'Materials *with* Materiality?' *Archaeological Discourses* 14(1): 2–23.

Knappett, Carl and Lambros Malafouris. 2008. 'Material and Nonhuman Agency: An Introduction', in C. Knappett and L. Malafouris (eds), *Material Agency: Towards a Non-Anthropocentric Approach.* New York: Springer Books, ix–xix.

Kooijman, Simon. 1972. *Tapa in Polynesia.* Honolulu, Hawaii: Bishop Museum Press.

Kopytoff, Igor. 1986. 'Cultural Biography of Things: Commoditization as Process', in A. Appadurai (ed.), *The Social Life of Things: Commodities in Cultural Perspective.* Cambridge: Cambridge University Press, 64–94.

Kotler, Philip and Francoise Simon. 2003. *Building Global Biobrands: Taking Biotechnology to Market*. New York: Free Press.

Kreps, Christina. 2008. 'Appropriate Museology in Theory and Practice', *Museum Management and Curatorship* 23(1): 23–41.

Kuechler, Susanne. 1987. '*Malangan*: Art and Memory in a Melanesian Society', *Man* 22: 238–55.

———. 1997. 'Sacrificial Economy and its Objects: Rethinking Colonial Collecting in Oceania', *Journal of Material Culture* 2(1): 39–60.

———. 1999. 'Binding in the Pacific: Between Loops and Knots', *Oceania* 69(3): 145–56.

———. 2002. *Malanggan: Art, Memory and Sacrifice*. Oxford: Berg.

———. 2005. 'Why are there Quilts in Polynesia?', in S. Kuechler and D. Miller (eds), *Clothing as Material Culture*. Oxford: Berg, 175–91.

Kuechler, Susanne and Graeme Were. 2005. *Pacific Pattern*. London: Thames and Hudson.

Kwa'ioloa, Michael, and Ben Burt. 2001. *Na Masu'u Kia 'i Kwara'ae: Our Forest of Kwara'ae*. London: British Museum Press.

Labrum, Bronwyn. 2010. 'Material Histories in Australia and New Zealand: Interweaving Distinct Material and Social Domains', *History Compass* 8(8): 805–16.

Lai, Jessica C. 2014. *Indigenous Cultural Heritage and Intellectual Property Rights: Learning from the New Zealand Experience?* London: Springer International Publishing.

Latour, Bruno. 1993. *We Have Never Been Modern*, trans. C. Porter. Cambridge, MA: Harvard University Press.

———. 1996. *Aramis, or the Love of Technology*. Cambridge, MA: Harvard University Press.

Latour, Bruno and Steve Woolgar. 1979. *Laboratory Life: The Construction of Social Facts*. London: Sage.

Lave, Jean. 2011. *Apprenticeship in Critical Ethnographic Practice*. Chicago, IL: University of Chicago Press.

Lawrence, David Russell. 2014. *The Naturalist and His 'Beautiful Islands': Charles Morris Woodford in the Western Pacific*. Canberra: ANU Press.

Lemonnier, Pierre. 2012. *Mundane Objects: Materiality and Non-Verbal Communication*. Walnut Creek, CA: Left Coast Press.

Levi-Strauss, Claude. 1966. *The Savage Mind*. Chicago, IL: University of Chicago Press.

Lewis, Phillip H. 1969. *The Social Context of Art in Northern New Ireland*. Fieldiana: Anthropology, Vol. 58, Publication 1069. Chicago: Field Museum of Natural History.

———. 1979. 'Art in Changing New Ireland', in S.M. Mead (ed.), *Exploring the Visual Art of Oceania*. Honolulu: University of Hawai'i Press, 378–89.

Lindstrom, Lamont. 1993a. *Cargo Cult: Strange Stories of Desire from Melanesia and Beyond*. Honolulu: University of Hawai'i Press.

———. 1993b. 'Cargo Cult Culture: Toward a Genealogy of Melanesian "*Kastom*"', *Anthropological Forum* 6(4): 495–513.

Lindstrom, Lamont and Geoffrey M. White (eds). 1990. *Island Encounters: Black and White Memories of the Pacific War*. Washington, DC: Smithsonian Institution Press.

Lipset, David. 2005. 'Dead Canoes: The Fate of Agency in Twentieth-Century Murik Art', *Social Analysis* 49(1): 109–40.

———. 2013. 'Mobail: Moral Ambivalence and the Domestication of Mobile Telephones in Peri-urban Papua New Guinea', *Culture, Theory and Critique* 54(3): 335–54.

———. 2017. *Yabar: The Alienations of Murik Men in a Papua New Guinea Modernity*. New York: Springer.

Lipset, David and Paul Roscoe (eds). 2011. *Echoes of the Tambaran: Masculinity, History and the Subject in the Work of Donald F. Tuzin*. Canberra: ANU Press.

Lipset, David and Eric Kline Silverman (eds). 2016. *Mortuary Dialogues: Death Ritual and the Reproduction of Moral Community in Pacific Modernities*. Oxford: Berghahn.

Mackenzie, Maureen. 1991. *Androgynous Objects: String Bags and Gender in Central New Guinea*. Chur, Switzerland: Harwood Academic Publishers.

Mann, Rev Ira. J. 1919–1941. *Diaries and papers* PMB 630. Pacific Manuscripts Bureau, Australia National University, Canberra.

Marchand, Trevor H.J. (ed.). 2010. *Making Knowledge: Explorations of the Indissoluble Relation between Mind, Body and Environment*. Oxford: Wiley-Blackwell.

Martin, Keir. 2013. *The Death of the Big Men and the Rise of the Big Shots: Custom and Conflict in East New Britain*. Oxford: Berghahn.

Matisoo-Smith, Elizabeth et al. 2009. 'On the Rat Trail in Near Oceania: Applying the Commensal Model to the Question of the Lapita Colonization', *Pacific Science* 63(4): 465–75.

McCullough, Malcolm. 1996. *Abstracting Craft: The Practiced Digital Hand*. Cambridge, MA: MIT Press.

McTavish, Lianne. 2005. 'Visiting the Virtual Museum: Art and Experience Online', in J. Marstine (ed.), *New Museum Theory and Practice: An Introduction*. Oxford: Blackwell, 203–225.

Medway, Dominic and Gary Warnaby. 2014. 'What's in a Name? Place Branding and Toponymic Commodification', *Environment and Planning A* 46(1): 153–67.

Meikle, Jeffrey L. 1997. *American Plastic: A Cultural History*. New Brunswick, NJ: Rutgers University Press.

Miller, Daniel. 1987. *Material Culture and Mass Consumption*. Oxford: Basil Blackwell.

Miller, Daniel. (ed.). 2005. *Materiality*. Durham, NC: Duke University Press.

Miller, Daniel and Don Slater. 2000. *The Internet: An Ethnographic Approach*. Oxford: Berg.

Miodownik, Mark. 2015. 'Toward Designing new Sensoaesthetic Materials: The Role of Materials Libraries', in A. Drazin and S. Kuechler (eds), *The Social Life of Materials: Studies in Materials and Society*. London: Bloomsbury, 69–80.

Mirzoeff, Nicholas. 2011. *The Right to Look: A Counterhistory of Visuality*. Durham, NC: Duke University Press.

Morgan, Nigel, Annette Pritchard and Rachel Piggott. 2002. 'New Zealand, 100% Pure: The Creation of a Powerful Niche Destination Brand', *Journal of Brand Management* 9(4/5): 335–54.

Morphy, Howard. 2007. *Becoming Art: Exploring Cross-cultural Categories*. Oxford: Berg.

Mosko, Mark. 2009. 'The Fractal Yam: Botanical Imagery and Human Agency in the Trobriands', *Journal of the Royal Anthropological Institute* 15(4): 679–700.

Mueggler, Erik. 2011. *The Paper Road: Archive and Experience in the Botanical Exploration of West China and Tibet*. Berkeley, CA: University of California Press.

Munn, Nancy D. 1977. 'The Spatiotemporal Transformations of Gawa Canoes', *Journal de la Société des Océanistes* 54–55(33): 39–53.

———. 1992. *The Fame of Gawa: A Symbolic Study of Value Transformation in a Massim (Papua New Guinea) Society*. Durham, NC: Duke University Press.

Murray, John. 1838. *An Account of the Phormium Tenax, or, New Zealand Flax: Printed on Paper Made from its Leaves (Bleached) with a Postscript on Paper*. London: Relfe and Fletcher.

Nombo, Porer, and James Leach. 2010. *Reite Plants: An Ethnobotanical Study in Tok Pisin and English*. Canberra: ANU EPress.

Norman, Donald A. 1988. *The Psychology of Everyday Things*. New York: Basic Books.

Norris, Lucy. 2005. 'Cloth that Lies: The Secrets of Recycling in India', in S. Kuechler and D. Miller (eds), *Clothing as Material Culture*. Oxford: Berg, 83–105.

———. 2010. *Recycling Indian Clothing: Global Contexts of Reuse and Value*. Bloomington, IN: Indiana University Press.

O'Connor, Kaori. 2011. *Lycra: How a Fiber Shaped America*. London: Routledge.

O'Rourke Tim, Nick Flutter and Paul Memmott. 2010. 'Prototyping Spinifex Grass as Thermal Insulation in Arid Regions of Australia', in C. Murphy, S. Wake, D. Turner (eds), *On the Edge: 44th Annual Conference of the Australian and New Zealand Architectural Science Association ANZASCA, Auckland*. Auckland: Architectural Science Association.

Otto, Ton. 1992. 'The Ways of *kastam*: Tradition as Category and Practice in a Manus Village', *Oceania* 62(4): 263–83.

Parkinson, Richard. 2010 [1907]. *Thirty Years in the South Seas: Land and People, Customs and Traditions in the Bismarck Archipelago and on the German Solomon Islands*. Sydney: Sydney University Press.

Parry, Ross. 2007. *Recoding the Museum: Digital Heritage and the Technologies of Change*. London: Routledge.

Peekel, P.G. 1984. *Flora of the Bismarck Archipelago for Naturalists*, trans. E.E. Henty. Lae, Papua New Guinea: Office of Forests, Division of Botany, Papua New Guinea.

Peers, Laura and Alison K. Brown. 2003. *Museums and Source Communities: A Routledge Reader*. London: Routledge.

Pellizzi, Francesco. 1995. 'Editorial: Remains', *RES: Anthropology and Aesthetics* 27: 5–10.

Phillips, Ruth B. 2013. 'The Digital (R)evolution of Museum-Based Research', in R.B. Phillips (ed.), *Museum Pieces: Toward the Indigenization of Canadian Museums*. London: McGill-Queen's University Press, 277–96.

Pye, David. 1968. *The Nature and Art of Workmanship*. Cambridge: Cambridge University Press.

Rancière, Jacques. 2008. *The Future of the Image*. London: Verso.

Ray, S.H. 1892. 'Note on the People and Languages of New Ireland and Admiralty Islands', *The Journal of the Anthropological Institute of Great Britain and Ireland* 21: 3–13.

Rickard, Paul P. and Paul A. Cox. 1984. 'Custom Umbrellas (poro) from Pandanus in Solomon Islands', *Economic Botany* 38(3): 314–21.

Robbins, Joel. 2004. *Becoming Sinners: Christianity and Moral Torment in a Papua New Guinea Society*. Berkeley, CA: University of California Press.

Rowlands, Michael. 2002. 'Heritage and Cultural Property', in V. Buchli (ed.), *The Material Culture Reader*. Oxford: Berg, 105–14.

Rowley, Susan. 2013. 'The Reciprocal Research Network: The Development Process', *Museum Anthropology Review* 7 (1–2): 22–43.

Russell, T. 1948. 'The Culture of Marovo, British Solomon Islands', *The Journal of the Polynesian Society* 57(4): 306–29.

Schiebinger, Londa L. 2004. *Plants and Empire: Colonial Bioprospecting in the Atlantic World*. Cambridge, MA: Harvard University Press.

Schmid, Christin Kocher 1991. *Of People and Plants: A Botanical Ethnography of Nokopo Village, Madang and Morobe Provinces, Papua New Guinea*. Basel: Ethnologisches Seminar der Universität und Museum fur Völkerkunde.

Scion Annual Report 2011. Last accessed 17 March 2014 from: http://www.scionresearch.com/__data/assets/pdf_file/0003/35526/Scion-Annual-Report-2011-web.pdf.

Scion Annual Report 2013. Highlights. Last accessed 17 March 2014 from: http://www.scionresearch.com/__data/assets/pdf_file/0017/42443/ScionAnnualReport2013-Highlights.pdf.

Shaw, M.B., Bicking, G.W. and M.J. O'Leary. 1931. 'The Paper-Making Properties of Phormium Tenax (New Zealand flax)', *Bureau of Standards Journal of Research* 6(3). Research Paper 285 (RP285), 411–20.

Sheller, Mimi. 2014. *Aluminum Dreams: The Making of Light Modernity*. Cambridge, MA: The MIT Press.

Shove, Elizabeth, Matthew Watson, Martin Hand and Jack Ingram. 2007. *The Design of Everyday Life*. Oxford: Berg.

Sillitoe, Paul. 1983. *Roots of the Earth: Crops in the Highlands of Papua New Guinea*. Manchester: University of Manchester Press.

Silverman, Raymond A. (ed.). 2015. *Museum as Process: Translating Local and Global Knowledges*. London: Routledge.

Simpson, Moira G. 2005. 'Museums, World Heritage, and Interpretation: The Case of the Parthenon Marbles', in E. Close, M. Tsianikas and G. Frazis (eds), *Greek Research in Australia: Proceedings of the Biennial International*

Conference of Greek Studies, Flinders University April 2003. Adelaide: Flinders University Department of Languages – Modern Greek, 241–62.

Smith, Peter. 2008. *An Introduction to the Baha'i Faith*. Cambridge: University of Cambridge Press.

Somerville, Boyle T. 1897. 'Ethnographical Notes in New Georgia, Solomon Islands', *Journal of the Royal Anthropological Institute* 26: 357–412.

Srinivasan, Ramesh. 2012. 'Rethinking Digital Cultures and Divides: The Case for Reflective Media', *The Information Society* 28: 24–36.

Steinbach, Leonard. 2011. '3D or Not 3D? Is that a Question?', *Curator: The Museum Journal* 54(1): 41–54.

Strathern, Marilyn. 1979. 'The Self in Self-decoration', *Oceania* 49(4): 241–57.

———. 1988. *The Gender of the Gift: Problems with Women and Problems with Society in Melanesia*. Berkeley, CA: University of California Press.

———. 1990. 'Artefacts of History: Events and the Interpretation of Images', in J. Siikala (ed.), *Culture and History in the Pacific*. Helsinki: Transactions of the Finnish Anthropological Society, 25–44.

———. 1991. *Partial Connections*. Savage, MD: Rowman and Littlefield.

Strathern, Marilyn and Maurice Godelier (eds). 1991. *Big Men and Great Men: Personifications of Power in Melanesia*. Cambridge: Cambridge University Press.

Sully, Dean. (ed.). 2007. *Decolonising Conservation: Caring for Maori Meeting Houses Outside New Zealand*. Walnut Creek, CA: Left Coast Press.

Tallon, Loic and Kevin Walker (eds). 2008. *Digital Technologies and the Museum Experience: Handheld Guides and Other Media*. Lanham, MD: Altamira Press.

'The Utilisation of New Zealand Hemp Waste', *Bulletin of the Imperial Institute* 1919: XVII, 485–88.

Thomas, E.L.G. 1933. 'Northern Solomons: Pandanus Hood', *Man* 33: 40.

Thomas, Nicholas. 1991. *Entangled Objects: Exchange, Material Culture, and Colonialism in the Pacific*. Cambridge, MA: Harvard University Press.

———. 1995. *Oceanic Art*. London: Thames and Hudson.

———. 1999. 'The Case of the Misplaced Poncho: Speculations Concerning the History of Cloth in Polynesia', *Journal of Material Culture* 4(1): 5–20.

Tilley, Christopher. 2004. *The Materiality of Stone*. Oxford: Berg.

———. 2007. 'Materiality in Materials', *Archaeological Discourses* 14(1): 16–20.

Tolia-Kelly, Divya P. 2013. 'The Geographies of Cultural Geography III: Material Geographies, Vibrant Matters and Risking Surface Geographies', *Progress in Human Geography* 37(1): 153–60.

Tsing, Anna. 2005. *Friction: An Ethnography of Global Connection*. Princeton, NJ: Princeton University Press.

Tuzin, Donald F. 1997. *The Cassowary's Revenge: The Life and Death of Masculinity in a New Guinea Society*. Chicago: University of Chicago Press.

Van Dijck, Jose. 2007. *Mediated Memories in the Digital Age*. Stanford, CA: Stanford University Press.

Van Doorn, Niels. 2011. 'Digital Spaces, Material Traces: How Matter Comes to Matter in Online Performances of Gender, Sexuality and Embodiment', *Media, Culture and Society* 33(4): 531–47.

Verran, Helen and Michael Christie. 2007. 'Using/Designing Digital Technologies of Representation in Aboriginal Australian Knowledge Practices', *Human Technology* 3(2): 214–27.

Verran, Helen, Michael Christie, Bryce Anbins-King, Trevor Van Weeren and Wulumdhuna Yunupingu. 2007. 'Designing Digital Knowledge Management Tools with Aboriginal Australians', *Digital Creativity* 18(3): 129–42.

Wagner, Roy. 1991. 'The Fractal Person', in M. Godelier and M. Strathern (eds), *Big Men and Great Men: Personifications of Power in Melanesia*. Cambridge: Cambridge University Press, 159–73.

Waite, Deborah. 2000. 'An Artefact/image Text of Head-hunting Motifs', *The Journal of the Polynesian Society* 109(1): 115–44.

Weiner, A.B. 1989. 'Why Cloth?', in A.B. Weiner and J. Schneider (eds), *Cloth and Human Experience*. Washington DC: Smithsonian Institution Press, 33–72.

Welz, Gisela. 2003. 'The Cultural Swirl: Anthropological Perspectives on Innovation', *Global Networks* 3(3): 255–70.

Wendrich, Willemina. 1999. *The World According to Basketry*. Los Angeles: The Cotsen Institute of Archaeology Press.

Wengrow, David. 1998. 'The Changing Face of Clay: Continuity and Change in the Transition from Village to Urban Life in the Near East', *Antiquity* 72(278): 783–95.

Were, Graeme. 2005a. 'Pattern, Efficacy and Enterprise: On Fabricating Connections in Melanesia', in S. Kuechler and D. Miller (eds), *Clothing as Material Culture*. Oxford: Berg, 159–74.

———. 2005b. 'Thinking through Images: *Kastom* and the Coming of the Baha'is to Northern New Ireland, Papua New Guinea', *Journal of the Royal Anthropological Institute* 11(4): 659–76.

———. 2006. '*Kapkap*: The Art of Connecting in Island Melanesia', *Journal of Pacific Art* NS1: 27–35.

———. 2007. 'Fashioning Belief: The Case of the Baha'i Faith in Northern New Ireland', *Anthropological Forum* 17(3): 239–53.

———. 2008. 'Out of Touch? Digital Technologies, Ethnographic Objects and Sensory Orders', in H. Chatterjee (ed.), *Touch in Museums*. Oxford: Berg, 121–34.

———. 2010. *Lines that Connect: Rethinking Pattern and Mind in the Pacific*. Honolulu: University of Hawai'i Press.

———. 2013. 'On the Materials of Mats: Thinking through Design in a Melanesian Society', *Journal of the Royal Anthropological Institute* 19(3): 581–99.

West, Paige. 2014. '"Such a Site for Play, this Edge": Surfing, Tourism, and Modernist Fantasy in Papua New Guinea', *The Contemporary Pacific* 26(2): 411–32.

———. 2017. *Dispossession and the Environment: Rhetoric and Inequality in Papua New Guinea*. New York: Columbia University Press.

White, Geoffrey. M. 1993. 'Three Discourses of Custom', *Anthropological forum* 6(4): 475–94.

Woodford, Charles.M. 1909. 'The Canoes of the British Solomon Islands', *Journal of the Royal Anthropological Institute* 39: 506–16.

Worboys, Michael. 1990. 'The Imperial Institute: The State and the Development of the Natural Resources of the Colonial Empire, 1887–1923', in J.M. MacKenzie (ed.), *Imperialism and the Natural World*. Manchester: University of Manchester Press, 164–86.

Wright, Christopher. 2008. '"A Devil's Engine": Photography and Spirits in the Western Solomon Islands', *Visual Anthropology* 21(4): 364–80.

———. 2013. *The Echo of Things: The Lives of Photographs in the Solomon Islands*. Durham, NC: Duke University Press.

Young, Michael. 1997. 'Commemorating Missionaries Heroes: Local Christianity and Narratives of Nationalism in the South Pacific', in T. Otto and N. Thomas (eds), *Narratives of Nation in the South Pacific*. Amsterdam: Harwood Academic Publishers, 91–132.

Index

A

Aboriginal communities, Australian, 73, 148–49, 163
abulume, 33
additive technology
  of canoe, 16, 94–95, 98, 101, 107, 169
  scaling and, 16, 94–95, 98, 101, 182
affordances, 14
  mapping and, 29, 45–46
  materials innovation and, 29, 175
  Norman on, 29–30, 39, 46
  pandanus and, 45, 175, 181
  of plastic, 29
  theory of, 15, 28
African design, 90–92
agency, individualized, 43–44, 64–65, 178–79
agency, material, 18, 178
  Bennett and, 10, 70
  Gell on, 7–8
  holistic understanding of, 10–11
  Ingold on, 8–9
  materials innovation and, 72
  material turn and, 52
aitek (malangan carvers), 144–47, 155–56
Alpers, Svetlana, 172
amazaraas, 32
amotmot. *See* pandanus
araazira mat, 24–25, 55
  amotmot and, 38–40
  production of, 35–36
  as protective covering, 36–38, 40
archival practices, 73–74
arekrek (pandanus hat). *See* pandanus
Armbruster, Stefan, 159n6
Art and Agency (Gell), 7–8, 91
Arts and Crafts Movement, 5
aruaai basket, 57–59, 61, 63
  kastom and, 64
  mulai used for, 66
  sale of, 64–65
Ashby, Mike F., 53, 60, 177
assemblages, 181
  artefacts as, 133
  Bennett on, 50–51, 77, 179
  networked, 4
Australia
  Aboriginal communities in, 73, 148–49, 163
  Justice and Police Museum in, 143
  Queensland Museum in, 56, 150–51, 158, 186
  spinifex in, 73
awoiwoi. *See* pandanus

B

Baha'i, 134n2
  crafting practices and, 47n2, 93
  kastom and, 56–57, 116–18
  among Naliks, establishment of, 116–17
Ball, Philip, 10, 12, 73, 111, 176
  on computational, materials as, 86n2, 89

on made to measure materials, 6–7, 13
bamboo, 12–13
barkcloth (kapiak), 43. *See also* aruaai basket; baskets; cloth
colonialism and, 51–52
constraints and, 60
gender and, 15, 178–79
material identity of, 54–55, 61, 64–65
materiality of, 51, 54
mulai and, 66, 179
peles and, 61
production of, 61–63
revival of, 44–45, 52, 59, 64–65, 178–79
Barry, Andrew, 29, 176
baskets
Ingold on, 8, 26–27, 59–60
in Kavieng, 64–65
material identity of, 50, 60
Bell, F. Dillon, 68
Belting, Hans, 142
Bennett, Jane
on assemblages, 50–51, 77, 179
on latent individualism, 54
material agency and, 10, 70
on networked materials, 15
on vibrancy, 70, 77
Bensaude-Vincent, Bernadette, 7, 10, 176
Bicking, G.W., 76
bicycles, 12–13
big men societies, 108
Bijker, Wiebe E., 10
bikmaus, 121
bilum, 57
birua, 38
body painting, 132
Boivin, Nicole, 11
Bolton, Lissant, 93
Boluminski Highway, New Ireland, 21–22, 24, 31–32, 152
bonito, 103, 109n2
Borofsky, Robert, 163, 171
bowl, Eastern Solomon Islands, 101–3, 107–8
breadfruit tree (kapiak), 59–61
Bre-X gold scandal, 115, 134n1
bricoleur, 47n12, 182
British Museum, 186
pandanus artefacts in, 47n8, 47n11
Solomon Islands collection of, 93–94, 96–97, 103–5, 165–68, 171
Brockway, Lucile H., 69
Brooking, Tom, 78
Brown, Deidre, 142–43
Brown, George, 22
Burnett, Frank, 105–6, 108
bus (forest), 21–22
bus pipol (bush people), 22

C
Campbell, Shirley F., 110n4
Canada, First Nations of, 173n1
canoe, Melanesian
additive technology of, 16, 94–95, 98, 101, 107, 169
bonito and, 103, 109n2
in British Museum, 96, 165–68, 171
computational properties of, 99
construction of, 97–100, 164
dead, of Murik people, 131
dugout, subtractive technology of, 98
Europeans on, 97
food trough and, 105–6
Gawa, 98
houses for, 105–6
kula, 110n4
mana and, 100–101, 106
motifs of, 100, 110n4
scaling and, 16, 94–95, 101, 107, 109, 182
as symbol, 161
3D digital model of, 150, 161–73
tradition of, 163–64
types of, 96
Carr, D., 76, 78
Catholic missionaries, 22, 51, 116, 118
CD-ROM, 150, 152–53
cemetery enclosures, 119, 133
bikmaus, 121

kastom and, 120–21, 123
liana in, 122
maimai and, 120, 123
mortuary feasts and, 120, 122–23, 125
chiefly man. *See* maimai
Christie, Michael, 147–49, 162
clan cemeteries (rabaarau), 22, 127
clans (watbung), 31
clan totems (masalei), 23, 125
cloth, 50, 132
colonialism and, 54, 180
gender and, 12
as introduced material, 11–12, 53–54, 180
kastom and, 56
missionaries and, 17, 51, 53–54, 56, 180
in New Ireland, history of, 51–52, 55–56
co-constitutive, materials as, 65, 176
Colchester, Chloe, 12, 54
colonialism
barkcloth and, 51–52
cloth and, 54, 180
German, 22, 31–32, 47n9, 67n2, 125
computation, material, 182
Ball on, 86n2, 89
of canoe, 16, 99, 109
ethnographic collections and, 93–95
Gell and, 91–92
scaling and, 90–92, 95, 108
congregational, agency as, 10, 70
Conkey, Margaret W., 8
Conn, Steven, 17, 141, 159
Cook, James (Captain Cook), 76
copra, 31–32, 64
co-productive, materials as, 3, 15, 29, 175–76
cosmetics, 82–84
Cox, Paul A., 47n8
Cruthers, N., 76, 78

D

Damon, Frederick H., 38–39, 99
Davenport, William H., 102–3, 107, 109n2
Deger, Jennifer, 184
DeLanda, Manuel, 69, 90
digital objects, 3D, 17–18, 149
Maori and, 142
production process of, 166–69
of Solomon Islands canoe, 150, 161–73
digital return, 140
Naliks and, 17, 156–58
in Solomon Islands, 17–18, 160–65, 169–73
digital technologies, 139
archivist and, 163
divisions, inequalities and, 162, 183–84
ethnographic collections and, 140–41, 158–59, 172–73
imaging, 17–18, 140–44, 146, 182
knowledge networks created by, 160
material histories and, 141, 143, 183–84
materiality of, 142–44, 158–59
mediation by, 141
museology and, 141, 148, 159
Nalik participation in, 148–50, 161, 184
Nalik revitalization and, 152
participatory, 148–50, 162
as recoding, 140–41, 159
stakeholders and, 141–42
traditional craft and, 168
Do Museums Still Need Objects? (Conn), 141
Duffield, A.J., 36–37
dugout canoe, 94, 96, 98
Dupont, 71

E

economic botany, 73, 134, 185–86
Edge-Partington, J., 104–5
effigies (malangan). *See* malangan
Eglash, Ron, 90–92
empathy
materials innovation and, 4

plant materials and, 4, 89–90, 92, 177, 181–82, 186
selecting materials with, 89, 177, 182
in workmanship, 92
enabling, materials as, 3, 178–79
ethnobotany, 18n1, 32, 59–61
ethnographic collections, 17, 96–97. *See also* British Museum
in Canada, First Nations and, 173n1
digital technologies and, 140–41, 158–59, 172–73
knowledge networks sustained by, 160–61
materials computation and, 93–95
participatory museology and, 141, 159
rethinking, digital technologies and, 158
source communities and, 140, 171
ethnomathematics, 90
expressivity, 69–70, 75, 85

F
faamatkibal, 31
Favero, Paolo, 143
flax. *See* harakeke
food trough, Melanesian
in British Museum, 94, 103–5
canoe and, 105–6
in feasting ritual, 105–6
scaling and, 94–95, 101, 104, 106–7, 109
subtractive technology of, 16, 94–95, 101
forces, field of, 59–60
forest (bus), 21–22
form, forces and, 59–60
Formica, 49, 66
fractal
in African design, 90–92
island Melanesian personhood as, 108–9
Melanesian canoe and trough instantiating, 109
Freedberg, David, 142
funerary rites, Nalik, 30–31, 33, 119
future fibres, 73
Fuyuge, 114

G
garden enclosures, Nalik, 123–26
Gawa, 98
Gell, Alfred
Art and Agency by, 7–8
on cognitive complexities, artefacts and, 71–72
on coherence, 85
on Marquesan art, 7–8, 91–92
on scaling, 91
on Zande hunting net, 175
gender, 6
barkcloth and, 15, 178–79
cloth and, 12
men's house and, 16
pandanus hat and, 47n14
of plants, 33, 47n13
Germany
Linden Museum in, 47n8
Naliks and colonialism of, 22, 31–32, 47n9, 67n2, 125
ges (malevolent spirits), 21
Gibson, James J., 15, 28–29
Gibson, Ross, 143
Godelier, Maurice, 108
gogo (pandanus hat). *See* pandanus
green
harakeke as, 79–84, 177
New Zealand as, 85, 180
Groves, W.C., 124
Guadalcanal, Solomon Islands, 47n8, 116
Gunn, Michael, 55

H
Haddon, Alfred C., 95, 100, 109n2
Hagen society, 112–13, 129
Hancock, Rodney, 117
handloom weaving, 24, 47n10
harakeke (New Zealand flax), 180–81
Bell and Young on, 68
changing use of, 74
in cosmetics, 82–84

expressivity of, 69, 75, 85
extracting, technology of, 68, 76–77, 86n1
as green material, 79–84, 177
history of, 68–69, 76–78, 85, 86n1
Maori and, 75–76, 82–85
material identity of, 77, 79
materials innovation and, 68–70, 72, 74–75, 85
networked materials and, 15–16
scaling and, 81
as surfboard material, 81
Harrison, Simon, 118
Hau'ofa, Epeli, 5
Hawkins, Gay, 70, 176, 183
Hector, J., 76–77, 86n1
heritagization, 13, 112, 131
Hess, Mona, 165
Highland Maya, Mexican, 170
Highlands, Papua New Guinea, 3, 47n11, 133
big men societies of, 108
bilum of, 57
body painting in, 132
Wola of, 47n13
Hirsch, Eric, 114
histories, material, 141, 143, 183–84
Holbraad, Martin, 113
Hornell, James, 94–95, 100, 109n2
Hviding, Edvard
on canoe, 95, 97, 99, 105, 161, 164
on tangovo, 99
3D digital imaging team and, 165

I

identity, material, 12–14
of barkcloth, 54–55, 61, 64–65
of baskets, 50, 60
environment of, 66–67
in flux, 52, 65–67
of harakeke, 77, 79
multidimensional, 53
of plastic, 53, 65, 79
imageness, digital, 143–44
Imperial Institute (London, United Kingdom), 68–69, 73
individualism, latent, 54
Ingold, Tim, 9–10, 75, 85
on basket-making, 8, 26–27, 59–60
ecological approach of, 46
on forces, field of, 8, 59–60
on material identities, 52
phenomenological approach of, 176–77
in-law (tambu), 128, 130, 135n5
innovation, material, 1, 5, 11–12, 111, 134
affordances and, 29, 175
as cognitive, 71–72
empathy in, 4
expressivity and, 69–70, 75
factors driving, 70, 72–74
harakeke and, 68–70, 72, 74–75, 85
made to measure materials and, 6–7, 13, 89
material agency and, 72
performance and, 112–13
of plastic, 70–71, 74
social context of, 174
as value-adding, 10
Western technoscience and, 4
its work (wok bilong em), 35

J

Jebb, Matthew, 32
Johnson, Kara, 53, 60, 177
Jones, J., 76, 78
Justice and Police Museum (Sydney, Australia), 143

K

Kabariu, Luke, 60
Kaeppler, Adrienne, 42
Kaminiel, Adam, 144, 147, 149–52
kapiak (barkcloth). *See* barkcloth
kapiak (breadfruit tree), 59–61
Kara people, 120, 145
Kastanis, Lazaros, 144
kastom, 24–25, 179
aruaai basket and, 64
Baha'i and, 56–57, 116–18
cemeteries and, 120–21, 123
cloth and, 56
men's house and, 127–30

missionaries and, 116, 134
origins of, 116–17
performance and, 66, 118
plant materials and, 118–19, 130, 134
religious competition over, 118
scaling and, 114–15
short-cut, 126
Kavavu, Demas, 146
Kavieng, Papua New Guinea, 30, 115, 126, 144
baskets in, 64–65
District Council of, 157
museum proposal for, 147
as port, 21, 43
Kingston, Sean, 148
Knappett, Carl, 8, 28, 46
Kombeng, Martin, 144, 147, 150–52, 157
Kossep, Tamun, 128–32
Kreps, Christina, 148
Kuechler, Susanne
on cemetery enclosures, 121–22
on clothing, adoption of, 56
on death, ritual and, 119
on introduced materials, 53
on Kara people, 120, 145
on malangan, 38, 145, 147
kula canoe, 110n4
kula shells, 133
Kuot-speaking people, 22

L

Laing, R., 76, 78
laminates, 49–50
Lemonnier, Pierre, 50, 119
Levi-Strauss, Claude, 23–24, 47n12, 182
Lewis, Phillip H., 124, 127
liana, 59, 122
lifeworld, 3, 8, 176, 178
Lihir, Papua New Guinea, 60, 130
Linden Museum, Germany, 47n8
Lipset, David, 131
Living Nature, 82–83
Lycra, 11, 53, 71, 74

M

Made to Measure (Ball), 6–7
made to measure materials, 11, 186
Ball and, 6–7, 12–13
materials innovation and, 6–7, 13, 89
magic, 32, 124
maimai (chiefly man), 38, 147
cemetery enclosures and, 120, 123
men's house and, 127–28
mortuary feasts and, 108
Nalik Mobile Museum project and, 144, 152, 157–58
Malafouris, Lambros, 8
malangan (effigies), 31, 37, 47n14, 55, 117
archiving, 147–57
carvers of, 144–47, 155–56
Kuechler on, 38, 145, 147
loss of, 154–57, 159n4
missionaries and, 116
mortuary feasts and, 57, 145
tradition of, recovering, 156–57
wawara, 33, 121
male power
materials and, 112, 115, 119, 123
objects, classification of, and, 158
performance and, 114, 132–33
malevolent spirits (ges), 21
mana, 100–101, 106–7
Maori
harakeke and, 75–76, 82–85
meeting houses of, 72
3D digital facsimiles and, 142
mapping, 177
affordances and, 29, 45–46
logical, 44
of Naliks, 30, 44–45
Marovo, New Georgia, 96, 99, 104
Marquesan art, 7–8, 91–92
masalei (clan totems), 23, 125
Massim, 38, 47n8
materials libraries, 4, 73–74, 111, 140, 184
material turn, in humanities, 52–55

McCullough, Malcolm, 168
Melanesia. *See specific topics*
men's house, Nalik, 16. *See also* gender
decline of, 126–27
kastom and, 127–30
maimai and, 127–28
Notsi, 127
plant materials in, 128–33, 179–80
Prime Minister Somare and, 128–31
meshworks, 9
Methodist missionaries, 22, 47n7, 51, 116–18
Mexico, 170
Mirzoeff, Nicholas, 141–42, 158
missionaries
Baha'i, 117
cloth and, 17, 51, 53–54, 56, 180
kastom and, 116, 134
malangan and, 116
Naliks and, 22, 31, 47n7, 51, 56, 114–18, 127
Tongan, 47n7
mon. *See* canoe, Melanesian
Morris, William, 5
mortuary feasts, Nalik, 22, 38, 124, 126. *See also* funerary rites, Nalik
cemetery enclosures and, 120, 122–23, 125
maimai and, 108
malangan and, 57, 145
pandanus and, 33, 37
Moxomaaf clan, 121
mulai, 66, 179
Munn, Nancy D., 98
Murik people, 131
Murray, John, 76
museology
appropriate, 148
participatory, 141, 159
Mussau, Papua New Guinea, 24–25, 47n9
Muyuw Island, 99

N

Nalik Mobile Museum project, 141, 143
awareness project for, 148–52
CD-ROMs of, 150, 152–53
implementation of, 152–56
maimai and, 144, 152, 157–58
return, recovery through, 156–58
Naliks. *See also* kastom; malangan; New Ireland; pandanus
araazira mats of, 24–25, 35–40, 55
aruaai basket of, 57–59, 61, 63–66
awoiwoi mats of, 40–45
Baha'i and, 47n2, 56–57, 93, 116–18
barkcloth of, 15, 43–45, 51–52, 54–55, 59–66, 178–79
breadfruit tree and, 59–61
cemeteries of, 22, 119–23, 125, 127, 133
coast and, 21–22, 125
Council of Chiefs for, 157
digital participation of, 148–50, 161, 184
digital return and, 17, 156–58
digital revitalization of, 152
faamatkibal of, 31
forest and, 21–24, 31–32, 47n3, 60, 125
funerary rites of, 30–31, 33, 119
garden enclosures of, 123–26
German colonialism and, 22, 31–32, 47n9, 67n2, 125
individualized agency among, 43–44, 64–65, 178–79
maimai of, 38, 108, 120, 123, 127–28, 144, 147, 152, 157–58
mapping of, 30, 44–45
masalei of, 23, 125
men's house of, 16, 126–33, 179–80
missionaries and, 22, 31, 47n7, 51, 56, 114–18, 127
mortuary feasts of, 22, 33, 37–38, 57, 108, 120, 122–26, 145
Moxomaaf clan of, 121
museum proposed for, 147–48
patriclans of, 25, 31, 38

performance and materials of, 113–15
plant knowledge of, 22–25, 32, 55, 133–34
plants understood by, 45–46
Prime Minister Somare and, 128–31
scaling and, 36, 114–15
society of, 30–32, 38–40
Near Eastern Neolithic society, 11
networked materials, 15–16
New Georgia, Solomon Islands
canoes of, 94–101, 103, 105–7, 109
food trough of, 94, 103–4, 107
mana in, 100–101, 106–7
New Hanover, Papua New Guinea, 47n14
New Ireland, Papua New Guinea
Boluminski Highway of, 21–22, 31–32, 152
cash-crop economy of, 64
cloth in, history of, 51–52, 55–56
Kavieng in, 21, 30, 43, 64–65, 115, 126, 144, 147, 157
mining royalties and, 130
mobile telecommunications in, 144–45, 150, 158
Notsi of, 124, 127, 155–56
surfing in, 21, 46n1
tatanua mask of, 56
Tigak area in, 47n8
New Zealand
commoditization in, of landscape, 79–80, 83–84, 180
flax industry in, 15, 75–78, 180
green branding of, 85, 180
100% Pure campaign for, 79, 82, 84
Pasifika t-shirt in, 54
Rotorua in, 80, 186
Scion in, 80–81
New Zealand flax. *See* harakeke
Norman, Donald A., 60, 63, 69
on affordances, 29–30, 39, 46
on design constraint, 72
on Gibson, J., 29
on mapping, 29–30, 44–45
Norway, 164–65, 169
Notsi, 124, 127, 155–56

O

observed decay, 175–76, 182
O'Connor, Kaori, 11, 53, 71
O'Leary, M.J., 76
100% Pure campaign, 79, 82, 84
operational realism, 40, 81, 85
Ortelia, 144

P

Pacific Alternatives project, 164
pandanus, 15
abulume, 33
affordances and, 45, 175, 181
amazaraas, 32
amotmot, 26, 33, 35–40, 45, 177
araazira mat of, 24–25, 35–40
avadin, 33
avaum, 35, 37
awoiwoi, 26, 40–45, 47n7
azafna, 33–34
differentiation of, 32–33
gender and, 47n14
hat of, 37, 47n14
mortuary feasts and, 33, 37
stitched, from Solomon Islands, 47n8, 47n11
wawara of, 33, 121
Papua New Guinea
Fuyuge in, 114
Gawa in, canoes of, 98
Highlands of, 3, 47n11, 47n13, 57, 108, 114, 132–33
Japanese occupation of, 23
Lihir in, 60, 130
Massim in, 38, 47n8
Port Moresby in, 43, 115, 119, 131
Prime Minister Somare of, 128–31
Parkinson, Richard, 47n14
Parry, Ross, 140
Pasifika t-shirt, 54
patriclan, Nalik, 25, 31, 38
pattern, personhood and, 44, 48n16
Peekel, Gerhard, 59, 61
peles (place), 56, 58, 61, 115
Pellizzi, Francesco, 170

performance, 176, 183
 kastom and, 118
 male power and, 114, 132–33
 materials innovation and, 112–13
 Naliks and, 113–15
 plant materials and, 113, 118–19, 133, 185–86
 product and, 133
personhood
 fractal, 108–9
 pattern and, 44, 48n16
 relational, 112–13
PET. *See* polyethylene terephthalate
phenomenological approaches, to materials, 26, 176–77
Phormium tenax. *See* harakeke
place (peles), 56, 58, 115
plank canoe (mon). *See* canoe, Melanesian
plant materials
 classification of, 18n1
 empathy with, 4, 89–90, 92, 177, 181–82, 186
 as enabling, 3
 as informational systems, 112
 kastom and, 118–19, 130, 134
 knowledge of, 22–25, 32, 55, 133–34, 139
 in men's house, 128–33, 179–80
 Naliks and, 22–25, 32, 45–46, 55, 133–34
 operational qualities of, 133
 performance and, 113, 118–19, 133, 185–86
 in scaling, 133
 Western technoscience and, 2–4, 6, 176
plants, gendering of, 33, 47n13
plastic, 3, 5
 affordances of, 29
 emergence of, 10–11
 material identity of, 53, 65, 79
 PET, 70–71, 74
 sociality of, 29
plastic water bottles, 70–71, 183
point cloud, 169
polyethylene terephthalate (PET), 70–71, 74
Port Moresby, Papua New Guinea, 43, 115, 119, 131
Potter, Emily, 70
Primal Earth, 83–84
The Psychology of Everyday Things (Norman), 29
pudding bowl. *See* food trough, Melanesian
Pukapuka atoll, 163, 171
Pye, David, 92, 177

Q

Queensland Museum (Brisbane, Australia), 56, 144, 150–51, 158, 186

R

rabaarau (clan cemeteries), 22, 127
Race, Kane, 70
Ray, Sidney H., 37
Reasons for Promoting the Cultivation of the New Zealand Flax (Bell and Young), 68
Reciprocal Research Network, Canada, 173n1
reconfiguration, of materials, 182–85
Rickard, Paul P., 47n8
Romilly, H.H., 56
Rotorua, New Zealand, 80, 186
Roviana, 104–5
Russell, T., 104

S

St Matthias Islands, Papua New Guinea. *See* Mussau, Papua New Guinea
scaling, 112. *See also* computation, material
 additive technology of, 16, 94–95, 98, 101, 182
 bowl and, 107
 food trough and, 94–95, 101, 104, 106–7, 109
 Gell on, 91
 harakeke and, 81

kastom and, 114–15
materials computation and, 90–92, 95, 108
Melanesian canoe and, 94–95, 101, 107, 109, 182
Naliks and, 36, 114–15
plant materials in, 133
in ritual, 91
Tsing on, 114–15, 134n1
scanning, 3D, 167–68
Scion, 80–81
selection, of materials, 26–28
empathy and, 89, 177, 182
mapping and, 30
Seventh Day Adventist Church, 25
Shaw, M.B., 76
Shove, Elizabeth, 3, 10, 29, 53, 65, 175
Sillitoe, Paul, 47n13
simulacra, 143
sociality, of materials, 28–29
social transformation, materials and, 11–12
Solomon Islands
bowls of, 101–3, 107–8
in British Museum, artefacts of, 93–94, 96–97, 103–4, 165–68, 171
canoes of, 94–101, 109n2, 150, 161, 163–73
digital return in, 17–18, 160–65, 169–73
food troughs of, 16, 94–95, 101, 103–7, 109
internet access in, 165
photographic images in, 170–71
Roviana in, 104–5
stitched pandanus from, 47n8, 47n11
Vella Lavella in, 164, 166, 169–71
Somare, Michael, 128–31
Somerville, H.B., 98
spinifex, 73
Strathern, Marilyn, 3, 108, 112, 114, 132–33
subtractive technology, 90, 92, 109
in bowl-making, 103
of dugout, 98
of food trough, 16, 94–95, 101
surfing
harakeke and, 81
in New Ireland, 21, 46n1

T

Tabar Islands people, 154–55
tambu (in-law), 128, 130, 135n5
tangovo, 99
tatanua mask, 56
tattooing, 91
technoscience, Western, 11, 91
materials innovation and, 4
plant materials and, 2–4, 6, 176
Tench Island, Papua New Guinea, 24, 47n10
Thomas, Nicholas, 11–12, 52, 54, 132
3D digital objects. *See* digital objects, 3D
Tigak area, New Ireland, 47n8
Tilley, Chris, 9–10, 46
tok pisin, 35, 127, 135n6
Tonga, 42
Tongan missionaries, 47n7
torching, 170–71
Trobriand Island, 110n4
trough. *See* food trough, Melanesian
Trubridge, David, 81–82
Tsing, Anna, 114–15, 134n1

U

University of Bergen, Norway, 164–65, 169
University of Queensland Anthropology Museum, 144, 150–51, 154, 186

V

vaazufnalik (wash the baby), 38–39
vabalos, 38–39
value-adding, 10
Vanuatu, 56, 61, 93
Vanuatu Culture Centre, 93
Vella Lavella, Western Solomon Islands, 164, 166, 169–71
Verran, Helen, 147–49, 162–63
vibrancy, 70, 77

W
Wagner, Roy, 108–9
war canoe. *See* canoe, Melanesian
wash the baby (vaazufnalik), 38
watbung (clans), 31
wawara, 33, 121
Weiner, A.B., 51–52, 55
Welz, Gisela, 70, 72
West, Paige, 46n1
White, Geoffrey M., 116
wok bilong em (its work), 35, 42
Wola, 47n13
Woodford, Charles M., 95, 97–99, 104–5
workmanship, 92
Wright, Chris, 170

Y
Young, Frederick, 68

Z
Zande hunting net, 175

www.ingramcontent.com/pod-product-compliance
Lightning Source LLC
Chambersburg PA
CBHW070620030426
42337CB00020B/3867
* 9 7 8 1 8 0 5 3 9 1 2 2 7 *